CON

Preface

Writing in the preface to his fine monograph *Alexander Glazunov: Russia's great musical conciliator* (1987), Simon Mundy regretted the absence of a full-length English biography of the composer, in the half-century that had elapsed since Glazunov's death in 1936. He offered his volume as 'an outline rather than a definitive statement'.[1] Despite the publication of Donald Venturini's highly informative *Alexander Glazounov: His Life and Works* (1992), the substantial biography that Mundy looked for, and that Glazunov both deserves and needs, is still to appear.

Why then offer another outline of this composer's life and work? As my degree is in English Literature and Philosophy, rather than in Music or Russian, I cannot offer anything else. However, from the moment I first heard Glazunov's Fifth Symphony as a child, with its rhythmic vitality and lyrical beauty, I have been fascinated by his compositions and increasingly interested in the man who created them. I can certainly echo the sentiments of the famous English composer, Eric Coates, when he writes, 'I have to thank Glazounov for giving me as much pleasure with his music as I have received from any other composer.'[2] I might also invoke the voice of William Golding and the justification which he provides for his travel book, *An Egyptian Journal*:

> But I felt a connection, an unusual sympathy. It became, absurdly enough, a feeling of responsibility as if I owed the country something though I had never been there. There is even the possibility that this book is an unsuccessful attempt to pay that debt.[3]

This short book then is my attempt to 'pay that debt' to Glazunov. In the early days of my enthusiasm I became aware of a disparity between the enjoyment I received from listening to his music and the patronising remarks that sometimes accompanied the mention of his name on the radio or in magazine and newspaper reviews. It has therefore been encouraging, in recent years, to note the emergence of a more balanced view on both the value of Glazunov's works and the character of the man himself. In line with this trend, I have attempted to provide an indication of the significant aspects of Glazunov's compositional style as it evolved. His personality, and the principles that governed his conduct, are also considered.

He certainly lived through turbulent times, even judged by the standards of Russian history. In giving an account of his life, I have suggested how the rich productivity of the first part of his career was followed by the years of revolution, war and famine in which he shouldered the heavy burden of responsibility for the administration of the St Petersburg / Petrograd / Leningrad Conservatory. Finally, I have attempted to provide some explanation to account for the dramatic decline that his reputation suffered in the middle decades of the twentieth century, before going on to suggest why a greater acquaintance with Glazunov's best works can be an enriching and thoroughly enjoyable experience.

Dates

Russia continued to follow the Julian calendar until February 1918, so when two dates are given for events which took place in Russia prior to this date, the first refers to the Julian calendar, the second to the Gregorian calendar, as in 29 July/10 August. The Julian Calendar was twelve days behind the Gregorian in the nineteenth century and thirteen days behind in the twentieth century.

Names

Over the years, Russian names have been transliterated in many different ways. I have followed the practice adopted by Francis Maes in *A History of Russian Music*. Therefore, I have 'Chaikovsky' rather than 'Tchaikovsky' but 'Alexander' instead of 'Aleksandr'. In quotations, I have retained the spelling of any Russian name that the author employed in the original text.

Chapter One

1865–82: Family history and youth

'It is impossible for me to busy myself with other things. I am possessed by music. If I could not compose, I would have the feeling of wasting my life.' Alexander Glazunov[1]

In the history of Western music, certain years have been particularly significant in terms of the composers they have produced. No doubt the most famous of all is 1685, as it witnessed the births of George Frederic Handel (23 February), Johann Sebastian Bach (21 March) and Domenico Scarlatti (26 October). However, rearrange the numbers into 1865 and another truly remarkable year is revealed – one which welcomed into the world Carl Nielsen and Alberic Magnard (both on 9 June), Jean Sibelius (8 December) and the subject of the present monograph, Alexander Konstantinovich Glazunov (29 July/10 August).

By the time of Glazunov's birth, his family had already made a significant contribution to Russian culture. This can probably be dated to the reign of Catherine the Great (1762–96) when, in 1782, the composer's great-grandfather, Ivan (1765–1831), joined his elder brother, Matvey (1757–1830), in starting up a book selling and publishing enterprise in Moscow. At the time it was a bold venture, but one that was in tune with Catherine's advocacy of cultural ideas derived from the French Enlightenment. This forward-looking approach enabled a relatively small but significant middle class to establish itself in the commercial and intellectual life of Russia.[2]

As early as 1783–4 there were signs that the firm was prospering, as Ivan moved to St Petersburg to open a new outlet of the book shop and, in 1790, it was decided that he should run the St Petersburg branch as an independent enterprise. Nonetheless, despite Catherine's more liberal stance, the brothers still needed to tread carefully. At one point they did fall foul of the authorities when they printed works expressing opinions that did not meet with the approval of the ruling order. This episode is revealing in that it provides an early indication of the family's liberal political stance – one that will be significant when considering the composer's dealings with various governments, both Tsarist and Communist.

Ivan's son, Ilya (1786–1849) was able to build on his father's success and the reputation of the business was further enhanced by the publication of major Russian writers such as Lermontov. Firmly established on St Petersburg's magnificent Nevsky Prospect, Ilya also brought out various editions of Russia's greatest poet, Alexander Pushkin, including, in 1836, 5,000 copies of *Eugene Onegin,* for which he paid the poet 10,500 roubles.[3]

Ilya's two sons, Ivan (1826–89) and Konstantin (1829–1914), the father of Alexander, were therefore born into a prosperous family that was establishing a significant reputation as one of the leading representatives of the St Petersburg bourgeoisie. Much of Konstantin's energies were naturally taken up with running the family business but, in his hours of leisure, he devoted time to playing the violin. In 1863 he married Elena Pavlovna Turigina (1846–1925) whose family also belonged to the upper middle class. Although a very gifted pianist, she was too shy ever to perform in public. Alexander, born in 1865, was the first of their four children: two years later a daughter, Elena, entered the family, followed by two brothers, Dmitri and Mikhail, in 1869 and 1870 respectively. The apartment at No. 76 Kazanskaya (later Plechanova) Ulitsa had been in the family for many years and the composer would remain in residence there until he left Russia in 1928.[4] The Glazunov home, therefore, provided a stable, secure and cultured environment – one that was ideally suited to the development of the youth's talent. Writing of Glazunov's home circumstances, Montagu-Nathan comments:

Glazunov's father,
Konstantin Ilyich Glazunov

Glazunov's mother, Elena Pavlovna
Glazunova (née Turigina)

> Belonging to a family long established in one of the most dignified of commercial pursuits, he was brought up in surroundings that differ from those of an ancient aristocratic family only in that the qualities that won the distinction conferred were still to be observed in the daily pursuit of affairs.[5]

As Herbert Günther has suggested, Glazunov appears to have inherited a kind and even-tempered nature from his violin playing father, while his mother may well have provided the powerful creative impulse that was soon to manifest itself. Photographs of the composer as a boy reveal a very smartly dressed but rather serious looking young man, with an intense gaze. Even in later life he had a habit of speaking quietly[6] and he was known as a person who very rarely lost his temper.

When Rimsky-Korsakov first met the fourteen-year-old Glazunov, he described him as 'a charming boy, with beautiful eyes'.[7] Interestingly, the name *Glazunov* is probably derived from the Russian word '*glaz*' meaning 'eyes' and its extension '*glazun*' may have originally suggested something like 'large eyes'.[8] It is certainly noticeable that, when leading artists such as Ilya Repin and Valentin Serov came to paint or to sketch Glazunov, they focused the viewer's attention on the composer's searching gaze.

His first introduction to music was provided by the highly talented piano playing of his mother. Even at this stage Glazunov's remarkable memory for the sounds he heard was apparent. Recollecting his youth, he explained that he 'loved listening to his mother playing, and absorbed it so deeply that he often got up at night to experience again, in memory, the music he had heard'.[9] Throughout his life, Glazunov would provide many other examples of his remarkable memory for music. As a child he also demonstrated an early talent for drawing, although, significantly, his subjects often involved musicians such as a French horn player, a timpanist and a conductor – drawings that are indeed prophetic, as they depict some of the performing skills he would go on to develop in later life.

It was soon clear that more formal instruction in piano and music theory was needed, so Glazunov's early musical education was entrusted to Narziss Elenkovsky. At one time he had been a professor at the St Petersburg Conservatory and, in the summer of 1877, he joined the Glazunov family on holiday in the countryside at Gatchina. In addition to giving Glazunov piano lessons, he introduced his pupil to the theory of harmony, and encouraged the young man's early ventures into composition. In the summer of 1878, for example, Glazunov embarked on a short-lived attempt to write an opera based on the Persian legend of *Rustam and Sohrab*.

A significant moment in these lessons occurred when Elenkovsky introduced Glazunov to Balakirev's *Islamey,* an evocative piano piece based on two melodies Balakirev had heard while staying in the Caucasus region and another theme the composer had noted down from an Armenian actor.[10] When, in subsequent lessons, he played over pieces by Rimsky-Korsakov and Borodin, he can hardly have imagined that, in a few years' time, these famous composers would be his colleagues and friends.

Of course, Glazunov's education was by no means limited to music. At home, he had lessons in French and German from visiting teachers and, throughout his life, he remained fluent in both languages. Later he was enrolled in the Realschule No. 2, an institution that specialised in the sciences and modern languages. Glazunov did well at the school and, judging by the high marks he received for attentiveness and behaviour, he appears to have been a conscientious pupil. However, because he possessed perfect pitch, he could not tolerate the terrible singing lessons and he was not above a little harmless subterfuge to escape from them: by deliberately singing out of tune he was excused from the classes that were torturing him.[11]

The year 1879 was a significant one both in terms of Glazunov's development as a person and as a musician. In the summer months he experienced foreign travel for the first time when the family went on holiday to Bad Kissingen, in Germany. Glazunov was delighted by the little orchestra attached to the hotel and soon struck up friendly relations with the instrumentalists. Later the family moved on to Paris, giving Glazunov his first view of a city that would play a major part in his musical career.

The departure of Elenkovsky from St Petersburg was also to have important consequences. Initially it led to Glazunov's mother turning to Miliy Balakirev (1837–1910) to continue her own music lessons. Balakirev was a brilliantly talented, charismatic, if somewhat domineering figure who, by the 1860s, had gathered around him a small group of composers: César Cui (1835–1918), Modest Musorgsky (1839–81), Nikolai Rimsky-Korsakov (1844–1908) and Alexander

Borodin (1833–87). Inspired by the example of Glinka (1804–57), they were dedicated to the idea of developing a distinctively Russian style of music.

The members of the Balakirev group are variously referred to as 'the Mighty Handful', (a term derived from the Russian '*moguchaya kuchka*'), 'the *Kuchka*', 'the Five' or the 'New Russian School'. In the early years of their association the members of the group were highly suspicious of the type of academic training that was provided by the various conservatories and music schools that flourished throughout the rest of Europe and, at least initially, not one of them could be described as a professional musician: Balakirev was forced to earn a living, for a time, as an official on the Warsaw railway; Musorgsky, as a young man, served in the Preobrazhensky Guards before entering the civil service; Cui became a Professor at the St Petersburg Academy of Military Engineering where he was a recognised authority on fortifications; Rimsky-Korsakov followed a family tradition by serving as a naval cadet and officer, while Borodin pursued a highly successful career as a Professor of Chemistry at the Medical and Surgical Academy in St Petersburg.

Supported enthusiastically by the critic, Vladimir Stasov, who first coined the phrase '*moguchaya kuchka*' in an article of 1867, they set themselves in opposition to the more cosmopolitan and Western focused approach of the outstanding piano virtuoso, composer and administrator, Anton Rubinstein (1829–94), who had founded the St Petersburg Conservatory in 1862. In the same year, Balakirev was one of the prime movers in helping to establish the Free School of Music as an alternative to the conservatory curriculum established by Rubinstein. In the 1860s and 1870s these contrasting views led to a great deal of highly acrimonious – and generally pointless – debate. In 1865, for example, Cui unfairly described Rimsky-Korsakov's E flat minor symphony as the first Russian symphony, even although he was well aware that Rubinstein had already composed three works in the genre: No. 1 in F (1850), No. 2 in C *The Ocean* (1851) and No. 3 in A (1854–55).

In retrospect, it can be seen that the divisions between the two factions were not always as clear cut as was sometimes claimed. While it is undoubtedly true that Balakirev and his followers valued 'indigenous' elements, such as Russian folk song and Orthodox Ecclesiastical chants, their music still owed a significant debt to the Western symphonic tradition. When discussing Balakirev's orchestral compositions, for example, Francis Maes explains that, 'Despite all his attacks on German academicism, his technique continued to reflect the symphonic approach of the German tradition.'[12] On the other hand, Rubinstein eventually started to make use of Russian folk tunes in some of his most important works, such as his last two symphonies: No. 5 in G minor, known as *The Russian,* and No. 6 in A minor. In any case, as Orlando Figes makes clear, 'Russia was too complex, too socially divided, too politically diverse, too ill-defined geographically, and perhaps too big, for a single culture to be passed off as the national heritage…' And, as he later goes on to observe, 'We are inclined to consign Russia's artists, writers and composers to the cultural ghetto of a "national school" and to judge them, not as individuals, but by how far they conform to this stereotype.'[13] It was perfectly possible, in other words, to be a successful Russian composer without having to remain within the narrow orbit of the Mighty Handful.

At the time, however, the fact that Glazunov was discovered by Balakirev meant that he was regarded as a recruit to the ranks of the Nationalist composers. This happened when Glazunov's mother showed Balakirev some of her son's efforts in composition. Suitably impressed, Balakirev then suggested that the fourteen-year-old Glazunov should start lessons with Rimsky-Korsakov. Indeed, the meeting with Rimsky-Korsakov was one of the defining moments of the young man's life. Of this first encounter Glazunov later wrote: 'You can imagine with what youthful excitement I anticipated my first meeting with Rimsky-Korsakov. I was in awe of his creative work and utterly believed in his artistic authority.'[14] Lessons, which lasted for only an hour, took place once a week, on a Sunday, and started on 23 December 1879/4 January 1880. It should also be noted that they were discontinued during the holidays. In his autobiography *My Musical Life,* Rimsky-Korsakov recalls the early stages of their association:

> Elementary theory… proved unnecessary for him, as he had a superior ear… After a few lessons in harmony I took him directly into counterpoint… His musical development progressed not by the day, but literally by the hour.[15]

In due course the relationship between teacher and pupil evolved into one of lasting friendship and respect. In one of the early lessons, Rimsky-Korsakov presented his new acquaintance with some string quartets by Haydn and this encouraged Glazunov to compose his first essays in a genre to which he would later contribute some of his most attractive music. The five pieces for string quartet, composed between 1879 and 1881, already demonstrate a real feeling for the medium. Taken together they almost constitute a suite, with a Lento and Intermezzo from 1879, a Scherzo in E composed in August 1880, another Scherzo in C from October of the same year and a Scherzo *alla ongaressa* (in the Hungarian style), from 1881.[16]

It was the orchestra that was soon to become the centre of Glazunov's activity as a composer, however. As noted above, he had been delighted by the spa orchestra that he heard in Germany[17] and soon he was engaged in orchestrating a number of his early piano pieces, some of which would appear later in his *Characteristic Suite*. Remarkably, by the end of 1881, he was working on the *Overture on Greek Themes No. 1,* the *Overture on Greek Themes* No. 2, in addition to embarking on his Symphony in E.

Glazunov himself gives an account of his work on the symphony that was shortly to bring his name to the attention of the Russian musical world. Started in 1880, when he was still fifteen, he continued to work on the score during the summer of 1881 while on holiday in Finland so that, by the autumn of the same year, he was able to present the third movement (*Adagio*) to Balakirev. He later explained that Balakirev was satisfied with what had been written but, characteristically, suggested the addition of a few bars between the two main sections of the *Adagio*. Glazunov was happy to adopt the older composer's advice.[18]

Completed by the end of 1881, he was fortunate in having to wait only until the following spring for its first performance. Many other composers would no doubt have been envious of the éclat with which Glazunov's career was launched. At the same time, it should be noted that this opportunity had been presented to him because both Balakirev and Rimsky-Korsakov were convinced of the real merit of his symphony. Dedicated to Rimsky-Korsakov, the work was first performed under the direction of Balakirev, on 17 March/29 March, 1882, at the second concert in the season presented by the Free School of Music.

Rimsky-Korsakov provides a vivid account of the events surrounding the symphony's premiere:

> That was truly a day of rejoicing for all of us, the St Petersburg active workers of the young Russian school. Youthful in inspiration, but mature in technique and form, the symphony reaped great success… The audience was astonished when the composer, in a 'Gymnasium' (school) uniform, appeared in response to calls for him.[19]

Clearly the members of the Mighty Handful were delighted by Glazunov's début, as it indicated that a significant new talent had joined their ranks. Cui, in his review of the symphony, described it as 'frightening in its precocious maturity'.[20] Balakirev also dubbed Glazunov as the 'little Glinka' – a significant compliment bearing in mind Balakirev's veneration for 'the father of Russian music'.[21] Another key figure from this group was Alexander Borodin who had recently been introduced to Glazunov. He also 'warmly congratulated the young and talented composer'.[22]

Naturally enough, not everyone responded with the same enthusiasm and there appeared in the press a cartoon of Glazunov as a suckling baby. Rimsky-Korsakov was aware of rumours, circulating in St Petersburg, that the symphony had been commissioned by Glazunov's wealthy parents and then passed off as their son's work. Of course, as more of the young man's compositions appeared over the coming years, such ill-natured remarks were shown to be entirely groundless, but they do serve to reveal the degree of genuine surprise created by his achievement. Summing up his response to the first appearance of his pupil before the public, Rimsky-Korsakov observes: 'This symphony was the first of a series of original compositions by the highly gifted artist and indefatigable worker, compositions which gradually spread also to western Europe and came to be the finest adornments of contemporary musical literature.'[23]

It is instructive to consider the extent to which Glazunov's First Symphony deserves the praise that it received. The work was more than likely to meet with the approval of the members of the Mighty Handful, as Glazunov makes use of two folk themes, both of Polish origin: one in the trio of the Scherzo and the other as the opening theme of the Finale. He had heard the gardeners singing these melodies when he was holidaying at a dacha in Druskenik, near the Polish border.[24] As a result, the symphony is sometimes referred to as *The Slavonic* ('*Slavyanskaya*'), although this title does not appear in the score. Simon Mundy makes a perceptive point when he suggests that by the 1880s the tensions within the Mighty Handful meant that they were becoming less and less cohesive as a group. Musorgsky had died in the previous year and Borodin and Rimsky-Korsakov were moving away from Balakirev's influence. So Glazunov seemed, if only briefly, to unite them in a shared enthusiasm and some of this optimism no doubt accounts for their positive assessment of the symphony.[25]

Glazunov in the early 1880s

The conservatory-trained composers then based in Moscow, such as Chaikovsky (1840–93) and Sergey Taneyev (1856–1915), were also interested in the arrival of a new voice in Russian music but they were perhaps able to view Glazunov's early efforts in a more dispassionate way. One criticism which they aimed at the members of the Balakirev group was their habit of simply repeating a theme or motif, rather than genuinely developing it. This weakness is certainly apparent in Glazunov's Finale, where, in the central section of the movement, the musical argument is almost entirely static, as if the composer is merely marking time until the arrival of the recapitulation.[26] The opening theme of the *Adagio* is also somewhat lacking in character. It cannot be compared, in terms of quality, with the melodies that make the *Andantino* of Borodin's Symphony No. 1 in E flat major or the *Adagio* of Chaikovsky's Symphony No. 1 in G minor, so memorable.

At the same time the First Symphony of Glazunov displays, at its best, an engaging freshness and vitality. It is significant that the form of the first movement is very assured, with its telling contrast between the buoyant rhythm of the first theme and the flowing elegance of the second subject. The energy of the music builds up towards the end of the movement, so that the final chords are reached with a genuine sense of fulfilment. As the music critic Y. D. Engel wrote of Glazunov's achievement in this piece, 'he knows where he wants to go and how to get there'.[27]

Another undoubted success is the Scherzo. From the vigorous chords of its opening, underpinning the dashing strings, to the rather humorous use of the perky little Polish theme in the trio, this movement is a complete success in itself and it stands at the head of a long line of brilliantly imaginative scherzos that would flow from his pen over the following decades.

It is therefore fair to say that Glazunov had started his career with an impressive symphony. If not entirely successful, it is nonetheless the work of someone who thinks naturally in terms of symphonic structure. It is also remarkable to consider that, on the day following its first performance, Glazunov was back in school. His teacher addressed him as 'Composer Glazunov' when he called him out to complete a mathematical problem on the board.[28]

Rimsky-Korsakov's description of his pupil as an 'indefatigable worker' was no exaggeration, as the young composer was quick to follow up the success of his symphony by producing, later in the year, the String Quartet No. 1 in D, Op. 1. The first performance of the piece involved some of the finest string players in St Petersburg, including Leopold Auer, to whom, many years later, he would dedicate his Violin Concerto.

At the end of the performance, Glazunov was led out onto the stage, to receive the applause of the audience, by no less a figure than Anton Rubinstein. Rubinstein was certainly one of the most important musicians in the history of nineteenth century Russian music, and his involvement, in addition to that of Balakirev, in the early stages of Glazunov's career would later lead some critics, such as A.V. Ossovsky, to suggest that Glazunov played a role in reconciling the conflicting factions in Russian music: the Western orientated group, led by Rubinstein, and the Nationalist followers of Balakirev. Ossovsky would later write, in his biography of the composer:

> 'Glazunov has effected a reconciliation between the Russian music of his time and western music. In this he has played an even more decisive part than Tchaikovsky, who was in the thick of the struggle between the two tendencies and therefore psychologically incapacitated from playing the part of peacemaker.'[29]

While there is no doubt an element of truth in this view, it is only fair to point out that Glazunov may simply have appeared on the scene at a time when the conflict between the two factions had all but run its course and the old divisions were starting to fade into irrelevance.

The critical reception of the First Quartet was similar to the various reviews that appeared in the wake of the First Symphony, with some fulsome praise coming from the members of the Mighty Handful. Stasov wrote, for example, that the piece was, 'Masterly in form and even more remarkable for its inspired musical ideas',[30] while Cui added that in 'the Quartet we find the same talent and the same maturity as in the First Symphony but even more astonishing is the technical knowledge and experience'.[31] The appearance of this work in print was also the occasion for what is perhaps Chaikovsky's first significant reference to Glazunov. In a letter to his brother, Modest, of 12/24 September 1883, he writes:

> In Kiev I bought Glazounov's quartet and am pleasantly surprised. In spite of imitating [Rimsky-]Korsakov, in spite of an irritating habit of not developing his themes but confining himself to repeating it (sic) in a thousand different ways, in spite of neglecting the melody and chasing solely after harmonic curiosities, one senses real talent.[32]

Chaikovsky is undoubtedly justified in criticising Glazunov's inability to transform his ideas. This is a very marked feature, for example, of the central section of the quartet's opening *Allegro Moderato,* as Glazunov takes his second theme and sends it on a tour of various keys, without in any way changing its character. At the same time, the search for what Chaikovsky calls 'harmonic curiosities' might well be seen as a virtue, particularly in so young a composer, as he attempts to increase the expressive range of his music. The pensive and introspective mood of the principal melody in the third movement *Andante* is also genuinely beautiful and it provides an early example of the attractive lyricism that is to be found in the best works of Glazunov's maturity.

The interest shown in his first compositions by many of the leading Russian musicians of the day would soon lead to significant developments in Glazunov's career – developments that would, in time, have an impact on the future progress of Russian music.

Chapter two

1883–84: Expanding horizons

A member of the audience at the first performance of Glazunov's symphony was the wealthy timber merchant Mitrofan Petrovich Belyayev (1836–1904). As the owner of vast tracts of forest to the north-east of St Petersburg, Belyayev was a man of considerable wealth, which enabled him to pursue his love of music. He was a capable viola player and, on Friday evenings, friends would gather at his home to play through string quartets and to enjoy each other's company in the convivial setting provided by their generous host.

Writing about Belyayev many years later, Glazunov recalled that he had first met him at an orchestral rehearsal of the symphony, shortly before its premiere in St Petersburg. The piece had so impressed Belyayev that he decided to travel to Moscow to hear it again, where it was to be conducted by Rimsky-Korsakov as part of a concert given at the All-Russian Exposition. In his account of these events Rimsky-Korsakov recollected that, before he started to work with the orchestra, he was approached by the imposing figure of Belyayev who explained to him that he desired to attend all the rehearsals of Glazunov's symphony, in addition to its Moscow premiere. And so began Rimsky-Korsakov's friendship with this 'remarkable man who subsequently was of such enormous consequence to Russian music'.[1]

Belyayev, fired by enthusiasm for Glazunov's talent, set about supporting it in practical ways: in time, these would include sponsoring concerts that would feature Glazunov's compositions and setting up a firm to publish these works. There can be no doubt that all of this activity placed him in a very fortunate, if not a unique, position. However, it is one thing to be presented with great opportunities and another thing entirely to take full advantage of them. It would have been so easy for Glazunov to adopt the life of the gifted dilettante, relying on his financial security and comfortable surroundings to pursue a thoroughly pleasant, if somewhat idle, life. It is therefore noticeable that, from the outset, he approached his musical vocation with single-minded determination.

Even at this early stage in his career, the compositions that followed the Symphony and the String Quartet give an indication of how Glazunov's talent would develop over the coming years. His first piano work, for example, is a suite based on the theme 'Sascha'. 'Sascha' is the diminutive form of his first name, Alexander, and by employing German notation, in which S = E flat and H = B natural, a short theme is created: E flat, A, E flat, C, B, A. Glazunov explores the potential of this motif with striking resourcefulness through the five main sections of the work: 1. Introduction 2. Prelude 3. Scherzo 4. Nocturne 5. Waltz. The Nocturne, in particular, is a poetic and touching variation, somewhat in the manner of Borodin. The ability to develop melodies through thematic transformation would remain a highly significant element in Glazunov's compositional make up. It is certainly a more prominent feature of his work when compared with the compositions of Balakirev, Borodin or Rimsky-Korsakov, and so it can be identified as one of the ways in which Glazunov made a distinctive contribution to the development of Russian music in the nineteenth century.

Early signs of this creativity in developing ideas can also be found in the orchestral pieces that he composed at much the same time as the piano suite. By 1883, for example, his two overtures on Greek themes had received their first performances. Glazunov had discovered the tunes in a collection of 30 Greek melodies published by the French composer and scholar, Louis-Albert Bourgault-Ducoudray (1840–1910). Works based on folk songs had been central to the musical programme of the Mighty Handful who were strongly influenced by Glinka's treatment of two Russian folk songs in his orchestral fantasy *Kamarinskaya,* as well as his two overtures on Spanish themes: the *Jota Aragonesa* and *Recollections of a Summer Night in Madrid.* Glazunov's mentors composed important works following Glinka's example. Particularly significant in this respect are two pieces by Balakirev: the *Overture on the Themes of three Russian Songs* and the symphonic poem *Rus* [*Russia*]. Rimsky-Korsakov also contributed to the genre with his *Fantasia on Serbian Themes* and his *Overture on Russian Themes.*

Glazunov was therefore able to draw on the advice and example of both composers when he embarked on his two overtures. Each composition has three contrasting themes, as in Balakirev's *Rus* but, if Glazunov displays no particular originality in the overall structure of the overtures, he does explore the potential of this material in a highly creative manner. There is real imagination, for example, in the way that he sheds new light on the Greek melodies by varying both their rhythmic outline and their orchestration. A case in point is the graceful third theme of the First Overture. This is initially presented by a solo oboe but is later transformed into a delightfully jaunty march, with the woodwind and brass sections supported by a brisk rhythmic figure on the side drum.

The *First Overture on Three Greek Themes* was dedicated to Anton Rubinstein, who conducted it at a concert given by the Russian Musical Society early in 1883, although its premiere appears to have been given by Rimsky-Korsakov at a concert in Moscow on 16/28 November, 1882.[2] It was followed a few months later by the first performance of the Second Overture. On this occasion, the work was conducted by its dedicatee, Balakirev. It marked the last occasion on which Glazunov appeared in front of an audience in his school uniform, as he graduated from the Realschule No. 2 in May 1883.[3] Both compositions were well received and helped to confirm Glazunov's quickly growing reputation but, with these performances, the relatively short period of Balakirev's direct influence over Glazunov was drawing to a close and, as Rimsky-Korsakov notes, the intimacy of their connection gradually faded over the next few years.[4]

The arrival of Belyayev on the scene was the main reason for this new dynamic in Glazunov's relationships with his musical friends. Balakirev was always keen to exert his authority over his protégés and he certainly resented the ever-increasing influence of Belyayev over the direction of Glazunov's career. Glazunov had gone against Balakirev's advice by allowing Belyayev to arrange matters connected with the publication of the symphony. Later, Rimsky-Korsakov reveals that Belyayev refused to sponsor the concerts of Balakirev's Free School of Music, as he had his own concert projects in mind.[5] And so, as the Mighty Handful ceased to exist as a unified entity, a new group started to gather around Belyayev.

Having received so much early encouragement it is little wonder that Glazunov's creativity continued to find expression in a series of orchestral works, including the *Serenade No.1,* Op. 7, the *Elegy to the Memory of a Hero,* Op. 8 and the *Characteristic Suite*. He also made sketches for a Second Symphony, in E flat major, but his ideas changed significantly before this composition was ready for performance.

In the meantime, Belyayev decided to organise a concert of Glazunov's music on 27 March/8 April 1884. Described as a 'rehearsal', the event took place in the hall of the Petropavlovsky School and Belyayev hired the opera orchestra for the occasion. Originally Glazunov himself was to conduct part of the programme but Rimsky-Korsakov, fearing that the young man's inexperience with the baton would damage his standing with the orchestra, dissuaded him from making the attempt. In the end, Rimsky-Korsakov conducted the programme in collaboration with G. O. Dütsch.

At this concert Belyayev wanted to hear the symphony again, as well as a new orchestral piece, the *Characteristic Suite,* which, after revision, would appear as Glazunov's Opus 9. It is made up of seven movements: 1. Introduction 2. Intermezzo 3. Carnaval 4. Pastorale 5.

Danse Orientale 6. Élégie and 7. Cortège. The Suite contains some ideas from 1881 which actually pre-date the Symphony, a fact which may well account for the influence of Borodin in the rhythmic suppleness of the second movement's trio section, while Balakirev's orchestral colouring is apparent in the lively Oriental dance. Rimsky-Korsakov found this piece to be 'very odd and savage' and, again using his influence, had it excluded from the performance. However, to modern ears, this brightly coloured movement, with its sinuous melody, is unlikely to sound either 'odd' or 'savage'.[6]

More importantly, the appearance of distinctive aspects of Glazunov's musical personality can be detected in the way the composer links various movements of the Suite. This is noticeable in the use that is made of the work's stately opening theme to provide a degree of cohesion in what would otherwise be no more than a collection of independent genre pieces. This melody appears again, briefly, in the second movement (Intermezzo) and the fourth movement (Pastorale) before re-emerging as an important element in the transition from the Élégie into the Cortège finale. Here the quiet and melancholy nature of its original presentation is transformed into a joyful march. Many years later a Glazunov pupil, Nikolai Malko, recalled a conversation he had with the composer in which Glazunov recollected the excitement he had experienced on hearing the *Characteristic Suite* for the first time:

> The court orchestra played his *Suite* in a closed rehearsal. He listened enraptured and did not hear any false notes. 'And there were so many! Afterward I went into the street. It was March, chilly, and the streets were full of puddles… but for me everything was so beautiful.'[7]

Not content with this, Belyayev devised a plan to expand the horizons of the young composer by taking him on a tour of Europe. So, in May 1884, Glazunov, in the company of Belyayev and his wife, travelled through Germany, France and Spain. Spain was especially attractive to Glazunov because of its vivid folk music and its associations with Glinka, who had stayed in the country between 1845 and 1847. When in Seville, Belyayev and Glazunov visited the district known as Triana. There they were delighted with the folk music they heard and Glazunov took the opportunity to note down some distinctive phrases employed by the local musicians. This first-hand knowledge no doubt contributed to the success of the pieces in the Spanish style that he wrote in later years: the *Alla Spagnuola* movement from the *Five Novelettes*, the *Spanish Serenade* for Cello and Orchestra and the Spanish Dance from the ballet *Raymonda*.[8]

The young composer was also a great admirer of the music of Franz Liszt and the meeting with the great man in Weimar was clearly the main focus of the expedition. On first being introduced to the world-renowned composer and pianist, Glazunov was understandably nervous. His initial awkwardness soon passed, however, smoothed over by the fact that he could converse with Liszt in French and German.[9]

It was through the influence of Liszt that Glazunov's symphony was performed in Weimar. For many years, Liszt had enjoyed friendly relations with members of the New Russian School, dating from his acquaintance with Glinka which had started in 1843. As one of the most influential and progressive musicians of the nineteenth century, Liszt appreciated the fresh approach, especially in terms of harmony and rhythm, that he found in the works of his Russian colleagues. The emergence of the youthful Glazunov from this group was therefore more than likely to meet with Liszt's kindly attention.

Glazunov sat behind Liszt during the rehearsal of the symphony, and noted how he applauded after each movement and commented on details of the work which he liked. Although the orchestra, conducted by Carl Muller Hartung, had not played particularly well during the rehearsal, Glazunov was relieved that the performance in the evening was more successful.[10] Afterwards he was warmly congratulated by a number of

German music critics who were happy to welcome the début of the young Russian symphonist. The European trip had certainly provided him with some stimulating experiences, leaving him with much to ponder when he returned to Russia at the end of July.

Once back in St Petersburg, Glazunov became involved in a lively round of activities. He was now in regular attendance at Belyayev's musical gatherings, held without fail on Friday evenings. Belyayev played the viola in the string quartet which formed the core of the evening's performances and Rimsky-Korsakov recalls how, 'Towards the winter of 1883–4 Byelayev's Fridays became rather well attended.'[11] In addition to Glazunov and Rimsky-Korsakov, regular guests now included important figures such as Borodin and Anatoliy Lyadov (1855–1914).

It was the custom to start the evening by playing through some string quartets by the Viennese masters – Haydn, Mozart and Beethoven – followed by works of a more recent vintage, including pieces by Glazunov. By 1886 these would include the String Quartet No. 1 in D, the String Quartet No. 2 in F and the *Five Novelettes*. In addition to his own compositions for string quartet, he arranged a great many works by other composers to be played by this ensemble, ranging from fugues by Bach to songs by Grieg.[12]

Belyayev always provided lavish suppers, 'laced with abundant libations' in Rimsky-Korsakov's phrase, after which more music would be played. This provided the composers with an opportunity to gain some initial reactions to pieces on which they were still engaged. In these performances, Glazunov would sometimes play the cello part himself and new compositions would be 'baptised' with bottles of champagne. There can be little doubt that evenings spent in such talented and receptive company acted as a stimulus to Glazunov's creativity, a fine example of which is the String Quartet No. 2 in F, Op. 10.

This is the first of a number of works that Glazunov dedicated to his patron. It was played at one of Belyayev's Friday gatherings in

November 1884, followed shortly after by its first public performance at a quartet concert given under the auspices of the Russian Musical Society. This work provides clear indications of the progress Glazunov had made in the short time since the completion of his First String Quartet only two years earlier. In the opening movement, for example, the ideas are developed with greater confidence, generating a real sense of momentum. The bustling energy of the Scherzo is a feature of a movement that is more ambitious in scale, while the highlight of the work is the beautiful *Adagio molto* in which Glazunov strikes a deeper expressive note than he had hitherto achieved. The contrasting rhythms of the Finale's two principal themes help to provide a bright, cheerful conclusion to a fine quartet.

The young composer was also making progress in his study of musical instruments – one of the skills which enabled him to achieve mastery in the art of orchestration. As Irving Kolodin points out, in addition to his training as a pianist, Glazunov went on to learn several other instruments including the clarinet, French horn, trombone, and cello.[13]

In this respect, his talent was perhaps most noticeable in his ability to play the French horn. He was fortunate to receive lessons from the first horn of the Mariyinsky Theatre Orchestra, Fyodor Franke. Following these studies Glazunov wrote some attractive short pieces for the instrument, including early versions of the *Serenade No. 2*, Op. 11 and the *Idylle,* Op. 14, No. 1. The later *Rêverie*, for French horn, Op. 24, reveals fully Glazunov's understanding of the instrument's character. It also demonstrates the ability, which he shared with composers such as Saint-Saëns, to create beautifully crafted miniatures.[14]

Years later he could still astound an orchestra with his skill on this instrument. The anecdote about Glazunov and the French horn player is related here by Prokofiev:

Four important figures in Glazunov's musical life: Rimsky-Korsakov (top left), Lyadov (top right), Liszt (bottom left) and Chaikovsky (bottom right)

> This man came up to Glazunov during rehearsal and complained that a certain note in the score was unplayable. In silence, Glazunov held out his hand for the instrument, put it to his lips, fingered it for some time without making a sound, then blew the note. He handed the horn back to the player without a word.[15]

It is also interesting to note that, although Glazunov was never a piano virtuoso, he did have a remarkable, if somewhat unconventional, facility on the instrument. An insight into his ability in later years is provided by Nikolai Malko, who records this intriguing account of the composer at the keyboard:

> he could play the most difficult passages, however exacting they might be, as if he had seven fingers on each hand. His fingers executed everything correctly. Moreover, I remember how once he illustrated something on the piano while holding a cigar between his fingers. He just never made a mistake. This ability was, of course, connected with his phenomenal inner pitch (hearing). This pitch and inner hearing, this ability to read with his eyes even the most intricate scores and notice the most hidden things, was truly remarkable.[16]

Glazunov was now connected to a rich network of musical friendships and associations. His compositions were receiving the financial support of Belyayev and, in the press, his works enjoyed the advocacy of critics such as Stasov. In an important essay of 1883, entitled 'Twenty-Five Years of Russian Art', Stasov developed his ideas on Glazunov more fully:

> The principal characteristics of his music thus far are an incredibly vast sweep, power, inspiration, wondrous beauty, rich fantasy, sometimes humour, sadness, passion, and always amazing clarity and freedom of form. The only defect in his writing is occasional repetitiveness and overabundance of detail, clearly the consequence of an excessively inflamed youthful imagination... It seems certain that he will one day be the leader of our nationalist composers.[17]

Stasov was right to suggest that Glazunov would become one of Russia's leading composers but his assertion that he would be a Nationalist composer is more questionable. Given the nature of his early musical influences, it was inevitable that he would compose in the manner of the Mighty Handful and he certainly produced some very fine pieces in this style. Nonetheless, over the next few years it became increasingly apparent to him that, to develop fully as a composer, he would need to adopt a different approach. He had learned a great deal from Balakirev and Rimsky-Korsakov but, in the end, he realised that they could not help him to achieve his ambition of becoming an important composer of symphonies.

Some of these tensions can perhaps be noted in Balakirev's negative reaction to Glazunov's orchestral fantasy *The Forest* in C sharp minor, which was started in 1882 and later published as his Opus 19, in 1887. It may be that the profusion of ideas in the piece made Balakirev feel that it lacked a logical plan. However, the quality of the themes, allied to the vividness of the orchestral textures, enable Glazunov to capture the somewhat sinister atmosphere of folktale and legend. In the words of M. D. Calvocoressi, *The Forest* is filled 'with... evocations of the fairies, goblins, dwarfs, and giants of Slavonic mythology'.[18]

From its mysterious and richly orchestrated introduction, through the rhythmic urgency of the music associated with the hunt, to the magical evocation of dawn, with which the work concludes, *The Forest* is an impressive addition to Glazunov's orchestral output. Indeed, the final section, with its delicate orchestral textures depicting bird songs, must rank with Musorgsky's Prelude to *Khovanshchina* as one of the most beautiful evocations of dawn in all of romantic Russian music.

A key figure who would help Glazunov to re-evaluate his style was Chaikovsky. Initially the Nationalist composers had been somewhat suspicious of him, as he was seen as a representative of Western tendencies in Russian music – someone who, in their opinion, belonged to the enemy camp. After all, Chaikovsky was one of the first graduates of the St Petersburg Conservatory which had been established by Anton Rubinstein. In time, however, he had impressed them with compositions such as his first two symphonies and Balakirev even provided Chaikovsky with detailed advice for the *Romeo and Juliet* fantasy overture and the *Manfred* symphony.

Glazunov first met Chaikovsky at Balakirev's home in January 1884, and provided his impressions of this meeting in his 1924 memoir of the great composer:

> Tchaikovsky's appearance soon made an end to the somewhat tense atmosphere of the guests, especially among the younger ones. Combining simplicity with dignity and refinement… he made the most favourable impression on virtually all those present. We heaved a sigh of relief. With his conversation he introduced a breath of fresh air into our somewhat musty atmosphere and freely talked of matters on which we had kept silent partly out of devotion, combined with a certain fear of Balakirev's authority and that of the other members of his circle.[19]

Glazunov's reference to Chaikovsky providing 'a breath of fresh air' is particularly significant, revealing, as it does, his openness to musical ideas that did not originate within the Balakirev group. During the evening, Glazunov played through on the piano one of his new orchestral works, a piece which he had provisionally called *Andantino.* As Chaikovsky's response to this composition was positive, Glazunov asked him to suggest a better title and, in due course, the piece was renamed *Lyric Poem* ('*Poème lyrique*'). It was published under this title as Glazunov's Opus. 12 and it is perhaps the most personal in style of his early works, with moments of intensity arising naturally out of the pensive atmosphere with which the piece opens and concludes. Clearly the flowing, melodic lines, and the warmth of expression, appealed to Chaikovsky and helped to establish more securely his interest in Glazunov. Later, the critic S. N. Kruglikov also expressed his approval of the *Lyric Poem,* perceptively describing it as:

> full of far from simple details and wholly distinctive harmonic features; and some chord combinations are straightforwardly so new as never to have been encountered before in anyone else's music. And how fascinatingly beautiful all this is… This is a superb composition, the fruit of truly happy inspiration.[20]

And so, in a matter of five years, Glazunov had emerged from his studies with Rimsky-Korsakov to become a significant figure on the Russian musical scene. Belyayev had dedicated his wealth to launching his favourite composer's career, and Glazunov's first compositions had received the friendly attention of major figures including Liszt and Chaikovsky. As a consequence, much was now expected of him.

Chapter three

1885–90: The path to creative independence

Glazunov's association with Chaikovsky developed over the next few years. On 20 May/1 June, 1885, for example, they met at the inauguration of the Glinka memorial at Smolensk and, in November of the same year, they came across each other again at the first concert in a new series: the Russian Symphony Concerts, sponsored by Belyayev. This series had grown out of the 'rehearsal' of Glazunov's works that had been arranged, at Belyayev's instigation, in the previous year. That first concert certainly had an attractive programme: Chaikovsky's symphonic poem *The Tempest*, Rimsky-Korsakov's Piano Concerto in C sharp minor and an important new work by Glazunov, the symphonic poem *Stenka Razin*, Op. 13.

Stenka Razin is unusual in Glazunov's output in that it is based on events from the life of a famous figure from Russian history: Stephan Timofeyevich Razin. This remarkable man was a Cossack from the Don region who, through the force of his personality, gathered around him a significant band of followers. Their activities in the Volga region posed serious problems not only to the authority of Tsar Alexis (ruled 1645–76) but also to that of the Shah of Persia. Razin was able to extend his control up the Volga, capturing towns on the way. However, although the number of his supporters grew, they were decisively defeated by the Tsar's army in October 1670. Razin was later captured, taken to Moscow and executed in 1671.

This episode in Russian history provided Glazunov with some dramatic material to which he responded with the full force of his youthful talent. The tone poem employs the folk tune known as the

Song of the Volga boatmen which he selected from Balakirev's collection of *40 Russian Folk Songs* published in 1866. The music critic and friend of Ravel, M. D. Calvocoressi noted that *Stenka Razin* is:

> one of the most close-knit tone poems inspired by a circumstantial programme… a consummate example of thoroughly traditional form, built almost entirely on the famous song of the Volga boatmen… the first two periods of which are used as subjects of the introduction and the allegro that follows, the third being kept in reserve for the peroration, and a Persian tune being used from the middle section onwards.[1]

Calvocoressi describes the structure as 'traditional', as the tone poem is cast in a sonata form movement with a slow introduction. At the same time, he is entirely justified in drawing attention to the admirable skill with which Glazunov develops the composition, largely from the first eight bars of the theme, even although the piece lasts for about a quarter of an hour in performance.

The introduction, with its dark string tones, conveys a sense of the vast, brooding expanse of the great Volga river, while the figure on the cellos outlines the key intervals of the folk song, before it appears in the sombre tone of the trombones. When the *Allegro con brio* section arrives, Glazunov places the theme in the lower voices of the orchestra, while the strings add variety with their vigorous semi-quaver decoration of the Volga boatmen melody.

The Oriental theme, introduced by the solo clarinet, represents a captive Persian Princess. At this point in the score Glazunov imaginatively transforms the opening of the Volga boatmen theme into the flute accompaniment to the Persian melody. This motif on the flutes, with its undulating character, conveys the lapping of waves against the sides of Razin's boat, in addition to connecting the two key elements of the work in a subtle way, so that, while the Persian tune provides contrast to the rigorous development of the Volga boatmen folk song, the accompaniment actually strengthens the thematic unity of the work.

In the final section of tone poem, the music suggests how the Cossack chieftain sacrifices the Princess by sinking his boat before leading a final assault upon the Tsar's army. The climax of the work is achieved by a build-up of tension towards the moment when the boat is sunk, the eerie stillness that follows it, and then the final powerful statement of the Volga boatmen theme – as Calvocoressi points out, the only appearance of the complete tune in the entire work. The brilliant coda in the major key seems to suggest that, although Razin was defeated, his reputation as an independent spirit – one who resisted authority and oppression – would live on. In fact, Glazunov later made an arrangement of the *Song of the Volga boatmen* during the disturbances of 1905 when its political message, of opposition to autocracy, was very clear.

Dedicated to his friend, Borodin, *Stenka Razin* is certainly one of Glazunov's finest achievements to date; in the words of Mundy, it has 'the energy and exuberance of Borodin at his best'.[2] Over the next few years it would significantly enhance Glazunov's reputation in the musical world beyond Russia's borders.

Another significant event in the development of his career occurred at this time: the establishment of the music publishing firm *M. P. Belaieff,* on 2 July 1885, in Leipzig. Belyayev had chosen Leipzig, a major European centre of musical activity, for various reasons: this was partly due to his desire to ensure high professional standards in music printing but he also clearly hoped that it would help to draw wider attention to new Russian compositions. Furthermore, Belyayev aimed to achieve greater copyright protection for composers, as Russia, unlike Germany, was not party to the copyright agreements in existence at the time – a situation that was perpetuated by the Russian government's decision not to sign the Berne convention in 1886.[3]

Belyayev was intent on presenting the works of his composers in the best possible light, so many of the front covers of his editions are rich in colour and ornate in design. Moreover, he issued all orchestral and chamber scores in three formats, so that, in addition to full score and parts, there was also a reduction for piano duet. The latter was particularly important in an age when domestic music making was still the most likely way for music lovers to become acquainted with new compositions.

Yet another example of Belyayev's seemingly endless enthusiasm and generosity was his decision to finance a series of annual prizes, to the amount of 3,000 roubles each year. Known as the Glinka Prizes, as Belyayev kept his sponsorship a secret, they were presented for the best new Russian compositions. Although the awards were often given to the St Petersburg composers, such as Rimsky-Korsakov and Glazunov, they were by no means limited to Belyayev's own group. In the early days of this project Chaikovsky received 500 roubles for his *Romeo and Juliet* fantasy overture and, in future years, compositions by other prominent Moscow musicians such as Taneyev and Rachmaninoff were generously rewarded.

The composers who had already benefited so much from Belyayev's hospitality and support decided to convey their appreciation to their benefactor in a way that was most likely to appeal to him. So, to mark Belyayev's fiftieth birthday, on 10/22 February 1886, Rimsky-Korsakov, Lyadov, Borodin and Glazunov composed a String Quartet based on a theme derived from his name: *B-la-F* (B flat- A- F). Rimsky-Korsakov provided the opening movement, Lyadov the Scherzo, Borodin the delightful *Serenade in Spanish Style* and Glazunov the Finale, in which, as Peter Skans writes, he 'demonstrates his exceptional technical skill: there is no imaginable inversion of the Belyayev motif that he does not use'.[4]

Rimsky-Korsakov provides an account of the new quartet's first performance, noting how Belyayev's birthday 'was celebrated at a gathering of numerous friends, and accompanied with gigantic dining and wining on an equally heroic scale… The quartet was performed before the dinner, and the hero of the occasion was thoroughly delighted with the surprise we had given him.'[5]

The quartet is also interesting in that it demonstrates how the musical life of St Petersburg was evolving. Rimsky-Korsakov and Borodin, who had previously been closely associated with Balakirev, were now unquestionably members of the Belyayev group. It is also interesting to note that the composition of the *B-la-F Quartet*, which inevitably involved the four composers in discussions about their various responsibilities, indicates a degree of friendly and fruitful cooperation that is not exactly common in the history of Western music.

At this time, Glazunov had completed another work for String Quartet – one that also encapsulates the festive atmosphere of Belyayev's *Fridays*: the *Five Novelettes* for string quartet, Op. 15. The title for this suite was suggested to Glazunov by the distinguished German pianist and conductor, Hans von Bülow (1830–94). Although closely associated with Liszt and Wagner, he was in St Petersburg, in the 1885–6 season, conducting the concerts of the Russian Musical Society and establishing friendly relations with many of the leading Russian composers of the day.

The five movements of the *Novelettes* contain an attractive variety of folk styles. The effervescent first movement is headed *Alla Spagnuola* (in the Spanish style), with the pizzicato accompaniment suggesting the guitar of a Spanish serenade. This is followed by what is probably the most remarkable movement of the Suite: a brilliant *Orientale*. After these two lively numbers, the composer provides a contrast with the sonorous and introspective *Interludium in modo antico*. Here the fine counterpoint and the Dorian mode help to create a mood of monastic contemplation, evoking the atmosphere of an earlier time. The last two movements are an elegant *Waltz* and a lively *All' Ungharese* (Hungarian dance). Edwin Evans successfully captures the spirit of these pieces when he describes them as 'delightfully and picturesquely scored… Scarcely anything so bright as this had ever been written for string quartet.'[6]

Much of Glazunov's energy during 1886, however, was taken up with the completion of his Second Symphony, Op. 16. He had noted down various ideas for a symphony in E flat major not long after finishing his First Symphony in 1881 but as it turned out his thoughts took a very different turn. For one thing, he adopted the unusual tonality of F sharp minor, as the symphony's home key, a fact which indicates something of the boldness of his conception. Haydn's Symphony No. 45, known as the *Farewell*, provides a very rare example of another symphony in the same key.

The Second Symphony was to be dedicated to Liszt in token of Glazunov's appreciation for the encouragement he had received from this illustrious musician but, as Liszt died before its completion, it is dedicated to his memory. Glazunov decided to use the method of thematic transformation that Liszt had championed in works such as his *Faust Symphon*y and the Second Piano Concerto. In these compositions the development of one theme provides much of the basic material for the entire work. As we have already observed, Glazunov, from virtually the beginning of his career, showed a marked interest in this method of exploring his musical ideas. Applying this technique to a substantial work, such as a symphony, however, was an altogether more challenging enterprise.

His decision to adopt this approach clearly indicates that he was not content to produce another piece on the scale of the First Symphony and his ambition was applauded by his colleagues, including Borodin, who were in a position to hear the composer play over his ideas as they developed. It is sometimes suggested that everything came very easily to Glazunov and that his facility for composition was, in the end, as much a handicap as a benefit. This view has certainly been overstated, as it ignores the considerable creative effort that went into the production of a major piece such as his Second Symphony.

Evidence that the compositional process placed a degree of strain upon the still youthful composer can be traced in a number of letters he sent to his musical friends at this time. In the summer of 1886 he was in Helsingfors (Helsinki) and in a letter to Belyayev he explains, 'First I want to work on the Second Symphony, which is not giving me any peace.' Later he writes to Stasov complaining about 'fatigue' after completing the orchestration of the first movement and, in another letter to the same correspondent, he reacts to the news of Liszt's death, on 31 July, 1886, stating that it 'took away my desire to continue it; also there was not much desire there to begin with, rather a feeling of somehow not believing in myself, the result of being here almost all alone.'[7] At the very least these remarks should make critics a little more cautious when they feel inclined to suggest that, for Glazunov, the process of composition was always effortless and unproblematic.

The first performance of the Second Symphony took place on 24 October/4 November, at the Fourth Russian Symphony Concert. In his essay on Glazunov as a composer of symphonies, Engel suggests:

> In comparison with the First, the Second Symphony… represents a huge step forward as regards the composer's musical development… In this symphony the twenty-year-old composer comes before us as a real master already, with broad and free musical horizons. Flair has turned into confidence, while firmness of step has become boldness and the ability to take the bull by the horns.[8]

The symphony opens with an introductory *Andante maestoso*, in which the brass announces an arresting, fanfare-like theme, marked *energico.* Much of the musical argument that follows, is derived from what is essentially a seven-bar melody. When the main section of the movement is reached (*Allegro*), the theme is speeded up and presented initially by the woodwind. The second subject, more flowing and expansive in character, provides the necessary contrast to the rhythmic drive of the work's principal idea.

Engel's comment about Glazunov's progress since the completion of the First Symphony is borne out by the imaginative exploration of the work's principal idea. With the arrival of the first movement's recapitulation, for example, Glazunov springs a surprise. Instead of simply presenting the theme as it appeared at the start of the *Allegro*, he varies it, by lengthening the notes, and marking the passage *Sostenuto e pesante*. This powerfully creates a sense of the melody's continuing development, something which would be lacking in a more conventional restatement of the material.

The second movement, marked *Andante*, is one of Glazunov's most attractive, as it now allows the lyrical potential of the symphony's central theme to be fully realised in a series of rhapsodic variations. When it is presented on the cor anglais, for example, it has a melancholy and introspective character which is in marked contrast to its appearance in the first movement.

The Scherzo which follows (*Allegro vivace*) opens with an arresting theme which is remarkable for its irregular rhythm, achieved by placing accents on what would normally be weak beats in the bar. In contrast, the trio provides a further elaboration of the symphony's initial idea, this time in a smoothly flowing melody which rises to a richly orchestrated climax before the restatement of the Scherzo's themes.

The Finale opens with a slow introduction that is based on yet another variant of the symphony's principal idea. Its rather rugged quality promises well when the main *Allegro* section of the movement is reached. However, the energy of this passage is dissipated too soon, and the transition to a section, marked *Moderato,* sounds unusually awkward for Glazunov. The more song-like melody that is introduced here does have a somewhat unconventional rhythm but it cannot be said that it is particularly memorable. Indeed, despite some arresting moments, the overall impression left by the Finale is that it is more manufactured than truly inspired.

Despite these shortcomings, it must be acknowledged that no

other Russian composer in the nineteenth century had created such an impressive edifice largely on the basis of one short theme and, although not all the ideas are equally engaging, Glazunov's imagination is arrestingly inventive in the first three movements. Over the next few years, this work certainly helped to spread his reputation well beyond the concert halls of St Petersburg and Moscow.

Glazunov also marked the passing of Liszt in his *Elegy: Une pensée a François Liszt*, Op. 17, for Cello and Piano. Throughout his career he would produce compositions of the *In Memoriam* type and they always seem to have summoned something particularly fine from him.[9]

A much more unexpected death, and one much nearer to home, was to make a very significant impact on Glazunov's life over the next few years. While attending a fancy dress ball at the Sushchinsky lecture room on 15/27 February 1887, Alexander Borodin suddenly collapsed and died from a burst artery in the heart. This brilliant, multi-talented, and thoroughly amiable man was an enormous loss not only to his family and friends but also to all the causes he served with so much energy and in such a remarkably selfless manner.

Borodin's professional career as a chemist meant that much of his time was taken up with work in the laboratory, teaching and administration. Apart from his research into the condensation reaction of aldehydes, he was instrumental in establishing medical courses for women. Inevitably this left him very little time for composition. He once told his friends that, to write music, he had to be too ill to fulfil his professional duties but not so ill that he could not compose.

As soon as Stasov informed Rimsky-Korsakov of Borodin's death, they went to the latter's apartment, collected all his manuscripts, including the unfinished epic opera, *Prince Igor*, and took them back to Rimsky-Korsakov's house. After Borodin's burial in the Nevsky Monastery, Rimsky-Korsakov and Glazunov went through all the manuscripts and together decided to 'finish, orchestrate and set in order' all that they could and to prepare these compositions for publication.

The most demanding aspect of their work was undoubtedly the responsibility they shared in completing *Prince Igor*, the masterpiece on which Borodin had been working since 1869.[10]

They next decided on the following division of labour: Glazunov would complete Act Three, for which there was the 'smallest bulk of composed music' and write down the overture from memory which he had heard 'played so often by the composer'. The scale of the task facing both Rimsky-Korsakov and Glazunov should not be underestimated. As Marina Malkiel and Anna Barry point out: 'An extraordinary 1,680 bars, including the well-known Overture, were composed entirely by Glazounov, who was further responsible for orchestrating 157 of the 710 pages of full score.'[11]

There is an anecdote relating to the overture in Serge Dianin's book on Borodin. One day Glazunov asked Borodin to play him the overture but Borodin declined, saying, 'Please excuse me, old fellow, I'm so tired of it.' Glazunov then asked Borodin's permission to play the overture himself. According to Borodin, Glazunov's performance was 'accurate to the last note'.[12] It seems fair then to assume that Glazunov was well aware of Borodin's general intentions as far as the overture was concerned. At the same time his own explanation of his work on *Prince Igor,* produced at the request of Stasov, indicates that there was still some composing to be done, as he explained that the overture was worked out:

> '*roughly* [my italics] according with Borodin's plan. I took the themes from the corresponding numbers of the opera and was fortunate enough to find the canonic ending of the second subject among the composer's sketches. I slightly altered the fanfares for the overture. (The fanfares after the words, 'Sound, trumpets!' belong entirely to Borodin. The idea of the fanfares is preserved in the overture, but I changed their sequence.) The bass progression in the

> middle I found noted down on a scrap of paper, and the combination of the two themes (Igor's aria and a phrase from the trio) was also discovered among the composer's papers. A few bars at the very end were composed by me.[13]

Reflecting on these matters Serge Dianin came to the conclusion that 'Glazunov remembered perfectly the composer's improvisations of the overture, and that his modest disclaimer merely reflects his meticulous honesty, together with the fact that certain minor alterations were introduced into the work in its final formulation.'[14]

Whatever the case, the overture is certainly one of the most memorable parts of the score.

The completion of Act Three was undoubtedly a much more difficult task for Glazunov, as there was not even a libretto prepared for it by the time of the Borodin's death. This was provided by Rimsky-Korsakov. Glazunov could then draw on (a) his knowledge of Borodin's style, (b) memories of hearing Borodin improvise at the piano and (c) other music Borodin had written, to create a version of the missing act. It should also be remembered that, as Borodin did not start the process of composition at the beginning of *Prince Igor* and work his way methodically through the opera, it seems fair to assume that he would have dealt first with those aspects of the scenario that appealed to him most, such as the Polovtsian Dances, leaving other aspects of the opera, including the whole of Act Three, for completion at a later date.

Work on the opera absorbed Rimsky-Korsakov and Glazunov for the better part of the next year-and-a-half. The score was completed on 1/12 March 1888 and, following extensive proof reading, published by Belyayev in October that same year. It then had to wait until 23 October/4 November 1890, for its first performancc which took place at the Mariyinsky Theatre in St Petersburg. The entire project certainly reflected the love and admiration that Rimsky-Korsakov and Glazunov felt for Borodin and, while their approach to editing their friend's work may seem somewhat cavalier by modern academic standards, in the words of Malkiel and Barry, 'The musical world has always unanimously acknowledged its debt to Rimsky and Glazounov for rescuing *Igor* from oblivion...'[15]

Glazunov has also to be thanked for preserving the two movements of Borodin's unfinished Third Symphony in A minor. Remarkably, on Borodin's death, nothing of the first movement existed on paper. Rimsky-Korsakov notes that 'For the first movement there existed an unrecorded exposition of the themes, which Glazunov remembered by heart.'[16] This account is largely confirmed by Dianin who writes that Glazunov 'had written down the whole of the first movement from memory', although Rimsky-Korsakov's version would tend to suggest that Glazunov had a good deal of work to do on the development section and the recapitulation, using Borodin's themes.[17]

Glazunov was also aware that Borodin had planned to orchestrate the Scherzo in D major, originally scored for string quartet, so that it could be included in the symphony. The theme for the trio section was taken from music that Borodin originally intended for *Prince Igor* – as the *Merchants' Tale* – before abandoning the idea. Dianin again provides valuable information here by noting that, 'It was the composer's own intention that Glazunov should carry out the necessary adaptation.'[18]

On the second anniversary of Borodin's death, Glazunov and Rimsky-Korsakov were part of a small group who met up in Borodin's apartment, to commemorate the life of their old friend by playing excerpts from his music.[19]

Although Glazunov was not able to devote time to his own compositions when working on Borodin's scores, his activity soon resumed once the proof reading had been completed. By the end of May 1888, he had finished a *Mazurka* in G for orchestra, Opus 18. Further evidence of his attraction to dance movements is provided by his *Prelude and Two Mazurkas*, Op. 25 for solo piano which, with the *Barcarolle and Novelette*, Op. 22 and the Three Études, Op. 31 constitute an attractive group of shorter works for the instrument.[20]

Much of his creative energy in the period 1887-8, however, went into two pieces of chamber music: the Suite for String Quartet, Op. 35 and the String Quartet No. 3, in G, Op. 26, known as the *Slavonic* (*Quatuor Slave*). The Suite consists of five movements but it is on a larger scale than the *Five Novelettes*. The second and third movements – the *Scherzo* and the *Orientale* – are by far and away the most appealing in the set. As Günther explains, when Glazunov was on holiday in the Crimea, in 1887, working on the orchestration of the Overture to *Prince Igor*, he had enjoyed exploring the countryside around Magarag. Here he heard the singing of the Crimean Tartars and he even learned to sing in the 'Eastern' manner himself. The fruits of these experiences can be heard in the intriguing *Orientale,* with its unusual rhythms and arresting harmonies.[21]

As for the other movements, the work opens with an imposing *Introduction and Fugue*. A finely crafted movement, it provides an indication of the increasing importance of counterpoint in Glazunov's compositions. Following the *Orientale,* however, there is a not particularly characterful set of variations. The Fourth Variation, *Pensieroso*, for example, is not sufficiently differentiated from the Second Variation, *Mistico*. Even the concluding waltz hardly finds Glazunov at his best, as there is too much repetition of a simple three-note rhythmic figure.

Altogether more successful is the Third String Quartet. Unlike his other works in this genre, it was assembled from pieces written at different times, although a listener is unlikely to be aware of this, as the four movements sit together remarkably well.

The first movement, marked *Moderato*, was composed in April 1886, and originally intended for performance at the Glazunov household, on one of their Thursday night gatherings and originally entitled *Chetverka* (Thursday), before appearing at one of Belyayev's Fridays. It has a most engaging character – inward and thoughtful – with a telling *pizzicato* restatement of the main theme. This is followed by an *Interludium*, dating from July 1886. Based on a gently rocking theme, the instruments weave together, creating a meditative, ecclesiastical atmosphere. Glazunov then increases the tempo with an *Alla Mazurka* movement finished by November 1887. With its lively rhythms, including sudden changes of tempo, this fresh-sounding scherzo takes the listener from the introverted nature of the first two movements towards the extrovert high spirits of the *Allegro moderato* finale, entitled *Slavonic Festival* (*Une fête Slave*), the most ambitious movement he had as yet written for string quartet. It is in the form of a rondo with, as Iosif Raiskin points out, a number of dance themes which include 'a Russian trepak, Czech polka, Polish krakowiak and Ukrainian gopak'.[22] Per Skans sums up the movement well when he writes of the 'dance-like melodies following each other virtually without pause for breath, creating a dance suite full of zest and *joie de vivre*'.[23]

Glazunov later orchestrated the finale, as an independent orchestral piece, *Slavonic Festival*, Op. 26 bis. However, the very demands that he places upon the players, in the original version for string quartet, add to the excitement of the music. At this time, he also contributed the first movement of a second collaborative string quartet dedicated to Belyayev. The loss of Borodin meant that it has only three movements. Known as the *Name Day Quartet* (*Jour de Fête*), Glazunov provided the first movement (*Christmas Singers*), Lyadov the second (*Song of Praise*) and Rimsky-Korsakov the third (*Khorovod*). All three movements have a decided Nationalist character, providing the piece with a strong sense of stylistic unity.

The silver wedding anniversary of the composer's parents provided another happy stimulus for composition. This event was celebrated with the customary dinners and many of the leading figures in the musical life of St Petersburg, including Balakirev, Rimsky-Korsakov and Stasov, called to convey their greetings. As a touching gift to his parents, Glazunov wrote his orchestral *Wedding March*, Op. 21, the first of a number of pieces of the cortège type that he would produce to mark various anniversaries. Joyful and celebratory in character, it exemplifies

Glazunov's skill in creating highly appealing short orchestral works.

In an age when composers were generally expected to perform their own compositions – sometimes as soloists, sometimes as conductors – Belyayev was keen to see Glazunov take up the baton and conduct his own orchestral pieces. His enthusiasm was shared by his protégé, although Rimsky-Korsakov had initially advised caution. However, on 22 October/ 3 November 1888, Glazunov conducted for the first time, choosing his *Lyric Poem* for his début. Describing this event in a letter to his friend, S. N. Kruglikov, he wrote: 'I was somewhat nervous, perhaps because the audience was very small, and perhaps because of a lack of confidence in myself then. Of course, when I came out on stage the baton was shaking in my hand, but I soon got hold of myself and no one else noticed…'[24]

Rimsky-Korsakov provides an interesting, and far from partial, account of his favourite pupil's performance:

> His first essays in this field were by no means brilliant. Slow by nature, maladroit and clumsy of movement, the maestro, speaking slowly and in a low voice, manifestly displayed little ability either for conducting rehearsals or for swaying the orchestra during a concert performance. Nevertheless, the consciousness of the great merits of his compositions induced the orchestra to aid rather than obstruct him.[25]

Having overcome his initial nervousness, Glazunov would continue to conduct orchestras throughout the rest of his career. Wolfgang Eggerking makes an insightful point about the importance of conducting to Glazunov as a composer, when he suggests that it enabled him to develop an even more refined appreciation for orchestral timbres in his own compositions.[26] It is certainly the case that the orchestral pieces he produced over the next few years – such as *The Sea*, the *Oriental Rhapsody* and *The Kremlin* – demonstrate, apart from various other qualities, a high level of mastery in terms of orchestral colour.

The imaginative exploitation of orchestral resources was also very much in the minds of Rimsky-Korsakov and Glazunov when they attended the first Russian performances of Wagner's *Ring des Nibelungen,* at the Mariyinsky Theatre in St Petersburg. Four cycles of the operas were given between 27 February/11 March and 21 March/2 April 1889. Both composers attended the rehearsals, attentively following the score. As Rimsky-Korsakov observes, they were impressed by Wagner's technique of orchestration and thereafter started to employ Wagnerian devices in the instrumentation of their own works.[27]

Glazunov acknowledges his debt to Wagner in his next major work, the orchestral fantasy *The Sea*, Op. 28, by dedicating it to his memory. He provided a programme for his tone poem in which he describes how a man, sitting by the sea shore, witnesses that arrival of a sudden storm. The arch-like structure of the piece – calm-storm-calm – is one that was also favoured by Sibelius in some of his greatest works, such as *Pohjola's Daughter* and *The Oceanides*.

Glazunov employs enhanced instrumental forces in this tone poem. The woodwind, brass and percussion sections are notably enlarged and, with the use of devices such as woodwind tremolos and trombone glissandi, he is clearly responding to the excitement of hearing Wagner's orchestra. At the same time the principal melody of the piece has a lyrical quality that is very characteristic of Glazunov, as is the manner in which themes are combined when the central climax is reached – a powerful and joyous part of the score and one which certainly captures the awe-inspiring power of the storm.[28] In terms of Russian music, Glazunov's evocation of the sea merits a place beside Rubinstein's *Ocean Symphony*, Chaikovsky's *The Tempest* and Rimsky-Korsakov's S*adko* and *Sheherazade*.

When Rimsky-Korsakov was writing *Sheherazade,* which he dedicated to Glazunov, the latter was engaged on his own depiction of the East, the *Oriental Rhapsody,* Op. 29. He again provided a brief programme for the piece, which is divided into five sections:

(1) *Evening. The town sleeps. The watchman's call. Song of the young improviser.* (2) *Dance of the young men and girls.* (3) *An old man's ballad.* (4) *Fanfares. Return of the victorious troops. General triumph.* (5) *Celebration of the warriors. The young improviser appears in the middle of the dance. Unbridled orgy.*

As M. D. Calvocoessi suggests, 'There is a wealth of telling imagery and poetic suggestions in the exciting *Eastern Rhapsody*.'[29] Evening is beautifully evoked with the overlapping horn calls, leading to a passionate melody for the young improviser. Dynamic rhythms then dominate in the *Dance of the young men and girls*, before the richly scored melancholy of the following *ballad*. Ringing fanfares, derived from the opening horn calls, announce the surging climax of the work. Here, in addition to the vivid orchestral textures, Glazunov characteristically heightens the sense of a finale by bringing back melodies from earlier in the *Rhapsody* and combining them in freshly imagined ways. The high level of craftsmanship displayed here provides the work with an exhilarating conclusion.

This group of orchestral compositions, which occupied Glazunov towards the end of the first phase of his development, culminates in the symphonic picture *The Kremlin,* Op. 30. It is dedicated to the memory of Musorgsky and the titles of its three movements reveal that it was Glazunov's intention to depict various aspects of Russian life: (1) *Folk Festival* (2) *In the Monastery* (3) *Meeting and Entrance of the Prince.*

As with the other tone poems, the orchestra is large, including enhanced woodwind and percussion sections. The use of frequently varied rhythms successfully creates a picture of different groups of people assembling in the bustling scene of the opening movement's *Folk Festival.* The effect is enhanced by the bright C major tonality and the imaginative scoring. Contrast is provided in the second movement, which opens and closes with a solemn chant, while the central section depicts a religious procession. A particularly telling detail is found in the delicate evocation of the striking of small bells, which accompany the steady tread of the monks. After this mood of hushed contemplation, the finale resoundingly presents the entrance of the Prince into the Kremlin. The sense of power and grandeur in the scene is fully captured in this magnificent movement, uniting vigorous rhythmic patterns with orchestral brilliance.

Inspired by the example of Musorgsky, Glazunov provided in *The Kremlin* one of his most overtly Nationalist works but, despite the fact that he would always be able to employ the type of orchestral colour associated with his teachers, this was really a point of culmination, rather than a stepping stone to further development. He realised that he had done all that he could with the battery of techniques that Glinka and the Mighty Handful had created. If he wanted to make progress as a composer of symphonies, in particular, he had to forge a new path. While the important symphonic works that he produced over the next few years do not represent a complete break with the past, they do show that Glazunov was re-evaluating his style and looking to Russia's greatest composer, Chaikovsky, to indicate the way ahead.

In the summer of 1889, between the completion of *The Sea* and the *Oriental Rhapsody*, Glazunov travelled to Paris where Belyayev had sponsored two concerts at the Paris Exposition. Rimsky-Korsakov was entrusted with conducting the orchestral items on both programmes, with the exception of the two works by Glazunov – *Stenka Razin* and the Symphony No. 2 – which were conducted by the composer. Given the importance of these concerts in alerting Western audiences to the recent developments in Russian music, the decision to ask Glazunov to conduct certainly indicates confidence in his ability both as conductor and composer.

The concerts took place at the Trocadero on consecutive Saturdays, 22 June and 29 June, at two o'clock in the afternoon – *Précises*, as the French announcement rather elegantly puts it. In the first concert, with the sole exception of Chaikovsky, the programme focuses on the St Petersburg composers:

Glinka	*Ruslan and Ludmila* overture
Borodin	*In the Steppes of Central Asia*
Chaikovsky	Piano Concerto No. 1 in B flat minor – first movement (Nikolai Lavrov, soloist)
Rimsky-Korsakov	Symphony No. 2 *Antar*
	Interval
Balakirev	*Overture on the Themes of three Russian Songs*
Cui	*Overture Solonnelle*
Cui and Lyadov	Piano Pieces
Dargomïzhsky	*Finnish Fantasy*
Glazunov	*Stenka Razin*

Both Glazunov and Rimsky-Korsakov were impressed by the French orchestral players. Glazunov remarked on their professionalism and friendliness, sensing that French musicians were genuinely interested in performing the recent works of the New Russian School. In addition, many important French composers attended the rehearsals and the concerts: in this context Glazunov mentions Delibes, Debussy, Messager, Massenet and the elderly Thomas.[30] He goes on to say that 'Delibes had listened with great attention and was enraptured by *Antar*, *Stenka* and *Central Asia.*' Glazunov was also honoured by an invitation to the home of Gabriel Fauré and, at the offices of the newspaper *Paris*, his *Stenka Razin* was played again, by Pugno and Messager, this time in a four-hand piano arrangement.

The programme of the second concert was also of a substantial nature, with Chaikovsky again as the only 'outsider':

Glazunov	Symphony No. 2 in F sharp minor
Rimsky-Korsakov	Piano Concerto in C sharp minor (Lavrov, soloist)
Glinka	*Kamarinskaya, Fantasy on Russian Themes*
	Interval

Borodin	*Polovtsian March* and *Dances*
Musorgsky	*Night on Bald Mountain*
Balakirev, Chaikovsky, & Blumenfeld	Piano pieces (Lavrov)
Lyadov	First Scherzo for orchestra
Rimsky-Korsakov	*Capriccio Espagnole*

All this attention seems very satisfactory for the cause of Russian music in Paris but Rimsky-Korsakov felt that Belyayev had not advertised the concerts sufficiently – particularly considering the great number of events with which they were competing. Nonetheless, he did acknowledge that the relatively small audience had responded enthusiastically to the music of the Russian visitors.[31] Glazunov struck a more positive note in a letter to his friend Kruglikov where he commented that the audience for the second concert was much larger and that, all in all, Belyayev's enterprise amounted to a festival of Russian music.[32]

Although Glazunov's compositions were listened to with interest and warmly applauded in Paris, he was by no means immune from disappointments and setbacks. For one thing, he had already been attacked in the musical press by, of all people, César Cui. The origin for this critical assault may well lie in Balakirev's disquiet at the growing influence of the Belyayev group, with his ideas finding expression in Cui's article entitled *The Results of the Russian Symphony Concerts. Fathers and Sons*, published in the *Musical Review* of 9 January/ 21 January 1888. Here, Cui singles out the composer he had previously praised: 'Glazunov stands head and shoulders above the other sons in strength of talent and technical perfection, and therefore I shall have Glazunov's works primarily in mind in what follows.'[33]

The *Fathers and Sons* of Cui's title is a reference to Turgenev's novel in which generational conflict is used to explore the tensions within Russian society during the 1850s. For Cui, the *Fathers* are the composers of the older generation, such as Chaikovsky and the Mighty Handful, while the *Sons* are the new generation, exemplified by Glazunov. His criticism identifies what he calls 'three fundamental shortcomings': thematic inventiveness, harmony and programme music.

It is certainly true that Glazunov can hardly match the melodic invention of Chaikovsky and Borodin – but then very few other nineteenth century composers could claim to do this either, especially if they had been composing for fewer than ten years. In fact, the best years of Glazunov's 'thematic inventiveness' lay ahead of him, particularly in the orchestral music and ballets of his maturity.

Cui also expresses the concern that Glazunov is too experimental in his use of harmony and that 'seeking after new, unprecedented, original harmonisations has engulfed everything else'. This criticism may seem strange to modern readers, as the accusation of being too adventurous is one that is rarely aimed at Glazunov. As already suggested, in the discussion of the First String Quartet, it is surely necessary for young composers to experiment with harmony, as part of their attempt to develop an individual style. In any case, no one listening to a piece such as the beautiful *Lyric Poem* is likely to feel that, even at this stage in his career, Glazunov has sacrificed melody in his pursuit of 'original harmonisations'.

Cui's critique concludes with the question of programme music. For him, programme music is legitimate as long as the programme is of a general nature. He cites for approval Rimsky-Korsakov's *Antar* in which, in three separate movements, the music depicts vengeance, power and love – all general emotions. The weakness of Cui's argument here is that it completely fails to account for the success of the first movement of *Antar,* which follows an extremely detailed programme: the hero, Antar, wanders in the desert of Sham, by the ruins of Palmyra, when he is startled by the sudden appearance of a gazelle, pursued by a giant bird. When Antar chases off the giant bird, the gazelle turns into the Princess Gul-Nazar… and so on.

It is hardly fair for Cui then to criticise Glazunov's programme for *The Forest,* which is much less precise than the plan Rimsky-Korsakov followed in *Antar*. In fact, some of the very greatest tone poems have quite detailed programmes, such as the one Sibelius employed in *Pohjola's Daughter.* Surely what matters here is the extent to which the programmes inspire the creative imagination of composers, followed by their ability to create musically convincing structures from the literary or pictorial source material. Glazunov is careful to ensure that the wealth of themes in *The Forest,* for example, does not lead to a sense of shapelessness, as the piece is organised as a sonata form movement framed by a slow introduction, depicting the mysterious forest at night, and a peaceful coda, evoking the beauty of the dawn.

Stuart Campbell points out that Stasov was so angry with Cui that he published an article highlighting 'musically contradictory viewpoints, all expressed by Cui, and charging him with giving solace to the conservative foes of the New Russian School to which both Cui and Stasov had given their allegiance'.[34] Although these carping comments about Glazunov are not, in the final analysis, particularly telling, they do demonstrate that he could expect negative criticism even from those within the milieu of the St Petersburg composers. They certainly belie the assertion that he was spoiled by all the flattering attention he received. A typical example of this view is provided by Richard Leonard who claims that Glazunov's music made its way in the world 'without antagonism'.[35]

Rimsky-Korsakov also provides another reason not to overestimate Glazunov's success, in the first decade of his activity as a composer, when he indicates that the Russian Symphony Concerts were not particularly popular. Writing of the 1889–90 season he notes:

> It had been and became thereafter a custom to give invariably at least one composition by Glazunov at each Russian Symphony concert. The productive author gave no occasion for breaking this rule, and the public began to grow more and more accustomed to his name and appreciative of his talent. Yet his name did not draw audiences…[36]

Glazunov himself was also very disappointed by the reaction to his *Oriental Rhapsody*. Following its premiere on 8/20 January 1890, he wrote to Chaikovsky:

> Last week some unfortunate things happened with my new composition *Oriental Rhapsody*. In the first place, almost none of my close friends liked it, which hurt me very much. Secondly, it was not successful at the concert. All this was so painful for me because I did not share the opinions expressed to me and, on the contrary, at the first rehearsal was almost ecstatic.[37]

Chaikovsky replied tactfully to the effect that at least Glazunov had friends who gave him their honest opinion, rather than colleagues who simply provided polite but insincere compliments. Nonetheless, Glazunov's disappointment is very clear and, considering the quality of the work in question, entirely understandable.

Despite these setbacks, he was about to take a significant step forward with the composition of his Symphony No. 3 in D major, Op. 33. As Mundy explains, 'Glazunov was growing out of his teachers' clothes and the symphonic maturity of Tchaikovsky was opening up new possibilities for his own development.'[38]

Dedicated to Chaikovsky, the Third Symphony was performed under the direction of Lyadov at a Russian Symphony concert on 27 November/8 December 1890. The opening movement (*Allegro*) is bright and vigorous. The buoyant character of its first theme is effectively contrasted with the wistful nature of the minor key second subject, a beautiful melody which Glazunov develops with increasing intensity as the movement unfolds. Hc is now able to extend these ideas into genuine symphonic paragraphs, rather than resorting to the device of simply repeating his themes in a number of keys. A particularly fine moment occurs when the minor key melody appears for the last time, providing a passionate resolution of the musical argument, before the movement concludes with a brilliant and joyful coda.

The Scherzo (*Vivace*) which follows is one of Glazunov's finest, overflowing with invention and high spirits and delighting the listener with unexpected timbres and rhythms. To enhance the aural appeal of his score, Glazunov adds a glockenspiel to the orchestra, although even more significant is the originality with which his ideas are presented. Throughout the movement, for example, the main theme is constantly varied in key, orchestration and, most importantly, in rhythm, so that the listener is regularly surprised by its subtly changing character. Havergal Brian, the eminent English composer and critic, captures the essence of this 'fascinating Scherzo' very well when he observes that '…by reason of its rapidity and shape, [it] creates the physical impression of spreading like a comet's tail'.[39]

The third movement (*Andante*) in C sharp minor, reveals a still youthful composer searching for greater emotional depth. It has a romantic, brooding character that occasionally seems to look forward to Rachmaninoff. Indeed, Engel suggests that it is: 'one of Glazunov's not very frequent specimens of genuine *appassionato*. A profound and powerful chromatic melody works up by expanding and developing a vigorous passion, which in its heartfelt quality is not inferior to the finest inspirations of Tchaikovsky…'[40]

The comparison with Chaikovsky does seem to overstate the case here, although the principal theme, to which Engel refers, certainly has an appealing quality. At the same time the really fine lyrical melody that arrives when the tempo quickens (*poco piu mosso*) is surely capable of a much fuller treatment than it receives. The problem is compounded by the fact that the second half of the movement has nothing particularly new to say about the material that has already been presented; it appears only to provide a melancholy echo of what has gone before, leaving the real climax of the movement at the end of the first section.

The Finale (*Allegro Moderato*) is also not entirely successful, suffering from what Stasov had identified as Glazunov's tendency towards 'occasional repetitiveness and overabundance of detail'.[41] The opening idea has plenty of rhythmic impetus but in this respect it belongs more to his origins as a pupil of the Mighty Handful. If the first three movements suggest that Glazunov is close to finding his own voice as a composer, the Finale reveals that he has not yet fully integrated all the elements that will later become natural aspects of his own style.

Having acknowledged these relative weaknesses, it should be observed that, even here, there is evidence of a new creative path, as he is not simply prepared to repeat what had been achieved by the older generation of Russian composers. This can be seen in the way he sets about combining rondo form (in which the main theme alternates with contrasting episodes), and variation form (in which a melody undergoes an increasingly complex transformation). As the movement unfolds, for example, he takes the rugged rhythm of the main theme and, at one point, transforms it into a sinuous and chromatic fugal subject. Later, towards the end of the movement, it finally appears in augmented notes in the brass, followed by the woodwind and strings combining to suggest the peeling of bells. While these imaginative developments do not entirely save the movement, they certainly provide some indication of what Glazunov would be able to achieve when, following the example of Chaikovsky, he had learned to exercise greater control over his ideas.

Despite some disappointments, the first decade of Glazunov's activity as a composer had certainly brought him a degree of success. In a remarkably short time he had established himself as a composer with a growing international reputation. Gerald Abraham draws attention to relatively early works such as the symphonic poem *Stenka Razin* (1885) and the symphonic picture *The Kremlin* (1890), expressing the opinion that they 'suggested the advent of a considerable master…'.[42] The early promise he had shown was now being fulfilled, but the composition of his greatest works still lay ahead.

Chapter four

1891–96: Maturity

The period of Glazunov's most fruitful association with Chaikovsky occurred in the early 1890s. Following a more extended visit to St Petersburg in 1891, Russia's most famous composer became much better acquainted with the members of the Belyayev group and, in the remaining years of his life, he often participated in their friendly gatherings. With the conclusion of the evening's musical programme, Chaikovsky, accompanied by Glazunov, Lyadov and others, would often make their way to a restaurant, remaining there sometimes until three o'clock in the morning. As Rimsky-Korsakov somewhat wryly observes, few could keep up with Chaikovsky in terms of the amount of alcohol he could consume- while still retaining full possession of all his faculties![1]

Rimsky-Korsakov, Glazunov and Lyadov

The correspondence that passed between Glazunov and Chaikovsky at this time contains a clear sense of the respect that they entertained for each other. As already noted, Glazunov confided his disappointment to Chaikovsky at the negative reaction to the *Oriental Rhapsody* and received Chaikovsky's sympathetic response. That the elder composer gave some serious consideration to his young colleague's development is borne out by the letter he wrote to Glazunov on 30 January/11 February 1890, explaining that he thought very highly of his ability as a composer:

> But I do not know yet what to tell you. In many respects you are a puzzle to me. You have genius, but something prevents you from developing into breadth and depth. One expects of you extraordinary things, but this expectation is fulfilled only in a certain measure. One would like to help you in the full unfolding of your talents… but before I decide to talk to you concretely, I shall have to think. How would it be if you are to develop exactly as your nature demands and I simply do not understand you?[2]

It is worth remembering that when Chaikovsky wrote this letter, Glazunov was still only twenty-four years old. Unfortunately, the older composer did not live long enough to become acquainted with the works of Glazunov's maturity: he never heard a performance of the Third Symphony, although Glazunov played the work for him on the piano, and he died before the Fourth Symphony was completed. Perhaps when Chaikovsky suggests that 'something' is holding Glazunov back, he may be referring tactfully to Glazunov's use of the techniques employed by the Nationalist composers. He may well have detected that Glazunov was not yet entirely himself in the music he was writing.

Chaikovsky's point that Glazunov may in fact have been developing according to the 'demands' of his own 'nature' seems insightful. Perhaps, in the end, it was really the marked difference in their temperaments that led to Chaikovsky's perception of Glazunov as a 'puzzle': at the risk of oversimplifying, it could be suggested that the Dionysian personality of Chaikovsky was in marked contrast to the Apollonian characteristics of Glazunov's nature.

It is also interesting to note that, in his reply to Chaikovsky, Glazunov wrote, 'Your letter has given me great delight since you express sympathy in it to an extent rarely shown to me by anybody else.'[3] The tone of this remark undermines the assertion that Glazunov had become too self-confident and complacent, as a result of his early success. A typical example of this view was expressed by Gerald Abraham when he suggested that it fell to Glazunov's lot to lead the Nationalist movement in 'its comfortable, self-satisfied slide into ignominious mediocrity'.[4] In fact, his attention to the older composer's comments reveal that Glazunov, far from being 'comfortable' and 'self-satisfied', was deeply grateful for Chaikovsky's interest in his career. Clearly the younger composer was still searching for the way ahead and looking to Chaikovsky for advice and sympathy.

Many years later, Glazunov revealed that he had once asked Chaikovsky what he considered to be the main defects of his (Glazunov's) compositions, to which his friend replied: '… a certain lengthiness and absence of pauses'. Glazunov went on to add that he 'always valued his opinion, and remembered his words. Even in my late work I tried to live by them.'[5] In this respect it can be noted that, in comparison to the Third Symphony, the ideas in the Fourth are presented with much greater economy. Chaikovsky's advice and, more importantly, his example, were already having a beneficial effect on Glazunov's compositions.

In the period between the Third and Fourth Symphonies, he produced a number of short orchestral works that reflect the emergence of his mature style. One of the first is the short tone poem *Spring*, Op. 34, from 1891. The over-elaboration of detail that is apparent in at least some of the later parts of the Third Symphony is completely absent from this exceptionally beautiful piece. As M. D. Calvocoressi observes, it 'has a charm quite its own'.[6] Glazunov was inspired by a poem of Fyodor Tyutchev and, with its delicate evocation of spring breezes and bird calls, it conveys the wonderful freshness of the Russian spring, following the long, harsh winter. The translucent orchestral textures, compact structure and free flowing lyricism reveal the true essence of Glazunov's musical personality.

A very different world is evoked in the brilliant *Carnaval Overture*, Op. 45, with its driving rhythms and dancing melodies. The use of a solo organ in the work's reflective middle section, with its suggestion of gentle melancholy at the heart of the festivities, is an imaginative touch. This piece was clearly a favourite with Sir Henry Wood, as he conducted twenty performances of it at the Promenade Concerts between 1897 and 1940. Glazunov was perhaps unfortunate, however, in that he wrote his *Carnaval Overture* in 1892, only a year after Dvořák produced his masterpiece with the same title. Even so, Glazunov's overture is certainly worthy of revival, as it is a vivid and entertaining piece, overflowing with melody and high spirits.

In the same year, thanks to the advocacy of Chaikovsky, Glazunov received a commission for an orchestral march to be played at the opening of the Chicago Exposition of 1893. Chaikovsky was originally approached to fulfil the request but when he declined, he recommended Glazunov in his place. This thoughtful gesture provided the younger composer with a useful opportunity to make his name better known in the New World. The *Triumphal March* for orchestra and chorus (ad lib), Op. 40, combines an elegant theme, in Glazunov's best cortège manner, with the famous American song, *John Brown's Body*. Although no more than an occasional piece, Glazunov orchestrates these contrasting themes, with some colourful writing for woodwind and brass, before bringing them together at the climax of the march. He was no doubt gratified to learn that, when it was performed at the opening ceremony of the Exposition at 3pm on Wednesday, 7 June, it was very well received by the American public.[7]

Working with an American theme was a novelty for Glazunov but, from childhood, he had been acquainted with the music of Chopin. His affection for the Polish master is reflected in his next orchestral work, the *Chopiniana Suite*, Op. 46, consisting of orchestrations of four pieces by Chopin: the *Polonaise* in A, Op. 40 No. 1, the *Nocturne* in F, Op. 15 No. 1, the *Mazurka* in D minor, Op. 50 No. 3 and the *Tarentelle* in A, Op. 43. While any attempt to orchestrate such quintessentially refined piano music is unlikely to meet with approval in all circles, it was a project that absorbed Glazunov and he certainly valued this composition highly. Later, in 1908, Michel Fokine used the suite for a ballet of the same name, having asked Glazunov to orchestrate an additional item: Chopin's W*altz* in C sharp minor, Op. 64 No. 2.[8]

Bearing in mind his admiration for Chopin and Chaikovsky, it is hardly surprising that Glazunov became increasingly interested in creating music associated with the dance. In particular, it is noticeable how many waltzes he wrote in 1892-3. The orchestral Concert Waltz No. 1 in D, Op. 47, is a beautifully crafted work with memorable themes and an appealing elegance. If César Cui was still concerned about the quality of Glazunov's melodic invention then surely this infectiously attractive sequence of waltzes would have put his mind at rest. In addition to the stylish orchestration, the skill with which Glazunov spins variations on the principal melody marks out this Concert Waltz as a superior example of the genre.

Nowhere is his interest in the waltz more apparent during the early years of the 1890s, however, than in his piano music. The Little Waltz in D, Op. 36 of 1892, was followed, in 1893, by the Grand Concert Waltz in E flat, Op. 41, the Salon Waltz in C, Op. 43 and the Three Miniatures (Pastorale, Polka and Waltz), Op. 42. In the shorter waltzes Glazunov evokes, with great refinement, the world of the cultivated salon at the end of the nineteenth century before that milieu was swept away by war and revolution. The Grand Concert Waltz, as its title suggests, is a much more substantial piece. The wonderful way in which, from modest beginnings, the waltz grows and develops, becoming increasingly more elaborate and animated, is very characteristic of Glazunov's mature style.

Chamber music also continued to receive his attention in the period leading up to the Fourth Symphony. In 1891 he wrote the short, reflective piece *In modo religioso*, Op. 38, for Brass Quartet and, in 1892, the String Quintet, in A Major, Op. 39. Glazunov followed the example of Boccherini and Schubert, in adding a second cello to the standard string quartet, although his decision may also have been influenced by Borodin, who used the same combination in his String Quintet in F minor.

Glazunov's Quintet is a sunny composition, belonging to the spontaneous and good-natured world of Belyayev's chamber music evenings. At the same time, he demonstrates considerable skill in the way that textures and moods are contrasted throughout the work. After the richly scored *Allegro* of the first movement, for example, the listener's ear is refreshed by a Scherzo which employs delicate pizzicato. Then the rather plaintive and yearning quality of the third movement, *Andante sostenuto,* is offset by the energetic melody of the Finale. The lyrical theme which appears later in this movement is perhaps the loveliest in the whole work. Overall the grasp of balance and proportion in this piece is particularly impressive.

One significant consequence of Glazunov's rapid development as a composer was his close association with musicians of the older generation. In time, this would lead to his gradual isolation in the musical world but, even at this stage in his career, the premature death of Borodin had already robbed him of a valued friend and colleague. Another unexpected loss was to follow in 1893 when Chaikovsky died after contracting cholera.

Not long before his death, Chaikovsky confirmed his respect for Glazunov's talent when he mentioned him in an interview with the *Petersburg Gazette*:

> We have a great many talented young composers in Russia at the present time. Here in Petersburg there's Glazunov, in Moscow there are Arensky, Davydov (the nephew of our celebrated cellist), Rakhmaninov, who has written a splendid opera based on Pushkin's *The Gypsies*.[9]

When Chaikovsky came to St Petersburg to conduct the first performance of his Symphony No. 6 in B minor, Glazunov, Rimsky-Korsakov and Stasov were in the audience. After the concert Glazunov accompanied Chaikovsky to Palkin's restaurant. In the cab on their way there, as Glazunov later recollected, Chaikovsky 'complained bitterly' that his symphony 'had not been much of a success and that the musicians seemed to dislike it.' Glazunov observed that Chaikovsky 'always tended to be disappointed after the first performance of his works, but this time he was pleased with his offspring.'[10]

At Palkin's restaurant they dined with a group of leading figures from Belyayev's set, including Blumenfeld and Lyadov, as well as the music critic Herman Laroche. On 20 October/1 November, Glazunov again met up with Chaikovsky when the latter was dining at Leiner's restaurant. Vladimir Napravnik provides an account of the conversation between the two composers, revealing the musical bond that existed between them:

> Alexander Glazunov joined our table and spoke to Pyotr Ilyich about his most recent work, sketching several chords on a scrap of paper to show their resolution. Fascinated with the conversation, Pyotr Ilyich for his part also sketched several examples of especially interesting aural combinations.[11]

Chaikovsky then invited some of his friends, including Glazunov, to visit him the next day. When Glazunov arrived late on the following afternoon, however, he found that Chaikovsky was very unwell and asked to be left alone. After much suffering, the great composer died on 25 October/6 November. Glazunov would never forget Chaikovsky who, in his opinion, 'always conducted himself with great dignity and confidence'.[12]

It is possible that the chords Glazunov showed Chaikovsky at their meeting in Leiner's restaurant came from his Symphony No. 4, in E flat major, Op. 48, for with this work Glazunov appeared, without question, as a mature symphonist.

Completed on 22 November/4 December 1893, its first performance, under the direction of Rimsky-Korsakov, soon followed on 10/22 January 1894. Dedicated to Anton Rubinstein, the structure of the work is somewhat unusual in that it is cast in three movements, the first and the third of which are preceded by slow introductions. It opens in E flat minor with a long-breathed melody of great beauty, played on the cor anglais, before it is taken up by the strings. This then leads to the main body of the allegro with a lively new theme, supported by syncopated rhythms. As the movement unfolds Glazunov develops all the ideas-including the opening melody, in a speeded-up version. The music has something of a pastoral atmosphere, with many woodwind solos, sometimes supported by a solo horn and Glazunov provides a strong sense of structural unity by ending the movement with the original melody and tempo of the introduction.

The short central movement is a delightfully scored Scherzo, with fleet-footed rhythms that suggest a hunting scene. The following trio is a fast waltz, in which the main theme on the strings is offset by some particularly delicate woodwind figuration. Full of sunshine, this Scherzo provides an excellent contrast to the two substantial, and thoroughly worked out, movements that surround it.

The slow introduction to the Finale creates a hushed, expectant atmosphere and, indeed, it soon leads to a lively burst of fanfares which herald the main body of the movement. What is truly impressive here is the way in which Glazunov draws the entire symphony together, by developing not only the new ideas introduced in the Finale but also by recalling all the melodies from the first two movements as well. His ability to explore his ideas afresh, by constantly finding out interesting new variations and combinations, is intriguing and exciting. He is no longer prepared to provide a simple succession of lively dance tunes, as he had done, for example, in the First Symphony. This is all accomplished with a wonderful sense of exhilaration and it represents a new high point in Glazunov's symphonic development. His achievement is well summed up by Mundy when he writes:

> The result is a symphony with the emphasis on thoughtful and thorough thematic development, with only a brief period of light relief at the centre. It not only shows Glazunov being considerably more daring with form than he had been in the past, it also suggests that the compositional process was something he was now taking less for granted.[13]

Glazunov's productivity in the 1890s is truly remarkable. In 1894, for example, he composed orchestral works of a contrasting nature. Some of these pieces are of a celebratory or a balletic character, such as the *Cortège Solennelle*, Op. 50, a tribute to his friend Vladimir Stasov, the *Concert Waltz No. 2* in F, Op. 51, dedicated to the conductor Nikolai Galkin and the orchestral suite *Scènes de Ballet*, Op. 52, inscribed to the orchestra of the Imperial Russian Opera. This suite is made up of eight movements. Following the lively *Preamble*, with its fanfares and jaunty melody, there is some delicate orchestral tracery in the *Marionttes* and *Scherzino* movements, as well as the intensely romantic melody of the *Pas d'Action*. Glazunov also provides some fine examples of the type of dances that were particularly popular in the nineteenth century: *Oriental*, *Mazurka*, *Waltz* and *Polonaise*. This thoroughly engaging suite represents Glazunov at his most genial and spontaneous.

In contrast, the orchestral fantasy *From Darkness Into Light,* Op. 53, dedicated to the great Italian composer and pianist, Ferruccio

Busoni, is a much more searching and thoughtful work, as befits its dedicatee. To make darkness audible, Glazunov presents a winding, chromatic theme in the lower registers of the orchestra. This rises to a powerful climax before the transition to light, represented by expansive diatonic melodies. Chromaticism is finally banished and the work ends resplendently in C major. With its effective use of contrast in harmony, melody and orchestration, this is one of the most striking of Glazunov's tone poems.

A similar movement from darkness into light is also apparent in his String Quartet No. 4 in A minor, Op. 64. In this work he strikes an altogether more serious note, in comparison to the earlier string quartets. Indeed, this struck Stasov so forcefully when Glazunov played the opening of the quartet to him on the piano, that he exclaimed, "'This is a cry of despair! What's happened with you?' Glazunov replied that he had 'composed the quartet under the impression of gloomy memories'."[14]

As Calvocoressi explains, Glazunov was attempting something new in terms of his compositional method here:

> In the fourth quartet (op. 64) he resorts, not to simple theme-transformations in the Lisztian manner, but to the 'cyclic' methods of the Frank-D'Indy school, according to which most of the themes are derived from a germ-cell or germ-cells given in the exposition of the opening movement.[15]

The solemn, pensive chords which open the quartet provide Glazunov with the 'germ cell' from which much of the work is derived. In the first movement, in particular, he achieves a greater degree of concentrated musical thought than hitherto, deriving some striking ideas from his opening cluster of chords, such as when the theme is presented by the use of double stopping in all four instruments to create a rich chordal texture and, in contrast, the delicate dance-like variation which appears later in the movement.[16]

The following *Andante* is essentially song-like in character, with ideas that are graceful and tinged with a gentle melancholy. The references to the theme from the first movement, moreover, help to maintain the work's unity and to highlight, yet again, the sheer inventiveness with which Glazunov handles his original material. The third movement, a Scherzo, marked *Vivace*, is one of Glazunov's most virtuosic, with its propulsive semi-quavers, and displaced accents. As Gerald Abraham notes, 'The scherzo is, incidentally, one of the most brilliant pieces of quartet-scoring ever written.'[17]

The Finale, marked *Allegro*, begins with the return of the pensive mood of the quartet's opening, before providing a further examination of the work's central 'germ cell'. This is not entirely on the same level as the other three movements, as the ideas derived here from the opening chords of the work are not as arresting. However, even allowing for the fact that the Finale fails to achieve the high level of creativity found in the other movements of the quartet, Glazunov produced, as Calvocoressi says, a work that is 'the genuine article' and a significant contribution to nineteenth century Russian chamber music.

Glazunov spent the summer months of 1895 in Germany, visiting Berlin, Leipzig, Dresden and Wiesbaden. Work on the Fifth Symphony, which had started in April, continued during his time in Germany but he also managed to do some sightseeing. The great cathedral of Cologne made a particularly strong impression on him.[18] During his time in Dresden he heard Beethoven's *Fidelio,* in addition to three operas by Wagner from the Ring Cycle: *Das Rheingold, Die Walkure* and *Siegfried.*

While Glazunov was in Germany, the tenth anniversary of the founding of Belyayev's publishing house occurred on 20 June/ 2 July, and, as a token of his gratitude to Belyayev, he sent the manuscript of a celebratory march, the *Cortège Solennelle* for piano, four hands, to a friend in St Petersburg, with the instruction that it should be delivered to Belyayev on the anniversary day.

The composition of the Symphony No. 5 in B flat major, Op. 55, sometimes referred to as the *Heroic*, was completed on his return to Russia and its first performance took place at the second Russian Symphony Concert on 5/17 February, in St Petersburg, with the composer conducting. It is dedicated to Sergey Taneyev, who was greatly admired both as a concert pianist, and as a master of counterpoint. Taneyev had been the Director of the Moscow Conservatory from 1885–89 and he was still a Professor of Counterpoint there when Glazunov became friendly with him. Initially the two men must have seemed to their contemporaries to be following radically different musical paths, with Glazunov representing St Petersburg and Nationalism, while Taneyev stood for Moscow and Cosmopolitanism. In time, Chaikovsky proved to be a link between the two men and Taneyev started to receive advice on orchestration from Glazunov, while Glazunov benefited from examining Taneyev's rigorous approach to the art of composition.[19]

This view is supported by Engel, when he writes of the Fifth Symphony, drawing attention to the 'calm, mature simplicity of its general plan and the mastery of its execution'.[20] There is, indeed, a tautness in the structure of the first movement, and an inventiveness in the development of its melodies, that make it particularly arresting. It is also one of the most joyful and spirited movements in his entire symphonic output.

In the Scherzo which follows, Glazunov's attention to contrasting sonorities is illustrated by his use of delicate textures, dominated by woodwind instruments. The lightness of touch here, which extends to the sparkling trio, is particularly effective coming after the resonant climax of the first movement.

Glazunov then reverts to a warmly scored sound world in the following *Andante.* Ushered in by the rich tones of the orchestral strings, this movement contains a beautiful and heartfelt theme, tinged with melancholy, which nonetheless rises to moments of expressive intensity. The lyrical flow of the music is interrupted in places, however, by abrupt brass chords – the telling juxtaposition of these elements adding significantly to the impact of the movement.

The following *Allegro Maestoso* finale represents Glazunov at his most extrovert. His skill in building up varying rhythmic patterns, helps to generate a thrilling sense of momentum as the movement unfolds. In this respect, it provides a contrast to the more loosely structured finales of the Second and Third Symphonies. Indeed, Glazunov's control of his ideas throughout the work suggest that he was approaching the pinnacle of his career as a composer.

His status as an important figure in the Russian cultural world was acknowledged by a commission which he received in 1895 to write a Cantata for the Coronation of Tsar Nicholas II. The new Tsar was crowned in Moscow's Assumption Cathedral on 14/26 May 1896 and Glazunov's Cantata for soloists, chorus and orchestra, Op. 56, was performed that same day in the Granovitaya Palace, in the presence of the royal family, leading officials and eminent foreign guests. The Tsar appears to have approved of the composition. To a text by Krylov, the Cantata is divided into seven sections. The best movements are probably the opening and closing choruses and the tenor aria, *A Prayer*. Elsewhere, the imagination and skill of Glazunov's instrumentation is unfortunately offset by the somewhat banal nature of the vocal writing. This is particularly true of the sixth movement, *Heaven and Earth*.

1896 also saw Glazunov engaged with what would prove to be two of his finest works: the three-act ballet, *Raymonda*, and the Sixth Symphony. Referring to these compositions, Rimsky-Korsakov, a man not given to exaggeration, observes that Glazunov: 'had by this time reached the gorgeous flowering of his enormous talent... His imagination as well as his astounding technique had attained at this time the highest point of their development.'[21]

Work on the ballet would not be completed until later in 1897, but his status as the most important Russian symphonist, following the death of Chaikovsky, was consolidated on 8/20 February of that year with the first performance of his Symphony No. 6 in C minor, Op. 58, at

Glazunov, with a quotation from the String Quintet, dated 1896

a Russian Symphony Concert in St Petersburg. It is dedicated to his friend, Felix Blumenfeld (1863–1931), who was a leading member of the Belyayev group, and a composer, pianist and conductor of note.

Together with the Fourth and Fifth Symphonies, the Sixth Symphony represents the fulfilment of the promise that Glazunov had shown earlier in his career. Havergal Brian, captures the essence of the first movement when he explains how:

> From the opening theme in the 'cellos and basses, the composer fixes the attention of the listener, never allowing it to flag. Thus is created the impression of a single-minded achievement: the very shape of the bass theme offers inexhaustible opportunities to a craftsman such as Glazounoff.[22]

The slow introduction contains both of the strongly contrasted main themes of the movement. Marked *misterioso,* it creates a sense of latent tension which is released in the following *Allegro passionato;* here the ebb and flow of the musical argument generates real power, as both themes are developed in a resourceful manner.

The second movement, one of the composer's most beautiful, creates variety by immediately establishing an atmosphere of calm reflection after the powerful conclusion of the *Allegro passionato*. Marked *Andante*, it consists of a theme of touching simplicity, followed by a series of seven vividly characterised variations: 1. *Allegretto moderato*, in which the theme is accompanied by chromatic harmonies; 2. *Allegretto*, with the oboe providing a rhythmically altered variant; 3. a *Scherzino*, consisting of a lively variation in 6/8 time, featuring the flute; 4. a *Fugato*, which introduces darker tones with mysteriously evolving counterpoint, leading to 5. the hushed beauty of a *Nocturne*, enhanced by the rich tones of the clarinet and strings; 6. is characterised by rapidly oscillating figures in the violins and violas, before the final variation 7. a *Finale,* featuring the brass section, the theme being transformed this time into an imposing chorale. The subdued ending leads into the third movement, *Intermezzo*.

As the second movement contains some fast, scherzo-like variations, Glazunov's *Intermezzo,* marked *Allegretto,* is more like a courtly dance from the eighteenth century – as seen through late nineteenth century eyes. Its refined orchestration, including the delicate instrumentation of the trio section, is genuinely charming while at the same time ensuring that the imposing unison opening of the Finale creates maximum impact.

In this Finale, Glazunov adopts the form of double variation, so that the two main themes alternate with each other, appearing in different guises throughout thc movement. In particular he exploits a favourite device, one that involves the deployment of a wide range of time signatures, so that the rhythmic pattern of the themes is always evolving. As in the first movement, the musical argument is free from any superfluous detail and so builds convincingly towards a triumphant conclusion. Glazunov has succeeded here in providing an imposing finale of sufficient power to balance the intense opening movement.

The new symphony made a strong impression on Rimsky-Korsakov who described it as 'wonderful'. As Chaikovsky suspected, Glazunov had indeed developed along the lines determined by his own creative nature and, as a result, he was able to make a rich and distinctive contribution to the evolution of the Russian symphony.

Just over a month after the first performance of his Sixth Symphony, Glazunov was involved in another premiere – this time as the conductor of Rachmaninoff's First Symphony in D minor.[23] This was a major event in the young Moscow composer's life and the failure of the performance left Rachmaninoff open to a vicious critical assault. This came in the form of a press review written by a characteristically acerbic Cui who, still fighting the battles of the past, started his review with the following remarks: 'If there's a conservatory in Hell, and one of its gifted pupils should be given the problem of writing a programmatic symphony on the Seven Plagues of Egypt, and if he should write a symphony resembling Mr Rachmaninoff's, his problem would have been carried out brilliantly…'[24]

This had a traumatic effect upon Rachmaninoff and it would be several years before his creativity revived. Writing to a friend, A. V. Zatayevich, in the aftermath of the premiere, he made the following observations:

> 'I am amazed – how can a man with the high talent of Glazunov conduct so badly? I speak not merely of his conducting technique (there's no use asking this of him), but of his musicianship. He feels nothing when he conducts – as if he understands nothing! … So I assume that the performance may have been the cause of the failure (I do not assert – I assume).'[25]

In the long run, it is Glazunov's reputation that has suffered more than that of Rachmaninoff, as a consequence of this performance. This is not so much because of what Rachmaninoff wrote – notice that even at the height of his depression following the symphony's performance, he expresses himself in a cautious manner – but because his wife, Natalia Alexandrovna, later claimed that Glazunov was drunk when he conducted the concert. Indeed, it would seem that this supposition has taken on the status of an established fact. It is therefore worth considering the matter in a little more detail.

That Glazunov conducted a poor performance is not in doubt. Rachmaninoff's view is confirmed, for example, by the critic Nikolai Findeisen who noted that the Symphony 'was not very successfully interpreted'.[26] At the same time, had the work received an excellent performance, it is perfectly possible that Cui would still have produced a negative review, as his hostility to composers who did not belong to the Nationalist circle was well known. In addition, it is important to note that not all of the critics reacted in such a negative way. For example, Findeisen himself went on to comment in his review that, despite its shortcomings, he found '… much beauty, novelty, and even inspiration' in both the first movement and the finale. Indeed, as he refers to 'the furious finale' in his article, it would seem that the performance must have conveyed at least something of the remarkable strength of this vivid and powerful music.[27]

Glazunov, in common with other members of the Belyayev group, had already been impressed by Rachmaninoff's early tone poem, *The Crag*, and he certainly thought well enough of the symphony, in the first place, to perform it. In a letter to Taneyev, he stated his generally positive opinion of the work: 'I have looked through Rachmaninoff's symphony, have found some slips of the pen, but on the whole I approve [of] it, especially the orchestration.'[28]

In this context, it is worth noting that one of the most successful aspects of the symphony is the skill with which Rachmaninoff develops its principal melody. As thematic transformation formed an important element in many of Glazunov's compositions, he would surely have been appreciative of this aspect of Rachmaninoff's score.

Mundy also makes the point that when Rachmaninoff's wife claimed that Glazunov was drunk, the accusation '…was surely an aspersion cast with hindsight. In later years he did indeed have a drink problem, but in 1897 he was at the height of his professional powers.'[29] It is just possible that Natalia Alexandrovna's claim may have been prompted by the fact that there would no doubt have been a good deal of drinking *after* the concert at the celebratory dinner that Belyayev had organised to honour Rachmaninoff.[30] Drinking after a concert, sometimes into the small hours of the morning, was a fairly common practice, as we have noted when Glazunov and Lyadov joined Chaikovsky to drink in a restaurant until three o'clock in the morning.

The absence of sufficient rehearsal time is in fact much more likely to have produced a poor performance rather than drunkenness on Glazunov's part. This problem was exacerbated by the presence on the same programme of another premiere – the *Valse-Fantasia* of Nikolai Artsybushev – in addition to a performance of Chaikovsky's tone poem *Fatum* which had not been heard since 1869.[31] Taking over a quarter of an hour in performance, *Fatum* therefore represented a third score with which the orchestra was unfamiliar. Glazunov revered Chaikovsky and, following the latter's death, he made efforts to reintroduce works by his old friend that had fallen into neglect. He had, for example, given the premiere, in 1896, of Chaikovsky's early overture *The Storm*, and the appearance of certain works by Chaikovsky in the M. P. Belaieff catalogue at this time must in part be due to Glazunov's influence. It seems highly improbable that he would have given anything other than his full attention to the performance of a work by Chaikovsky.

It is also worthwhile bearing in mind that Glazunov was extremely fond of conducting. This, of course, on its own, does not mean that he was talented in this sphere but it does undermine any suggestion that he approached the task with carelessness or indifference. The distinguished Russian conductor, Nikolai Malko, who had Rimsky-Korsakov, Lyadov and Glazunov as his teachers at the St Petersburg Conservatory, left some revealing anecdotes in his memoirs:

> And Glazounov loved, so very much, to conduct. He was not a professional conductor, but when he led the orchestra there was always something valuable to be gained from the point of view of conducting. Performing his own compositions he could impart to the orchestra precisely that which was characteristic of the work, and it would reach the musicians and through them the listener. When he conducted the works of other composers it was not interesting.[32]

Malko goes on to recount how, some years later, students from the St Petersburg Conservatory approached Glazunov simply to ask him for permission to hold a party in one of the Conservatory's halls. When they explained to Glazunov that there would be dancing – with a small orchestra and a conductor – he immediately replied, 'I accept'. The students had not expected the Director of the Conservatory to conduct their dance band but it is significant to observe the alacrity with which Glazunov responded to the idea.

Although the failure of Rachmaninoff's Symphony inevitably resulted in a period of strain in the relationship of the two composers, it did not lead to a complete breach. That same year Rachmaninoff completed a transcription, for piano duet, of Glazunov's Sixth Symphony. Moreover, Geoffrey Norris notes that, in 1906, Rachmaninoff 'was keen to perform' Glazunov's recently completed Eighth Symphony[33] and, in 1911, when Rachmaninoff gave a recital at the St Petersburg Conservatory, Glazunov warmly thanked him for his performance and suggested that all studies should be suspended for the rest of the day because a concert by Rachmaninoff was equivalent to a visit by a member of the Imperial family.[34] Later, in 1926, Rachmaninoff was responsible for greetings sent to Glazunov on his sixtieth birthday, much to the latter's delight.[35]

Their connection was still in evidence in the 1930s. The violinist Nathan Milstein attended a party after one of Rachmaninoff's concerts in Paris, and recollected that Rachmaninoff's 'friends were all there: the composers Glazunov, Medtner, Grechaninov…'[36]

Milstein also quotes Rachmaninoff referring to Glazunov as 'Sasha', the diminutive of his name, which would be used in conversation between friends. It seems then that, despite the setback of the D minor Symphony's premiere, the two men maintained a friendly and respectful association. In the short term, however, Rachmaninoff's creativity would experience a hiatus of a number of years, while Glazunov's music continued to spread his fame abroad.

Chapter five

1897–99: Ballet years

In 1897 Glazunov was invited to appear as a conductor in England for the first time. His Fifth Symphony had been introduced to a London audience, on 30 January, by Henry Wood and five months later Glazunov made his English début, conducting his Fourth Symphony.

The Musical Times, as Gerald Norris observes, had 'been subjected to rather more Russian music than it was prepared to stomach'. As a result, its review of Glazunov's Fourth Symphony is somewhat patronising, the music critic claiming to have a slight preference for the Fourth Symphony over the Fifth as, in his opinion, it sounded less Russian![1]

What the review reveals, interestingly, is that Glazunov is being judged on his reputation as a follower of the Mighty Handful. The reviewer appears totally unaware of the change that had occurred in Glazunov's style since the composition of his earlier works such as *Stenka Razin* and *The Kremlin*. It is also noticeable that he is completely unprepared to acknowledge the existence of beauty and craftsmanship in the Fourth Symphony when, in fact, the work's overall musical design is as sophisticated as anything produced by contemporary Western European composers. In truth it would not have mattered what Glazunov had written: he was considered to be a Russian of the Nationalist School and, as a consequence, *The Musical Times* had decided it was not going to be impressed.

To put these comments into context, it is revealing to note that the same journal was very dismissive of other important Russian works including Musorgsky's *Night on Bald Mountain,* Borodin's Second Symphony and Rimsky-Korsakov's *Sheherazade.*[2] Despite such opposition, Glazunov's music continued to be played in England, with another of the most admired conductors of the day, Hans Richter, introducing the Sixth Symphony, on 29 May 1899. This was the first of ten performances that Richter gave of this symphony during his career.[3]

Meanwhile, on his return to Russia, Glazunov continued to work on his first ballet, *Raymonda*.

The origin of the commission which he received to compose a ballet for the Imperial Theatres dates back to 1896 when, nine days after his *Coronation Cantata* was performed, there was another celebratory event at which the Tsar's orchestra played a waltz by Glazunov. In the audience on that occasion was Ivan Vsevolozhsky, the Director of Imperial Theatres. He was impressed by the waltz and wrote to the leading choreographer of the Mariyinsky Theatre, Marius Petipa, that Glazunov 'was born to compose ballets for us'.[4]

At that stage they already had the scenario for a new ballet called *Raymonda*. Set in the Middle Ages, at the time of the Crusades, it had been submitted to them by the writer, Lydia Pashkova. Glazunov worked on the ballet throughout 1897, following closely the instructions he received from the legendary Petipa, a Frenchman whose career at the Mariyinsky had started as long ago as 1847 when he appeared as a dancer. By 1858 Petipa had graduated to staging ballets and his influence on future generations of choreographers was profound. Most importantly, Petipa had worked with Chaikovsky on his last two ballets, *The Sleeping Beauty* and *The Nutcracker*, in which the music was on a far higher level than had previously been the case in Russian ballets and clearly Petipa and Vsevolozhsky felt that Glazunov could continue this significant trend. Jennifer Homans expresses this point well when she writes of Vsevolozhsky's influence on the direction of the famous choreographer's craft: 'he pried the ballet master away from Minkus and the predictable rhythms of made-to-order ballet music and pushed him toward the far more complex and Russian voices of Tchaikovsky and (later) Alexander Glazunov.'[5]

The highly romantic nature of the ballet, very much a product of the late nineteenth century, is readily revealed by a synopsis of the plot:

Act One, scene I, *La fête de Raymonda*, takes place in the castle of the splendidly named Countess Sybil de Doris. A birthday celebration is being held in honour of her niece, Raymonda, who is awaiting the return of her fiancé, Jean de Brienne, from the Crusades. The Countess explains to Raymonda that the statue in the garden is of the White Lady, who is acknowledged as the guardian of the family.

In the second scene, *Visions*, Raymonda falls asleep and dreams of her betrothed. However, her dream suddenly takes on a troubling character as the image of de Brienne is replaced by that of a Saracen knight. Raymonda awakens, alarmed by the nature of her dream.

In Act Two, *Cour d'Amour*, guests arrive at the castle in anticipation of the return of Jean de Brienne from the Crusades. Raymonda notices with alarm that amongst them is the Saracen knight from her dream. He is Abderakhman and it is immediately clear that, deeply in love with Raymonda, he intends to win her for himself. He orders his retinue, which includes jugglers, Arab boys, Saracens and Spanish dancers, to entertain Raymonda in a series of brilliant dances. Raymonda rejects his advances and, just at the point when Abderakhman is about to abduct her, Jean de Brienne arrives, accompanied by King Andrew II of Hungary. The King decides that the dispute between Raymonda's two lovers should be settled by single combat and, in the duel that follows, de Brienne is victorious, aided by an appearance of the White Lady.

The Third Act, *Le Festival de Noces*, is a celebration of the wedding of Jean de Brienne and Raymonda. The presence of King Andrew explains the range of Hungarian dances and variations that make up the act. The ballet's premiere took place on 7/19 January 1898, with Pierina Legnani in the title role, Sergey Legat as Jean de Brienne and Pavel Gerdt as Abderakhman. The conductor was the vastly experienced Riccardo Drigo.

Commenting on the plot of the ballet, Alexander Benois observes that the problem with *Raymonda* rests with 'the absurdity of the subject, of which nobody could ever make head or tail'.[6] Indeed, there is even an anecdote in Nikolai Malko's memoirs which might suggest that the confusion over the story extended to the ballet's choreographer and composer:

> Glazounov once asked Petipa, 'Do you know the plot of *Raymonda*?'
> 'No,' Petipa answered. 'Do you?'
> 'No,' Glazounov said, 'I don't either.'[7]

The significance of what is almost certainly a joke being shared by Glazunov and Petipa, however, should not be overemphasised. If there is a lack of clarity in the unfolding of the drama, it really only affects Act One – and probably centres on the appearance and significance of the White Lady rather than any other aspect of the scenario. Acts Two and Three are surely entirely comprehensible to audiences who are likely, in any case, to be more than familiar with the plot devices found in the ballets of Chaikovsky.

The enduring strength of the work is confirmed by the fact that *Raymonda* has continued to be a repertory piece for leading companies such as the Bolshoi and the Mariyinsky, from the time of its premiere up to the present day. A continuing fascination with the ballet is reflected in the number of different versions produced by some of the leading dancers and choreographers of the twentieth century, including George Balanchine, Rudolf Nureyev and Yuri Grigorovich. In particular there have been attempts to integrate the two male dancers more fully into the action. In the production presented by the Teatro alla Scala, Milan in 2011, however, Sergej Vikharev revived the choreography and staging of the original version, presenting Glazunov's score in full, with all the numbers in the correct order. The magnificence of this production should leave no doubt as to why *Raymonda* was an outstanding success for Petipa and Glazunov when it was first performed at the Mariyinsky Theatre in 1898.[8]

In fairness to Pashkova, and her exotic story, it must also be acknowledged that the scenario did appeal to Glazunov's imagination and it inspired him to compose some of his most melodious, colourful and vibrant music. The way, for example, in which the introduction to Act One unfolds and grows from its quiet beginning, reveals that the confident hand of a master of symphonic music is at work here. Glazunov also brings a rich Wagnerian harmony to movements such as the two *Entr'actes symphonic* at the end of Act One and the beginning of Act Three. Mention must also be made of the two great waltzes in Act One: the exhilarating *Grande Valse* and, in contrast, the delicate and atmospheric *Valse fantastique*.

In Act Two, the Grand Adagio, in which Abderakhman declares his love for Raymonda, contains music of great nobility, beauty and passion. It is also very evident that Glazunov was in his element when writing the dances for Abderakhman's retinue and, characteristically, he avoids simply repeating these themes when the dancers return in the *Bacchanal* towards the end of the Act, supplying, instead, a series of variations that help to create an atmosphere of increasing excitement. The resolution of Act Two, *Denouement et final*, in which the prominent fanfare theme from earlier in the ballet is combined with Jean de Brienne's theme, provides one of the great moments in Romantic ballet, the diatonic nature of the two melodies reasserting control over the more chromatic harmonies associated with Abderakhman which have hitherto characterised much of the Act.[9] In this way, the composer demonstrates his ability to shape the entire Act into a coherent musical unit, rather than simply providing a collection of attractive individual dances.

The *Entr'acte* to Act Three, as mentioned above, is dominated by a richly scored melody that introduces a series of lively dances in the Hungarian style. The virile rhythms of numbers such as the *Le cortège hongrois* and the *Danse des enfants* is successfully contrasted with the more melancholy and lyrical *Pas classique hongrois*, with its beautiful cor anglais solo, and *Variation IV* for Raymonda, in which the solo piano is used to suggest the rhythmic patterns characteristic of the cimbalon. The work's glowing apotheosis returns to the music which introduced the Act, with a final reference to the fanfare theme to provide a fitting peroration.

The great dancer and choreographer, George Balanchine wrote that 'Glazunov's music for *Raymonda* contains some of the finest ballet music we have.' Having danced, as one of the Arab boys, in Petipa's original version of the work, he went on to create two attractive ballets based on the Hungarian music from Act Three. Of the first, *Pas de Dix* (1955), he wrote, 'The music for this dance for ten (two principals plus four girls and four boys) is taken from a ballet score I have always liked since my student days in Russia, Glazunov's *Raymonda.*'[10]

Balanchine returned to the ballet once more with his *Raymonda Variations* (1961) and again his affection for Glazunov's score is clear in his comment that the 'music itself, its grand and generous manner, its joy and playfulness, was for me more than enough to carry the plot of the dances'.[11] Malko also pays *Raymonda* a great compliment when he describes the work as the 'queen of all ballets'[12] while Jennifer Homans writes of Glazunov's 'gorgeously Russian-inflected music'.[13]

After the successful premiere of *Raymonda*, Glazunov set about preparing a Suite from the ballet, which was published as his Opus 57a. Petipa was also highly pleased with the outcome of their first collaboration and so, with Glazunov in mind, he went on to create the scenario for a one-act ballet called *Ruses d'amour*. Set in the aristocratic world of eighteenth century France, it was inspired by the paintings of Watteau.

The plot, divided into eleven scenes, is very straightforward. The young and wealthy Duchess Isabelle has been betrothed from childhood to the far from wealthy Marquis Damise. They have never met and so, on hearing of his arrival, Isabelle decides to test his true feelings for her by swapping costumes with her serving maid, Marinette. Fulfilling the requirements of a favourite plot device, Damise falls in love with the disguised Isabelle and proposes that they elope. The truth of Isabelle's identity is then revealed and all ends happily.

As Alexander Benois writes, 'In *Ruses d'Amour* the eighteenth-century subject is graceful, but too light to be moving.'[14] This comment may stand as a reasonable overall assessment of the ballet, although the lightness of touch, apparent in the work's orchestration, is intelligently adapted to the stylised nature of the scenario. It is also worth observing that the historical setting of the ballet allowed Glazunov to compose dances characteristic of an earlier age: *Gavotte with Musette*, *Sarabande* and *Farandole*. This is something that clearly appealed to him, as he created examples of dances from the Baroque period from the very start of his career: a *Sarabande* for piano was one of his first attempts at composition. He also wrote a *Courante* for string quartet which he contributed to the music played at Belyayev's Friday gatherings, and a *Gavotte* for piano, Op. 49, No. 3. Glazunov's fondness for this type of movement may even have given a few hints to Prokofiev who, in turn, brought his own highly distinctive style to the genre.[15]

The sparkling orchestration of the scene with marionettes provides another noteworthy aspect of the score. Glazunov adapted this from his *Scènes de Ballet* suite and with piccolo, flutes, celeste, violin trills, harp, bells and triangle, it creates the kind of glittering orchestral texture that is more often associated with his friend, Lyadov. The *Grande Valse*, of scene eight, must also be one of the composer's most insouciant, while the *Grande pas de Fiancés*, in the form of a duo for violin and cello, contains music of great delicacy and refinement.

The premiere of *Ruses d'amour,* Op. 61, took place on 4/17 February 1900 at the Hermitage Theatre, to be followed on 7/21 February by the first performance of his last ballet, *The Seasons*, Op. 67.[16] Dedicated to Petipa, *The Seasons* has no plot to speak of, as Petipa had created a series of four tableaux in which the contrasting attributes of the seasons appear in turn.

Winter is introduced first with widely spaced chords between the woodwind, brass and strings, to create an atmosphere of frozen stillness before the principal theme is heard. Delicately scored dances then follow, representing *Frost*, *Ice*, *Hail* and *Snow*, the latter represented by a short waltz in which the oboe melody is enriched by some characteristic Glazunov counterpoint provided by the solo horn.

The harp is then prominent in the transition to *Spring,* which is ushered in with a lively melody, one which immediately communicates the freshness of the season. The other principal theme in this movement is of a more lyrical nature. First presented by a solo clarinet, the melody is varied and developed before an even richer transition appears to herald the arrival of *Summer*. Glazunov fills out the orchestral texture to convey the increasing warmth of the season.

The quality of Glazunov's melodic invention in this score can be further illustrated by the three themes which are heard at the start of *Summer*: the first melody, depicting a meadow in flower; the waltz of the Cornflowers and Poppies, with its delightful syncopations and counterpoint; and the rich lyricism of the following *Barcarolle*. The movement also contains a virtuosic clarinet solo, representing the *Spirit of the Corn* before the music becomes more agitated, as a group of *Satyrs* and *Fauns* try to capture the *Spirit*, their attempt being frustrated by the *Zephyr*.

Autumn opens with the jubilant *Bacchanal* theme, which is perhaps Glazunov's best-known melody. The movement is in the form of a rondo and, between statements of the *Bacchanal*, the other seasons reappear. Glazunov displays his customary fondness for presenting his ideas in newly imagined forms, by varying the restatements of the themes associated with *Winter*, *Spring* and *Summer*. The *Petit Adagio* which follows memorably encapsulates both the beauty and the bitter-sweet atmosphere of autumn. Glazunov later added the brief movement *The Satyr* which provides an effective transition from the *Adagio* to the final statement of the *Bacchanal* theme, now in a different rhythm. In the final *Apotheosis* the earth is shown surrounded by the constellations of stars.

It is strange that ballet companies seem to neglect this wonderful score, as it would make up an excellent programme, for example, with *The Nutcracker* by Chaikovsky. Nonetheless, the exceptional quality of the music has ensured that it lives on in the concert hall and in many fine recordings. As Robert Letellier writes, 'The music is inventive, fresh, attractive, and beautifully scored throughout.'[17] When the ballet was revived in 1907, *Spring* was danced by the young Anna Pavlova, who would later include *Autumn* in her own programmes. *Autumn* was also successful when it was included in *Une Nuit d'Egypte*, a ballet which Diaghilev concocted for his first Paris Season. It included music by Taneyev, Rimsky-Korsakov, Glinka and, at the suggestion of Alexander Benois, *Autumn* from *The Seasons*. In his *Reminiscences of the Russian Ballet*, Benois writes:

> I cannot refrain from boasting that the last number was my choice. It so happened that I went to see this ballet during the days of preparation for our Paris Season. I had seen it many times before, but on this occasion I especially appreciated the *Autumn Bacchanal*e. Pavlova was divine in it; further, it seemed to me that in the literature of choreographic music there were few pieces so exciting as this work of Glazunov's. The music of *Autumn* used in Paris for our version of *Une Nuit d'Egypte* also illustrated a bacchanale, and the success of that number must be attributed chiefly to the alluring rhythm and the intoxicating themes of the music.[18]

With so much creative energy going into the writing of ballet music it is remarkable that Glazunov found the time to compose in other forms but he did succeed in completing a dozen songs, his most concentrated focus on a genre that was never central to his output.[19] The two sets of

Six Romances, Op. 59 and Op. 60, contain settings of texts by Pushkin, in addition to Petrarch (in Russian translations by Korinfsky), and Maikov. Often reflecting the melancholy aspects of life and love, the best of them have an appealing lyrical quality, as in *The Muse*, and *When Your Eyes Meet Mine* from the Op. 59 set, or *The Nereid* and *Dream* from Op. 60. Glazunov's technical craftsmanship also enables to him maintain a skilful balance between voice and piano.

The years 1898-9 also saw the completion of three choral works: the *Festival Cantata for the Centenary of the Pavlovsk Institute*, Op. 63 (1898), the *Festival Cantata on the Centenary of Pushkin*, Op. 65 (1899), and the *Hymn to Pushkin* (1899), Op. 66. The splendid vigour of the opening chorus of the Pushkin Cantata may well reflect Glazunov's pride in the association between the great poet and the Glazunov family's publishing firm. Commissions, such as these celebratory cantatas, provide further evidence of Glazunov's stature as a major figure in the Russian musical world.

Of far greater musical significance, however, is another work that he composed during the successful first run of *Raymonda*: the String Quartet No. 5 in D minor, Op. 70. In a letter to Belyayev, Glazunov explained the origins of this piece: '… since I was somewhat tired of composing dance music I wanted to get into a completely different area of music. I also wanted to attempt, as much as possible, a purely quartet style, as compared to my first essays in the genre…'[20]

The Fifth Quartet is dedicated to Leopold Auer, the great violinist, who was a Professor at the St Petersburg Conservatory. Without question it is one of Glazunov's finest quartets, occupying a place in his chamber music output similar to that of the Sixth Symphony in his symphonic oeuvre. Cast in the traditional four movements – 1. *Andante-Allegro* 2. Scherzo (*Allegretto*) 3. *Adagio* 4. Finale (*Allegro*) – Glazunov creates a series of telling contrasts. The contrapuntal writing of the serious and expressive first movement is immediately juxtaposed with the playfulness of the Scherzo. The deeply felt Adagio which follows is, in turn, succeeded by the brilliant, perpetual motion of the Finale. As Iosif Raiskin writes, 'The Fifth Quartet is marked by unusual melodic richness, beauty and thematic expressiveness.'[21] It was first performed in St Petersburg on 30 December 1899/11 January 1900, as part of a quartet concert given by the Russian Music Society.

In 1899 Glazunov wrote another piece of a similarly serious nature, this time for the piano – his Prelude and Fugue in D minor, Op. 62. Dedicated to August Bernhard, the Director of the St Petersburg Conservatory, it can be seen as a musical calling card, as Glazunov joined the staff of the Conservatory in that year as a Professor of Instrumentation. This new engagement was to have a profound effect on the direction of his life in ways that can hardly have been apparent to him at the time – after all, he was joining an institution in which his close friends Rimsky-Korsakov and Lyadov were already prominent figures.

The D minor Prelude and Fugue is also significant in that it indicates a shift in Glazunov's approach to the composition of piano music. Hitherto his output for solo piano had been dominated by shorter works – albeit of a varying nature. Over the next few years he would write some of his finest music for the instrument. A number of nineteenth century Russian composers wrote fugues as a part of their standard musical education but when they include fugal passages in their creative work, the music often possesses an awkward, rather self-conscious character. For Glazunov, as for Taneyev, this was not the case, as thinking contrapuntally came naturally to both composers. The D minor Prelude and Fugue is a fine example of Glazunov's ability to create music that is not only technically impressive but also deeply personal. It is a dramatic and somewhat stormy piece which maintains a high level of energy and concentrated musical thought throughout. Significantly, it reveals that Glazunov could still draw on the established forms of Western music to fulfil his personal creative vision: in pieces such as the D minor Prelude and Fugue he explores a darker emotional landscape, in contrast to the joy and optimism that can be found in his great ballet scores.

Chapter six

1900–06: Conflict and achievement

At the dawn of the new century, Glazunov's letters indicate that he was engaged once again with the composition of a symphony. Writing to Belyayev in August 1900, he comments somewhat ruefully on the slow progress that he is making with this work.[1] In fact, Glazunov was in the middle of the most productive period of his career – certainly in terms of the quality of the music he was composing. 1900 saw the completion of two fine orchestral works: the gently reflective *Romantic Intermezzo*, Op. 69, and the *Overture Solennelle*, Op. 73, in which rigorous thematic development is combined with one of Glazunov most memorable melodies, to create what is surely his finest overture – a genuinely stirring piece.

It has already been noted that the world of the Middle Ages had a strong appeal to the romantic aspect of his imagination and, in the years following the composition of *Raymonda*, he drew further on this creative impulse. *The Minstrel's Song* (*Chant du Ménestrel)* for Cello and Orchestra, Op. 71, falls into this category. Written for the cellist, Alexander Verzhbilovich, it is a beautiful miniature in which the singing quality of the cello is fully exploited. The English cellist, Beatrice Harrison, makes an interesting comment on this composition in her memoirs, when she explains that it 'has always impressed me very deeply – it is so full of the utter sadness of life'.[2] Verzhbilovich apparently asked Glazunov to write a concerto for the cello but the composer did not take up the idea until many years later.

An even more significant work completed in 1900 is the Theme and Variations in F sharp minor for piano, Op. 72. The short melody, only seven bars in length, is a Finnish folk song and it clearly appealed to Glazunov as he was to use it again in his *Finnish Fantasy* for orchestra of 1909. It is in the piano variations, however, that this arresting theme receives its fullest treatment. Following the stark statement of the melody there are fifteen variations in which Glazunov's creativity really takes flight. Each variation conjures some distinctive aspect of the folk song and, as the variations grow in length and complexity, the work creates a powerful sense of cumulative energy.

Glazunov continued to focus on piano music in 1901, completing his two sonatas for the instrument. The same high level of invention is evident in the Piano Sonata No. 1, in B flat minor, Op. 74, which he dedicated to Rimsky-Korsakov's wife, Nadezhda. In this work he combines a bold, romantic spirit, with memorable themes, subtle elaboration of motifs and an imaginative grasp of structure. Commenting on Glazuvov's creative abilities in this piece, Professor Terry Greenawalt observes: 'This is where the genius of Glazounov lies – in building his melodic material from a single germ and in the skilful contrapuntal combining of themes.'[3]

The work was warmly welcomed by Glazunov's friends, including Taneyev, who wrote to the composer in a letter from December 1901:

> Dear Alexandr Konstantinovich!
>
> I have been wanting to write to you for a long time to thank you for sending me your B flat [minor] Sonata. I cannot help but rejoice that you so energetically (I heard that you have completed the Second Sonata) are composing piano sonatas, temporarily setting aside short piano pieces. Long forms have not outlived their time by far, and probably even our grandchildren will not exhaust the repertoire…
>
> I am extremely interested in your Second Sonata, and I would be extremely obliged to you if you would send it to me when it is finished.[4]

The Piano Sonata No. 2, in E minor, Op. 75, also has three movements but with a *Scherzo*, rather than an *Andante*, at the heart of the piece. Taneyev would surely have been struck with the Sonata's leaner textures and altogether darker tone, with the exhilarating Scherzo providing the element of contrast. In the Finale, Glazunov returns to the ideas of the opening movement, at one point presenting the first theme as a fugal subject, described by Ronald Stevenson as 'very powerful and architectonic'.[5] To resolve the tension, he modulates into E major and introduces a sonorous chorale, based remarkably on the opening theme of the *Scherzo*. This is certainly one of his most imaginative compositions- with a sense of his technique being pushed to the limits- and it clearly made a profound impression on Stasov who explained that, 'Glazounov's Sonata… moved me to the very depths of my soul. It has strength, passion, beauty and depth.' Stasov's reference to the sonata's 'depth' of expression is particularly significant as this is what Chaikovsky hoped to hear in his friend's music, as Glazunov's talent developed.[6]

With their combination of a high level of inspiration and a mastery of compositional techniques, the two sonatas and the Theme and Variations are masterpieces which constitute a valuable and distinctive addition to the literature for the instrument.

Following the completion of these important piano pieces, his attention turned to orchestral composition, including the *March on a Russian Theme*, Op. 76. Written at his dacha at Ozerki during the summer of 1901, it is dedicated to his friend N. I. Abramychev. Its lively, melodious and optimistic character may well be a reflection of Glazunov's relief at spending the summer away from his responsibilities at the St Petersburg Conservatory. It received its first performance in that city, on 3/16 February 1902, when it was conducted by Lyadov. The most important work to absorb his attention at this time, however, was the Seventh Symphony.

Glazunov had started work on the Symphony No. 7 in F major, Op. 77, in the summer of 1900, although it was not completed until the end of the following year. Dedicated to Belyayev, it was given its first performance, with the composer conducting, on 7/21 December 1901. It has a very different character in comparison to the Sixth Symphony and reveals that, although Glazunov remained loyal to the traditional forms, he showed considerable imagination in the way in which he exploited those structures.

The opening movement, *Allegro moderato*, with its invigorating, open air atmosphere has given rise to the work being described as Glazunov's *Pastoral Symphony.* Engel describes the two principal themes as 'shepherd's pipe' melodies and both are initially presented by the oboe, helping to give the music a genial, outdoor character throughout. This characteristic even prompted Prokofiev to pay Glazunov a rare compliment, when he wrote in his diary that 'in this work there is much that gives pleasure: the second subject of the first movement is positively splendid!'[7]

The following *Andante* opens with a solemn theme on the trombones. Its rhythm is somewhat reminiscent of a Sarabande and it immediately establishes the movement's dark, searching tone. A more chromatic idea is introduced by the strings and, from these two themes, and variants derived from them, Glazunov constructs a movement with a rich, contrapuntal texture, balanced by a theme of great lyrical beauty. It is probably Glazunov's finest slow movement to date, as the evolution of his interest in counterpoint is matched by a greater emotional depth.

The *Scherzo* which follows has tremendous energy, with something of the opening movement's pastoral character. This time the flute takes the lead, supported by the restless rhythm of the string accompaniment. A new, soaring theme is soon introduced by the oboe but, such is the forward momentum of the music, there seems to be no time here to state this melody in its complete form – Glazunov, in fact, holds this back until the last movement. Marked *Allegro maestoso* (*molto pesante*), the Finale is a remarkable *tour de force* as, in addition to the new material, all of the themes from the rest of the symphony reappear, often in new forms and in original combinations. Technical mastery and creative imagination come together here to create a highly original and exciting conclusion to the symphony. As Engel writes: 'Something extremely variegated results (a rondo with ten themes, a form never envisioned in theory), but interesting; to someone who has listened attentively to the preceding movements of the symphony, even rather integral to it.'[8]

It is worth noting that the Seventh Symphony also made a strong impression on Taneyev. In a letter to Glazunov he explains, rather touchingly, how:

> For several days now my life has been revitalised and enthusiasm, long absent, has returned. The reason for this is your new symphony. I have listened to it at all the main rehearsals and at the concert and played it with my students in the [Moscow] Conservatory and elsewhere, and at other times I have been thinking about the impressions that I gained, which I would like to discuss with you. In my opinion your symphony is a very remarkable composition.[9]

At the same period Glazunov's imagination was drawn once again to the world of the Middle Ages in two further evocative and tuneful orchestral scores: the *Ballade*, Op. 78, and the Suite *From the Middle Ages*, Op. 79. The Suite is in four movements, each depicting some aspect of Glazunov's romantic view of the distant past: 1. Prelude. The Castle on the Shore. The Isle of Love. 2. Scherzo. Danse macabre. 3. Serenade of the Troubadour. 4. The Crusaders.[10]

As it turned out, the dedication of the Seventh Symphony to Belyayev proved to be timely, as Glazunov's generous benefactor died from heart failure on 28 December 1903/10 January 1904. Intelligent, enterprising and forward-looking, Belyayev had made a highly significant contribution to the dissemination of Russian music, through his publishing house and the sponsorship of concerts at home and abroad. The list of Russian composers who benefited from his unstinting support is a long one, containing, in the words of Nicholas Slonimsky, 'a galaxy of Russian luminaries…' as well as a number of minor figures.[11]

Glazunov felt his loss deeply. Belyayev had been one of his most loyal supporters from the occasion, in 1882, when he heard the premiere of Glazunov's First Symphony. It was Belyayev who had arranged for the young composer's music to be published. He had also taken him abroad to see more of the world and to meet important musicians, such as Liszt and, later, many leading French composers. Perhaps, above all, there had been the enjoyable evenings at Belyayev's house – the famous *Fridays* – filled with music, friendship and lavish entertainment. If the opening of the new century found Glazunov at the pinnacle of his compositional career, it also marked the acceleration of the process already noted by which death would take from him many of his closest musical friends, leaving him an increasingly isolated figure by the time of the First World War.

Business-like as always, Belyayev had arranged that, after his family had been provided for, sufficient funds would remain, so that the various enterprises he had established in his lifetime could continue after his death. He entrusted Rimsky-Korsakov, Lyadov and Glazunov with the management of his legacy, so that they became responsible for selecting works to be published by the firm M. P. Belaieff, running the three Russian Symphony Concerts to be held each year, and awarding the prizes for new orchestral and chamber music compositions by Russian composers. A fund was also established to help with the living expenses of composers who were struggling financially. These enterprises continued to flourish up to the time of the Bolshevik Revolution in 1917.

To mark the passing of Belyayev, Rimsky-Korsakov, Lyadov and Glazunov all took part in a concert dedicated to his memory which was held on 19 February/3 March 1904. The first set of Glinka prizes following Belyayev's death were awarded on 27 November/9 December of that year, the date marking the anniversaries of the first performances of Glinka's two operas. The list of winners announced in 1904 is an extremely impressive one, even if, with the exception of Scriabin, it reveals the essentially conservative musical tastes of Rimsky-Korsakov, Glazunov and Lyadov:

Arensky: Piano Trio in D minor, Op. 32 (500 roubles)
Lyapunov: Piano Concerto in E flat minor, Op. 4 (500 roubles)
Rachmaninoff: Piano Concerto No. 2 in C minor, Op. 18 (500 roubles)
Scriabin: Piano Sonata No. 3, Op. 23 (300 roubles)
Scriabin: Piano Sonata No. 4, Op. 30 (200 roubles)
Taneyev: Symphony in C minor, Op. 12 (1,000 roubles).

In terms of composition, 1903 was almost entirely fallow, the first such year since the start of Glazunov's career in the early 1880s. In a letter to Rimsky-Korsakov, written in the late summer of 1903, he comments that, as yet, nothing had come of his ideas for a new symphony and a concerto.[12]

The symphony that Glazunov refers to here is his Eighth, in E flat major, which he would not complete until 1906. However, his Violin Concerto was finished in the following year. Although his rate of composition was slowing down at this time, Glazunov notes in the same letter that he was able to draw consolation from the fact that his conducting was improving: 'As bold as it may be on my part to admit it, I feel that I am making significant progress in my conducting: the orchestra listens to me and I don't have to tell them about shading, as they take their cues from my baton.'[13]

Glazunov's first venture into the genre of the concerto, the Violin Concerto, in A minor, Op. 82, is dedicated to Leopold Auer, who had a long association with the St Petersburg Conservatory, dating back to

1868. In his day, he was an outstanding soloist and, later, he became a famous teacher who played a significant role in developing the talents of some of the greatest violin virtuosi of the twentieth century, including Mischa Elman, Jascha Heifetz, Nathan Milstein and Efrem Zimbalist. As Solomon Volkov suggests, 'No wonder Glazunov dedicated his Violin Concerto to Auer. The similarities in their musical principles are noteworthy: a striving for grandeur and dignity. Both the composer and the teacher valued clarity of thought, neatness of detail, and technical perfection.'[14]

Although Glazunov took longer than usual over the composition of the Violin Concerto, even at times wondering if he should complete the work, it has long maintained a place in the concert repertoire and, although it cannot be compared in terms of musical interest with his mature symphonies, it does contain many key features of Glazunov's style: graceful melodic invention, skilful thematic transformation and imaginative orchestration. There is also a characteristically thoughtful approach to form, while remaining within the nineteenth century tradition of the one movement concerto established by Liszt. In Liszt's Second Piano Concerto, for example, the various movements follow each other in sequence but without a break between them. Glazunov adapts this procedure, placing the brief slow movement within the first movement then using the skilfully constructed cadenza to link the finale to the rest of the Concerto.

It was first performed in St Petersburg on 19 February/4 March 1905 with Auer himself as soloist and the composer conducting. Initially the critical response to the Concerto was not very favourable, with one reviewer suggesting that the 'author of *Raymonda* did not escape the fate of all talented artists: to produce, once in a while, a lame work'.[15]

Its fortunes soon changed though when it was taken up by Mischa Elman who gave the first London performance on 17 October, in the same year, with Sir Henry Wood conducting the Queen's Hall Orchestra. It was also Elman who, on 3 March 1910, introduced the work to

American audiences with Modest Altschuler, the latter conducting his own Russian Orchestra. When describing the concerto, Mundy suggests that, 'In the solo part Glazunov finds a romantic nostalgia in the *Andante sostenuto* akin to that of Elgar in his concerto of five years later, although the finale provides a chance for the sort of virtuoso display that characterises the Tchaikovsky.'[16]

The work has certainly been fortunate in enjoying the advocacy of violinists of the first rank. This is true from the time of its premiere, as it swiftly entered the repertoires of all of the great Auer pupils mentioned above. One of them, Nathan Milstein, has left an account of his performance of the concerto, under the composer's direction, at a concert in Odessa, organised to mark Glazunov's fiftieth birthday:

> Glazunov's violin concerto is a fresh, attractive work, brilliantly orchestrated (although the Rondo is a bit heavy). At the rehearsal I played something at the beginning of the concerto in my own way. Obviously I was a brazen boy – the presence of the composer did not intimidate me. Glazunov looked down at me through his pince-nez and murmured, 'Don't you like the way I wrote it?' I played it his way then, but when the rehearsal was over Glazunov turned to me and said, 'Play it any way you want!' Because he saw that my version was better.
>
> A wise and calm man, Glazunov. He was not afraid that his authority would somehow be undermined.[17]

In the world of Russian politics, however, the years of 1904–5 were ones in which authority was being severely challenged – the ramifications of which would not bypass the St Petersburg Conservatory. Russia had entered into a war with Japan, as the two empires vied for control over Korea. Russian forces subsequently suffered one defeat after another, the most startling of all being the naval battle of Tsushima Strait, in which the Russian Baltic fleet was all but destroyed in an afternoon. The authority of Nicholas II's government was further weakened when troops opened fire on a peaceful demonstration, led by Father George Gapon, as it approached the Winter Palace on 9/22 January 1905. Hundreds of unarmed demonstrators were killed and the day of the massacre was thereafter known as Bloody Sunday. This outrage caused widespread unrest throughout the country and, inevitably, the St Petersburg Conservatory became involved.

Nikolai Malko, has left this first hand account of these troubled times:

> In the Conservatory the events took an especially ominous turn when one of the students (a soldier in the music brigade by name of Manetz) cynically boasted in front of a group of students that he had taken part in the event [the Bloody Sunday massacre], even shooting at the crowd himself. The students, deeply provoked, demanded the expulsion of this Manetz from the conservatory.[18]

On 10/23 February, the students held a meeting at which they voted, by a considerable majority, to support a *Declaration of the Moscow Composers and Musicians* which had been published in the newspaper *Our Days*, on 3/16 February, calling for artistic and political freedom. They also resolved to go on strike and to demand that the St Petersburg Conservatory should be closed until September. On the following day there was a meeting of the Art Council of the Conservatory – a body made up of the Director, August Bernhard, and the leading professors on the teaching staff. Rimsky-Korsakov, supporting the students, stated his opinion that the Conservatory could not continue to function under present circumstances and to argue that the Art Council should be freed from the control of the government appointed Directorate of the Russian Musical Society (RMS), a view that he then expressed in an open letter to the editor of the daily newspaper, *Russia*.

This liberal stance was fully supported by Glazunov when he addressed the following remarks to Bernhard in a letter of 12/25 February:

> I implore you not to reveal the names of Conservatory students who attended their meeting to the Board of Education. Police measures have no place in a temple of art. What can be accomplished by handing lists of names to those bemedaled and beribboned generals who preside over the board? This would ruin the careers of many talented students. The Jews would particularly suffer, for they would probably be subjected to much harsher reprisals than the Christians. Eventually the Conservatory would have to be placed under administrative authority in which case many of its best teachers would probably resign.[19]

Tensions increased even further when, at a subsequent meeting of the Art Council, Bernhard severely criticised the open letter which Rimsky-Korsakov had written to the editor of *Russia* and insisted that the Conservatory would open on 16/29 March. On that day, the building was surrounded by police and over a hundred protesting students were arrested. With this further deterioration in the situation, Rimsky-Korsakov then wrote another open letter to the press, this time addressed to Bernhard, in which he deplored the fact that the students who had gone on strike could expect to be harshly treated by the police.[20]

At this stage the Conservatory was closed and, in a tone of magisterial detachment, Rimsky-Korsakov points out, 'more than a hundred pupils were expelled, Bernhard left, and I was dismissed from the ranks of professors of the Conservatory by the chief Directorate, without previous consultation with the Art Council'.[21] Bernhard had resigned at a meeting of the Directorate of the RMS and N. F. Solovyev was named as the interim director, although the Art Council had advanced

Glazunov's name as a candidate for this post.

Following Rimsky-Korsakov's sacking, Glazunov and Lyadov wrote to the Directorate of the St Petersburg branch of the RMS, informing them of their decision to resign from the Conservatory. Their joint statement was published in the 25 March/7 April edition of the newspaper *Russia*:

> Having learned of the dismissal of N. A. Rimsky-Korsakov, Distinguished Professor of the Petersburg Conservatory, we have the honour to inform the Directorate that, to our great regret, we cannot continue our pedagogical activity at that institution after this occurrence.[22]

Other distinguished professors followed suit, including Felix Blumenfeld, Anna Esipova and Alexander Verzhbilovich. Classes could not be resumed at the Conservatory and, at private meetings held at the Glazunov family apartment, it was decided by a large majority of the instructors to elect Glazunov as the director of a self-governing conservatory. Events, however, took a different turn and this idea was never realised.[23]

An incident, very typical of the times, occurred when a group of students decided to organise a performance of Rimsky-Korsakov's opera *Kashchey the Immortal* at Madame Kommissarzhevskaya's Theatre. Following the performance, which Glazunov conducted, on 27 March/ 9 April, Rimsky-Korsakov noted in his memoirs: 'I was called before the curtain, addresses from various societies and unions were read to me, and inflammatory speeches were delivered... The din and hubbub after each address and each speech were indescribable.'[24]

The police then intervened, ordering the curtain to be lowered and thereby forestalling the performance of the second part of the concert which was to have included a performance by Efrem Zimbalist. In a memorandum made soon afterwards Rimsky-Korsakov anticipated that he, Glazunov and Jewish students might expect to face 'considerable annoyance' in the wake of these events.

There were more political disturbances later in the year, with strikes and demonstrations in October. It was at this febrile time that Glazunov received a hurried request from the conductor, Alexander Siloti. Vladimir Stasov provides the following account in a letter to his brother, Dmitri, dated 20 October/2 November:

> The day before yesterday Siloti rushed to Glazunov and said: '*I have to* begin several concerts with the 'anthem' [God Save the Tsar], but *I don't want to*. I want to begin with something else. Do me a great favour, Sasha. Write immediately the boatman's chorus *Ei, ukhnem* [the *Song of the Volga boatmen*] for orchestra.' Glazunov did it – yesterday, for full orchestra, and today they played it.[25]

Glazunov had, of course, used this theme very imaginatively in his early tone poem *Stenka Razin*, so Siloti's request was a very natural one. Rimsky-Korsakov, who considered Glazunov's arrangement to be 'magnificent', also provided a revolutionary piece with his exhilarating version of the protest song, *Doobinooshka* [The Little Cudgel].[26]

Despite these major expressions of unrest, some progress was made with the organisation of the St Petersburg Conservatory. New rules were promulgated to the effect that the Art Council could appoint professors, and elect the director, without the interference of the Directorate of the RMS. At the first meeting of the Art Council carried out under the new rules, Glazunov was elected as director and the expelled students were reinstated. The students, however, refused to return to classes, as strikes were still being held at other institutions of higher education – one concession being that those who were about to graduate could sit their final examinations in May 1906.

It might be thought that matters would now settle down at the

Conservatory but, in such unsettled times, passions on both sides of the political divide were high and the conservative members of the Art Council ensured that Glazunov's appointment would introduce into his life an element of conflict and stress that he had not known before. Rimsky-Korsakov notes that the meetings proved to be 'stormy to the point of indecency'. In fact, at one of these sessions, Rimsky-Korsakov was so incensed that he left, vowing never to return. He was particularly upset because of the way in which Glazunov was being treated: 'The position of Glazunov, who was worshipped by the students, was a difficult one. The conservative group of instructors snarled at him like dogs, at every meeting.'[27]

Even the Directorate of the RMS seemed to revive, making life complicated for Glazunov, by applying financial pressure to the Conservatory. Once again, Rimsky-Korsakov gives a vivid idea of the strain that Glazunov was under at this time: 'He [Glazunov] was in despair, saw in my departure seeds of further disorders, and would not consent to go himself, expecting still to be of use to the institution.'[28]

It is significant that Glazunov resolved to stay on, despite all the conflict, because he believed that his presence could help the Conservatory through a difficult time. This is a particularly commendable decision as he had a peaceable nature and intensely disliked the idea of protesting about anything, as Rimsky-Korsakov observed to his friend, V. V. Yastrebtsev.[29] At this point in his career Glazunov was still sufficiently wealthy to have lived a comfortable life, detached from all the turmoil surrounding him. Yet when he resolved to accept the onerous role of director, he was already fully conscious of the problems and disputes with which he would have to deal. Rimsky-Korsakov, well aware of this, decided to stay on at the Conservatory as he knew that 'Glazunov's intentions were of the best, and it came hard to frustrate his plans.'[30]

Three months before his appointment as the director of the Conservatory, Glazunov had started work on what proved to be his last completed symphony – No. 8 in E flat major, Op. 83. It took him over a year to finish – from 17/30 July 1905 to 31 October/13 November 1906, a reflection no doubt of the chaotic times in which it was composed. Another reason may well be that Glazunov was also striving for greater expressive intensity in this work. Furthermore, earlier in the summer, he had been ill with tonsillitis. According to Yastrebtsev, this 'led to complications and an abscess in his ear, and even though his eardrum has been pierced, it is almost impossible for him to hear music'.[31] In the light of this unpleasant experience it is understandable that, in later years, he would become increasingly concerned about his hearing.

The Eighth certainly represents an imposing summation of Glazunov's career as a symphonist, combining a complete mastery of ideas with a darker, more unsettled mood – one that had been increasingly a feature of some his best works from the turn of the century onwards. The often-sombre tone of the symphony may well reflect, in part, his reaction to recent events but, as always in Glazunov's symphonies, there is no extra-musical programme. The composer conducted the first performance of the symphony at a Russian Symphony Concert on 8/21 December 1906.

The first movement, *Allegro moderato*, opens with an immediate sense of urgency, ushering in an expansive first subject. Much of the energy generated in this movement is derived from the highly focused development of this melody, including its immediate use in the transition to the second subject. This new theme, with its highly expressive falling and rising sequences, maintains, rather than relaxes, the tension, as it builds towards a powerful climax. Even although the home key is E flat major, the movement has a sombre character, so that its darkly scored final pianissimo bars leave the listener with a sense of unresolved tension.

The second movement, *Mesto*, intensifies the note of pathos that has been established in the first movement, the richly scored opening, with organ-like sonorities and insistent, unsettling rhythms preparing the way for a theme which is genuinely tragic in tone. The greater emotional depth is due in part to the large intervals between the notes of this melody and the related four note figure which is used to form a sequence rising in intensity. The other main theme of the movement is more lightly scored; it provides enough contrast to the opening idea, without detracting from the essential seriousness of the overall mood. The end of the movement, as David Nice suggests, 'is perhaps the most devastating thing Glazunov ever composed; here desolation becomes explicit for the only time in his works.'[32] This powerful music certainly made a profound impression on Glazunov's friends when he played it to them on the piano. Stasov, who died before the symphony was completed, said of this slow movement that it was 'something Glazunov had never done before. New, original into infinity. A great work!'[33]

The Scherzo, *Allegro*, which follows, is also very different in character when compared to the type of high spirited, dance-like movements audiences had come to expect from Glazunov. Taking up a triplet figure from the opening of the second movement – just one of the many subtleties found throughout the symphony – the Scherzo has great rhythmic drive. At times this gives it a somewhat sinister quality, which is entirely absent from the brilliant scherzos he wrote earlier in his career. In the headlong rush, there is no time for a conventional trio and the movement ends with an outburst of restless energy.

The frenetic conclusion to the Scherzo prepares the way for the beautiful and reflective opening of the Finale. Here a stately melody, imaginatively derived from a theme in the first movement, introduces the move towards a brighter conclusion to the work, even although the menacing triplet figure makes another appearance. The theme, like so many other ideas in the symphony, is developed in a rising sequence, giving it a striving character, as if it were reaching out of the darkness into the light. This leads to the main body of the movement, *Allegro moderato*, in which a very resolute figure, derived, in a highly original transformation, from the first melody of the slow movement, is contrasted with a more song-like idea, presented first on the clarinet. Glazunov then develops these themes and, while the Finale may lack the great sweeping melodies of a work such as the Second Symphony of Rachmaninoff, the coda provides the note of triumph towards which the symphony has been aiming. It is all the more powerful, as the music conveys the sense of a conflict that has to be resolved before the peroration is achieved. This composition is Glazunov's symphonic masterpiece, as it is both powerfully expressive and a thoroughly integrated work of art.

Its first performance took place on 9/22 December 1906, with the composer conducting. As already mentioned, Glazunov's friend and loyal supporter, V. V. Stasov, had died only two months earlier on 10/23 October. This outstanding critic, with his wide range of knowledge and boundless enthusiasm, had been an important supporter of the Nationalist composers. Indeed, he was probably the first and the most loyal advocate of Musorgsky's genius. As we have seen he had also welcomed Glazunov's appearance as a composer and, even although Glazunov had developed in ways that Stasov had not imagined in 1882, it is important to note that he admired the work of the mature artist even more than that of the youthful composer.

One of the works he particularly loved was the first movement of Glazunov's Fourth String Quartet. It is fitting then that, when Glazunov wrote his orchestral *Prelude in Memory of Stasov*, Op. 85, No. 1, the opening chords, with their poignant, falling intervals, are derived from the first bars of the earlier work. He also makes use of the theme *With Holy Repose* from the Orthodox Ritual. The *Prelude* was given its premiere at a Russian Symphony Concert, dedicated to Stasov's memory, on 11/24 November 1906. Yastrebtsev describes the composition as a 'very interesting and profound piece'.[34] The quality of the Prelude is also acknowledged by Calvocoressi when he writes that Glazunov 'strikes a new imaginative note' and goes on to add that it is a work 'rich in recondite poetic suggestiveness'.[35]

By this time, it was clear that Glazunov's early promise had been more than fulfilled in the major works of his maturity.

Gluzunov by Valentin Serov (1906),
from the collection of the Tretyakov Gallery, Moscow

Chapter seven

1907–17: An acknowledged master

The year 1907 was a particularly significant one for Glazunov as, to mark his silver jubilee as a composer on 27 January/9 February, a special concert was arranged in his honour, with the following programme:

Glazunov:	Symphony No. 1 in E major, Op. 5 (conducted by Rimsky-Korsakov)
Lyadov:	*Welcome to Glazunov*
Rimsky-Korsakov:	*Hail to Glazunov*
Glazunov:	Symphony No. 8 in E flat major, Op. 83 (conducted by Siloti)
Glazunov:	*Why are the voices silent*? Op. 27 No. 1, sung by Fyodor Chaliapin, with orchestral accompaniment.

This programme, with the contrasting character of the two symphonies, clearly indicates just how productive these years had been, not only in the wealth of music he had created but also in the way his style had evolved. The teenage Prokofiev attended the concert and his account brings out clearly the importance of the event:

> The Hall of Columns had a festive appearance… There were a great many delegations there to congratulate Glazunov, and they all brought wreaths or big baskets of flowers. Glazunov received them on the stage. They slowly filed up to him, passing behind the white columns and making a long queue that extended the entire length of the hall.[1]

Rimsky-Korsakov also noted that, 'The jubilee concert went off splendidly before a filled auditorium.'[2] Although he was too modest to mention the importance of his own role in the proceedings, this was noted in the touching description provided by the reviewer of the *Russian Musical Gazette*:

> Changing his usual way of walking into an unnaturally slowed gait that is meant to be solemn, he [Rimsky-Korsakov] slowly advances towards the fêted man at the head of the committee group. A few brief words: 'It has been resolved to establish a fellowship in your name,' a copy of the address is handed over, and then – the most magnificent and significant moment of the jubilee celebration – a long, prolonged, repeated kiss, with which Rimsky-Korsakov ended his greeting.[3]

Special performances to mark this anniversary also included a programme of Glazunov's ballets *The Seasons*, *Ruses d'amour* and Act Three of *Raymonda* at the Mariyinsky Theatre on 15/28 January, while, on the following day, two of his string quartets and the Second Piano Sonata were given at a special concert in the St Petersburg Conservatory. Taken together, these three events provided a fine survey of Glazunov's achievement as a composer, covering important pieces of symphonic, stage and chamber music.[4]

Given the troubled political scene, and the problems it had created at the Conservatory, Glazunov had little time to enjoy the applause surrounding the festivities. One aspect of his directorship of the institution that merits special attention is his attitude towards the students. One of them, Oscar Potoker, makes the following revealing remarks about him:

> The generosity, the consideration of that man! Sons of rich men are usually unable to sympathize with other people's need for money; they don't understand it. But Glazunov, who comes from a wealthy line of publishers, is the opposite. You should have seen him coming to the Conservatory in the morning or leaving it – trying to leave it – at night! The poor students fairly mobbed him, and he handed out bills [banknotes] like scraps of waste paper… 'Oh, your rent? Yes, yes, how much? Your tuition? Here, is this enough? A ticket for the opera tonight? Let me see – yes, I have one here.' He satisfied everybody. And always spoke to them in such a slow, modest voice, as if he were the one asking for the favour.[5]

This account is further illustrated by Sir Thomas Preston, who became a friend of Glazunov in the 1920s:

> Glazounoff's good nature and kindness were proverbial. In pre-revolutionary days the story goes that the much-beloved director of the conservatory of music used to wander about the corridors of the conservatory with his pockets stuffed with rouble notes, which he doled out in the most unostentatious manner to indigent students. In those days he never kept his salary from the conservatory: it was always given to his poorer musical friends.[6]

A typical example of Glazunov's generous and considerate treatment of Conservatory students can be found in the case of Oda Slobodskaya, who became, in later years, a famous Russian soprano. At the time when Slobodskaya was receiving singing lessons from Professor Natalya Iretskaya, she recalled that:

> The whole conservatory loved Glazunov. With his courtly clothes and kindly manner, even Madame Iretskaya had a soft spot for him. He was not forbidding and encouraged all the students to go directly to him with their troubles. He even gave them money at times, if they were having difficulties making ends meet, and this always came from his private income.[7]

One of Madame Iretskaya's rules was that her pupils were not allowed to sing professionally – an injunction that extended even to minor roles. She was therefore furious when she discovered that Slobodskaya was appearing as a flower maiden in a production of Wagner's *Parsifal* and demanded that she be expelled from the Conservatory. When the young singer appeared before Glazunov, he learned that she had disobeyed her teacher because she was desperately short of money. Instead of expelling her, Glazunov awarded her an allowance and took it upon himself to pacify an indignant Madame Iretskaya, with the result that she accepted Slobodskaya back into her class.[8]

Jewish students also benefited from Glazunov's determination to support all talented musicians – regardless of their social or racial origins. Anti-Semitism was a singularly ugly feature of life in Tsarist Russia. As we have already seen from his letter to Bernhard, Glazunov was well aware that Jewish students were likely to face particularly unpleasant reprisals from the authorities following the student strike of 1905. At that time there were, in any case, quotas on the number of Jewish students who were permitted to attend institutions of higher education: Nicolas Slonimsky, who was a student of Maximilian Steinberg and Vasiliy Kalafati at the St Petersburg Conservatory, gives a figure of three-and-a-half percent. The proportion of Jewish students taking classes at the Conservatory was far higher – indeed, Slonimsky states that over half the students there were Jewish.[9] However, as he was well aware, they could count on Glazunov's support: 'Glazunov… was a great admirer of

Jews; he used to remark about some non-Jewish Conservatory students that their playing was "disappointingly Christian.'"[10]

Solomon Volkov mentions a highly significant example of the director's defence of Jewish students – one which reveals that, although Glazunov disliked any form of conflict, he was prepared to defend his principles:

> Glazunov gave his patronage in every possible way to talented Jews. A Russian, he was even called 'King of the Jews'. Shostakovich told me about Glazunov's famous response to the inquiry from the Russian prime minister, Pyotr Stolypin, about the number of Jewish students at the Petersburg Conservatory: 'We don't keep count.'[11]

To put Glazunov's conduct into context, it is worth noting that, while he and Rimsky-Korsakov stood out honourably against anti-Semitism, this was certainly not the case with all Russian composers at that time. Balakirev, for example, who had been such a significant influence on Glazunov's early career, was described by Rimsky-Korsakov as 'an implacable Jew-hater',[12] while Richard Taruskin points out that – in addition to Balakirev – Glinka, Chaikovsky, Musorgsky and Stravinsky also held anti-Semitic views.[13] Clearly the unprejudiced stance adopted by Glazunov and Rimsky-Korsakov was not one that was universally shared.

In addition to his many administrative responsibilities, Glazunov continued to teach. Among the memoirs left by some outstanding musicians who were trained at the Conservatory, during the period of Glazunov's directorship, there are contrasting accounts as to how successful he was in this role. One of the most positive descriptions comes from the composer, Dimitri Tiomkin, who later found fame in Hollywood with his highly imaginative scores for films such as *High Noon* and *Lost Horizon*:

> Besides being an eminent composer, Glazunov was a superb teacher, a pedagogue both formidable and entertaining. He taught musical theory with a strict insistence on the niceties of part writing, the correctness of suspensions and modulations – and beware of consecutive fifths! He could be severe and scowl at mistakes, but on the whole he was a good-humored titan.
>
> Majestic in frock coat, he would stand at a blackboard lined with musical staves and write out the notes of a three-part counterpoint; and we, copying it on our music pads, were required to complete it by writing a fourth part. It was a kind of charade, a puzzle to be solved, and his manner was that of the amiable director of a game.[14]

On the other hand, Nikolai Malko describes Glazunov as 'a huge, fat, clumsy, and slow man who usually spoke very softly and deliberately…' and goes on to suggest that he 'belongs among those "pedagogues" who cannot teach, but from whom it is possible to learn'. Malko refines his point by stating that from 'Glazunov, students could not easily acquire the basic fundamentals'.[15]

What these two accounts suggest is that the more able the student, the more he or she could learn from Glazunov. In the case of Prokofiev, for example, Glazunov once made a suggestion about how the young composer could notate a particular rest in the score of the Finale of his early E minor Symphony. Of this advice Prokofiev remarked, 'I liked the suggestion and have used it ever since.'[16]

However, if Tiomkin and Malko entertained different opinions on the effectiveness of Glazunov's instruction, they had no doubt at all that they were being taught by an exceptionally gifted musician. Tiomkin says of Glazunov:

> His knowledge of music was vast, his memory prodigious, his ear infallible. After someone had played a sonata or a prelude and fugue, he might remark slyly, with his voice trailing off, 'In the third section, page seven, bar twenty-six, you neglected to play the F sharp,' and cock his head to one side and chuckle.[17]

In a similar vein, Malko notes that 'Glazounov's musical abilities were phenomenal; truly, he could be compared to no one. Everything was easy for him. His inner hearing (ear) was of such quality that he could perform amazing feats.'[18]

As the years unfolded, there can be no doubt that Glazunov felt the strain placed upon him by the burden of his responsibilities. In part, this manifested itself in periodic bouts of heavy drinking. Tiomkin was well aware of these episodes in Glazunov's life:

> … from time to time he would disappear and go into seclusion, and then we knew he was either composing or having a bout with the bottle. Ordinarily he didn't drink much, but he had occasional alcoholic interludes. When he did, he would come back to the Conservatory with boils on his neck.[19]

This pattern of behaviour is confirmed by Slobodskaya:

> Because of his kindness, Glazunov's indisposition was overlooked. He had fits of manic depression coupled with alcoholism. When the fit was upon him he would lock himself up in his study, with his servant carrying up bottle after bottle. He would refuse to eat or to see anyone. Then, when the sickness had passed, he would return to his duties and things would continue as normal.[20]

Despite these interruptions, Glazunov's involvement in the administration of the Conservatory was undoubtedly beneficial to the institution and its many students: he did what he could to secure its independence in the face of government pressure and he maintained a lively interest in the progress of its students, taking particular care over those talented young musicians who, for whatever reason, required additional support. Something of Glazunov's benign presence is perhaps reflected in this evocative description provided by Prokofiev:

> At the Conservatory, Glazunov always wore a frock coat... It sat amply on his bulky torso, and in one of its deep pockets he carried a big cigar case with ten big cigars in it. Glazunov would smoke one cigar after another, and when he walked through the hallways of the Conservatory he would leave the light aroma of a fine cigar behind him. We would sniff and say, 'The director has just passed this way.'[21]

A number of significant events later in 1907 helped to consolidate Glazunov's reputation as an established master, in this his anniversary year. In May he travelled to Paris, to take part in the magnificent festival of Russian music organised by Serge Diaghilev. The series of five concerts included a wide range of Russian composers, from Glinka to Scriabin.

This was Diaghilev's first major enterprise as a music impresario and he had to exert the full force of his charm to persuade Rimsky-Korsakov to undertake the journey to Paris. Diaghilev's efforts were rewarded, however, as Rimsky-Korsakov was warmly received as the doyen of Russian composers. Scriabin was also present to hear a performance of his Second Symphony, conducted by Nikisch, and Rachmaninoff appeared as soloist in his Second Piano Concerto and as conductor in his Cantata *Spring*.

Diaghilev had originally arranged with the famous Belgian violinist, Eugene Ysaye, to perform the solo part in Glazunov's Violin Concerto, for a fee of 2,000 francs, but the composer indicated that he preferred to include something other than the Concerto and so, on 26 May, at the fourth concert, Glazunov conducted his Suite *From the Middle Ages*. The fifth and final concert also included his *Lyric Poem*.[22] Summing up these events Boris Schwarz points out that, while the appearance of the leading Russian composers of the day ensured the artistic success of the concerts, it could not prevent their financial failure, leaving Diaghilev with debts of 100,000 francs.[23]

At this time Glazunov also received a number of honours from leading cultural and academic institutions – a reflection of his renown as a major composer. The French Academy named him as a Corresponding Member[24] and, following the series of Diaghilev concerts, he travelled to England where he was awarded honorary degrees in Doctor of Music by Cambridge University (12 June) and Oxford University (18 June).

Before these ceremonies took place, Glazunov visited the Royal College of Music on 6 June where his presence was marked with a concert of his works. He was naturally interested in the curriculum of the College, as his work in reforming the St Petersburg Conservatory continued, but he also found time to conduct the student orchestra in his *Raymonda Suite*, two songs for contralto and orchestra, sung by Dilys Jones, and the *Minstrel's Song,* played by Beatrice Harrison. The programme also contained a performance of the Seventh Symphony conducted by Sir Charles Villiers Stanford. *The Musical Times* noted that, 'The eminent Russian composer, who had a very cordial greeting, was greatly pleased with the interpretative excellence of the students at the Royal College of Music.'[25]

At Oxford, a speech was addressed to the Vice-Chancellor, outlining Glazunov's fitness to receive the honour which was to be bestowed upon him. This was written (in Latin) by Dr F. W. Bussell of Brasenose College but at the ceremony, it was delivered, in his own translation, by the University's Professor of Music, Sir Charles Hubert H. Parry. It contains some genuine insight into the nature of Glazunov's compositional style and clearly indicates, as such a speech must necessarily do, the respect and admiration which he enjoyed at what can be seen as the high watermark of his career. After outlining the origins of St Petersburg and Glazunov's early activity, it continues:

> Nor as a man did he fall short of the promise of his youth, but became notable for his industry as well as for his disposition. For in him we find at once many qualities united which in other composers are sometimes found scattered, a variety of melody, whether sweetness or cheerfulness or seriousness be desired, a strength and manliness of rhythm, and rich invention at once various and consistent, a mastery of resource, so that when he employed the orchestra some new and unexpected charms revealed themselves, a vigour and a judgment… so conjoined in him that he combines the vivacity of youth with the prudence of maturity.[26]

During his visit to the Universities, Glazunov was canvassed to approach Rimsky-Korsakov to see if he would be willing to travel to England to accept similar honours. In a letter of 27 June, Glazunov wrote to his old mentor from Folkstone, explaining that the ceremonial aspect of the event was not at all tiring and that, as a recipient of an honorary degree, he would not be required to make a speech.[27]

Rimsky-Korsakov indicated that he had no intention of accepting the honour and asked Glazunov to convey his decision to the Universities. In January 1908, however, both Rimsky-Korsakov and Glazunov, together with Balakirev and Cui, were elected honorary members of the Moscow Branch of the Russian Musical Society.[28]

Rimsky-Korsakov's declining health may well have been a factor in his decision not to travel to England. By the end of spring 1908, it was becoming increasingly evident that he was seriously ill, as he suffered two attacks of angina within the space of five days, the first occurring on 10/23

April. Following a week's rest in bed he seemed to regain his strength and he travelled with members of his family to Lyubensk on 21 May/3 June. Even so, he was unable to attend the marriage of his daughter, Natalya, to the composer Maximilian Steinberg on 4/17 June and, following a thunderstorm, he had a final attack and died on 8/21 June.[29]

At the time of his death, Rimsky-Korsakov was widely regarded as Russia's foremost composer but he was also one of Glazunov's closest colleagues, as well as being a loyal friend. Despite the disparity in their ages, their relationship had developed quickly from the very first lessons Glazunov received from Rimsky-Korsakov in 1879. It was therefore appropriate that, following a memorial service in the chapel of the St Petersburg Conservatory, Glazunov delivered a eulogy at his old teacher's grave. In his memoirs Yastrebtsev notes approvingly that Glazunov praised not only Rimsky-Korsakov's musical genius but also his inquiring intellect and his constant striving for the highest ideals.[30]

The nature of Glazunov's development as a composer made him, in effect, a contemporary of Rimsky-Korsakov rather than his successor. They had worked closely together for many years and they expressed similar views on what they considered to be the disturbing new trends that were increasingly emerging in the world of music at this time. They shared, for example, a strong antipathy to the music of Richard Strauss. Russian music was fortunate, however, in the sense that they complemented each other as composers. As Gerald Abraham observes:

> Looking back on Rimsky-Korsakov's work as a whole, one sees at once that the Korsakov who matters is Korsakov the opera-composer… Even the best of his concert-works for orchestra are hardly 'symphonic' in the true sense; their delightful material and magical scoring have deservedly won them a unique place in the repertoire, but they reveal the composer's lack of skill as a musical architect all too clearly.[31]

In contrast, Glazunov, who wrote no operas, demonstrated a very real talent for creating the type of symphonic architecture that held no appeal for Rimsky-Korsakov. Evidence for this can be found, for example, in the convincingly argued first movements of the mature symphonies and in the brilliantly conceived finales of these same works. Another revealing contrast is to be found in their chamber music, as Glazunov invested far more creative energy in the string quartet than his illustrious teacher.

It is true that, in certain areas, there is undoubtedly a similarity in the orchestral colour that the two men cultivated – a guild-like quality that is particularly noticeable in 'oriental' pieces, such as Rimsky-Korsakov's *Sheherazade* and Glazunov's *Oriental Rhapsody*. At the same time, this should not disguise the fact that the forms in which they expressed their finest ideas reveal that they had a very different approach to composition.

Glazunov also contributed a moving musical tribute to his old friend in the *Prelude in Memory of Rimsky-Korsakov* which, together with the *Prelude in Memory of* Stasov, forms his Opus 85. Noble and deeply felt, it reveals Glazunov's ability to capture a note of genuine pathos. It shares with works, such as the Eighth Symphony, a rich and dark orchestral texture, beauty of ideas and a profound seriousness of purpose. As Ateş Orga comments, 'its diatonically wistful E major Amen goes back hauntingly to the anchorage of *Sheherazade* and the 1880s'.[32]

The loss of Rimsky-Korsakov was particularly hard for Glazunov at a time when he was still struggling to organise the Conservatory and to deal with the innumerable problems that inevitably arose in his dealings with a reactionary Russian government. Before the end of 1908, however, he managed to complete two further orchestral scores, the first of which was *The Song of Destiny*, Op. 84. Described as a *Dramatic Overture*, it was Glazunov's last in this genre. In a work that appears to arise from a world riven with conflict, Glazunov employs the famous opening theme from Beethoven's Fifth Symphony but in a form in which its rhythm and harmony are altered. The ominous and, at times, forceful presentation of the 'Fate' theme is contrasted with another of those singing, expansive melodies, often with a tinge of melancholy, that are an appealing feature of his mature style.

Glazunov's fame at this stage in his career is also reflected in the fact that he was increasingly requested to provide incidental music for various theatrical productions. When Ida Rubinstein decided to present Oscar Wilde's play *Salomé*, she commissioned Glazunov to compose an *Introduction and Dance,* Opus 90. In his memoirs Alexander Benois provides some insight into the reaction of members of the Russian aristocracy, noting the disquiet caused by the idea of an actor representing John the Baptist on stage, as well as the expected unease at the prospect of Ida Rubinstein's nudity at the end of the Dance of the Seven Veils. This was seen to be particularly troubling as she belonged to a family with respectable bourgeois credentials. Benois goes on to explain, 'I have but a faint recollection of the rehearsal with Ida Rubinstein, and only remember the impression made on me by Glazunov's music which had been especially composed for the occasion.'[33]

In the event, Rubinstein's production was banned by the censor, although no such problems faced the music which received its first performance under the direction of the composer at a concert given in the St Petersburg Conservatory early in 1909.[34] In the *Introduction* Glazunov suggests the decadence and latent violence of King Herod's court with some highly charged chromaticism while, in contrast, there is a dignified theme, first introduced by the horns, representing John the Baptist. With the *Dance* Glazunov is able to draw on his long experience of composing music in an 'oriental' style. Here, however, there is a richness of musical content that is new – something that is particularly noticeable in the harmony and rhythm of the piece.

Glazunov's status as a leading figure in the cultural life of Russia is further demonstrated in the next commission he received – this time for an orchestral work to mark the hundredth anniversary of the birth of Nikolai Gogol, one of the most original and influential literary figures of his day. To celebrate this significant event, Glazunov wrote a truly splendid orchestral work: the *Prelude in Memory of Gogol*, Op. 87. Although he had been kept busy with his characteristically conscientious supervision of exams at the Conservatory, he still managed to complete the *Prelude* by 3/15 March 1909 and he conducted its premiere in the St Petersburg Conservatory on 20 March/1 April.

The piece opens in a trenchant manner, with strongly accented chords in a syncopated rhythm. The first of its two main themes has a plaintive, folk-like character, while the second is a particularly beautiful melody, reminiscent of the lyrical theme from *The Song of Destiny* overture. After both ideas are developed, Glazunov builds the Prelude towards a triumphant conclusion, the melancholy aspect of the opening giving way to a powerful and resolute statement of the two principal themes. With its brilliant orchestration and propulsive energy, it provides a fine tribute to one of the nineteenth century's greatest writers.

Later in 1909 Glazunov was at work on another orchestral composition – the *Finnish Fantasy*, Op. 88. This was the first of a small group of orchestral works inspired by the countryside and legends of Russia's northern neighbour. Throughout his life Glazunov had visited Finland. As far back as 1881 he had spent his summer in the resort of Sur-Mericki, working on his First Symphony,[35] while in the early years of the twentieth century he would regularly appear as the conductor of his own compositions in Helsingfors (Helsinki). He was much admired by the Finnish conductor and composer, Robert Kajanus, who, in addition to his advocacy of his fellow Finn, Sibelius, would frequently programme works by Russian composers. As Erik Twaststjerna notes, the most frequently performed of these composers was Glazunov.[36]

In addition to his knowledge of the Finnish countryside, Glazunov's aural imagination was perhaps intrigued by hearing recent works by Sibelius. In the year when he was working on the *Finnish Fantasy*, for example, Sibelius's tone poem *Night Ride and Sunrise* was given its premiere in St Petersburg under the baton of Alexander Siloti. After the performance Siloti wrote to Sibelius: 'Even Glazunov liked the piece (he told me at the rehearsal) and said it was "a very beautiful composition.'"[37]

Writing about the *Finnish Fantasy*, Nicholas Slonimsky notes that it is 'derived thematically from authentic Finnish sources and accoutred in sonorous Russian harmonies'.[38] Glazunov was always responsive to nature and the mysterious forests of the North seem to be reflected in the deep, rich colours with which the piece opens. The contrasting Finnish melodies – including the one he had used in his Piano Variations – are skilfully presented in various instrumental combinations before the work is crowned with a ringing statement of the Lutheran chorale *Ein' feste Burg ist unser Gott,* in acknowledgement of Finland's Protestant religious tradition.

Three years later, in 1912, Glazunov returned to the Finnish theme in the two short orchestral pieces which constitute his *Finnish Sketches* Op. 89. The first is called *From the Kalevala* while the second is entitled *Procession*. The great epic poem *The Kalevala* had provided Sibelius and others with the inspiration for many of their most distinctive works. Although Glazunov's horizons are much more modest here, the *Sketches* pay a gracious tribute to their dedicatee, Robert Kajanus. *From the Kalevala* is based on a short melody which is repeated throughout; variety is created by Glazunov's highly imaginative use of the orchestra, as each repetition of the melody is accompanied by some new combination of sounds. In a few minutes, the composer demonstrates his absolute mastery of instrumentation. *The Procession* is a darkly coloured and forceful march – much gloomier in mood than other *Cortège* movements of his. The stern heroes of Northern legend seem to be recalled here, although the work ends with a major key statement of the Lutheran chorale previously employed in the *Fantasy.*

The final, and most substantial, of the works which Glazunov composed on a Finnish subject is the *Karelian Legend*, Op. 99. It was completed in 1916 and first performed on 11 May 1918 with the composer conducting. The impetus to write the tone poem came to Glazunov when he was visiting Sortavala and Valamo. The legend referred to in the title concerns a young man who is irresistibly drawn deep down into the caverns under Koli, a mountain near the shores of lake Pielinen. Once there he is a witness to the devil worship practised in the underground kingdom. After his return from the caverns, he starts to give an account of what he has seen but a sudden gale sweeps him away under the mountain from which, this time, he never returns. These dramatic episodes are framed by the peaceful scenes of nature: the call of the cuckoo and the wind in the pine trees, echoing through the canyons.[39]

The *Karelian Legend* is a richly evocative piece, with attractive themes; Glazunov clearly revelled in the depiction of those elements of the story connected with nature, such as the rustling pines and the cuckoo's calls, in addition to capturing the more dramatic and sinister aspects of the narrative. It is also worth pointing out that, by writing these works at a time when the Finnish people were growing increasingly dissatisfied with the status of their country as a Grand Duchy of the Russian Empire, Glazunov was expressing his sympathy for their plight. Sibelius acknowledged as much when he noted in his diary for the day that marked Glazunov's fiftieth birthday: 'a toast for him, the friend of Finland!'[40]

Glazunov wrote only one major orchestral work following the completion of the *Karelain Legend*. The slowing down of his creativity, caused in part by the incessant demands placed upon him by his duties at the Conservatory, in conjunction with his awareness of the emergence of radical new voices in the world of composition, is also reflected in the fact that he started his Ninth Symphony in D minor in 1910 but only completed a piano sketch of the first movement. This work had been on his mind for some time, as he had mentioned that he would give some thought to his Eighth and Ninth Symphonies after finishing work on the Violin Concerto, in a letter to Rimsky-Korsakov, from August 1904.[41]

It was certainly unusual for Glazunov not to complete a work once he had embarked upon it. Some insight into the reason for this was later given by the critic, Mark Semyonov, who, after Glazunov's death, recollected a conversation he had with the composer in which Glazunov 'confessed that it was perhaps a dread of the mighty shadow cast by Beethoven that led him never to return to his Ninth'.[42]

Before Glazunov left the Soviet Union in 1928 he gave the piano sketch to Maximilian Steinberg. Following Steinberg's death, it was presented to the Leningrad Institute for Theatre, Music and Film by his widow, Natalya. Then, in 1947, Gavril Yudin learned of the score's existence and decided to orchestrate the piece. As he later explained:

> I felt it my duty and my tribute to Alexander Glazunov to breathe new life into the work, and resolved to edit and orchestrate the composition. Having finished this task, I presented the results of my labours early in 1948 to Dmitri Shostakovich, N. Y. Miaskovsky, Y. A. Shaporin, Reinhold Gliere, and S. N. Vasilenko. My editing and orchestration met with their unstinting approval. In the summer of 1986 I again reviewed the score and made several corrections in the instrumentation.[43]

It can only be regretted that Glazunov did not finish the Ninth Symphony. The one completed movement, by turns sombre and intense, gives an indication of how he could employ his mastery of compositional technique to explore a much darker sound world, reflecting a more troubled and uncertain response to life. The work opens with an *Adagio* introduction, its beautifully unfolding counterpoint leading to the main body of the movement, marked *Moderato*. Here the first theme from the introduction appears again in a new guise, later contrasted with a more song-like idea, described fittingly by Yudin as '… one of Glazunov's most felicitous melodic inspirations'.[44] With these themes he constructs a powerful and closely argued movement which eventually dies away, returning the listener to the work's subdued and melancholy opening.

Yudin has to be congratulated on his skill in orchestrating the sketch, thereby enabling audiences to hear Glazunov's last thoughts on the symphony. He conducted the premiere on 7 May 1948 in a radio broadcast, the first public performance following on 31 July 1948 when he directed the Leningrad Philharmonic.

Although the Ninth would remain unfinished, Glazunov did produce a major composition in 1910: the Piano Concerto No. 1 in F minor, Op. 92. As far back as 1889, he had started work on a piano concerto but the project was set aside, with some of the musical ideas finding their way into the Third Symphony. Once the composer was settled in his summer dacha at Ozerki, however, he created what would turn out to be his most substantial and, in certain respects, his most interesting concerto.

When working on the piece, Glazunov was very conscious of the fact that, although he possessed a remarkable facility at the keyboard, he was not a trained pianist, let alone a virtuoso such as Medtner, Rachmaninoff or Scriabin. He was therefore relieved to find that, when he showed his sketches to the work's dedicatee, Leopold Godowsky, the famous soloist had few suggestions to make concerning the piano part.[45]

Glazunov conducted the premiere of the Concerto on 24 February/ 9 March 1911, with Konstantin Igumnov as soloist. Two years later, on 28 August 1913, it was given for the first time in England at a Promenade Concert in which Alfred Quaife played the solo part and Sir Henry Wood directed the New Queen's Hall Orchestra. Indeed, up until the end of the Second World War, it received a number of performances in various Promenade seasons, featuring some interesting soloists: York Bowen (1920); Lev Pouishnoff (1921, 1922, 1930 & 1945); Stephen Wearing (1934) and Elena Glazunov (1938). The Concerto also enjoyed the advocacy of the great Russian pianist, Sviatoslav Richter, who made the first recording of the work with Kiril Kondrashin and the Moscow Youth Symphony Orchestra. Richter, who admired the expert construction of the piece, considered Glazunov to be 'an excellent composer, a musician who knew all there was to know and who had a great influence on the musical life of Russia.'[46]

The concerto, which is in two movements, is described by Donald Tovey as a 'delightful and compendious work'.[47] The first movement, *Allegro moderato*, contains three themes, all of which are developed with Glazunov's customary flair. This process gives the work a genuinely symphonic quality; the composer's aim is to explore his ideas and, therefore, he has no need to resort to mere pianistic virtuosity to create excitement.

The second movement is in the form of a theme with variations. Concerning the theme itself, Michel Stockhem has noted its 'aristocratic and discreetly Russian allure'[48] and the nine variations which follow find Glazunov on his very best form – Variation VI (*quasi una fantasia*) is particularly touching and beautiful. In Variation XI (*Finale*) the theme appears as a march and the three melodies from the first movement return to be woven impressively into the texture of this concluding variation, providing further evidence of Glazunov's powerful sense of musical architecture.

In the following year, 1912, Glazunov naturally played a significant role in the events to mark the fiftieth anniversary of the St Petersburg Conservatory, by writing a celebratory *Prelude – Cantata* for soloists, choir and orchestra, to words by Nikolai Sokolov. This occasional piece honours Anton Rubinstein, the founder of the Conservatory, by quoting from his Fourth Piano Concerto, and Chaikovsky, its most famous graduate, by employing a theme from his *Romeo and Juliet* fantasy overture. Increasingly ill at ease with recent trends in the musical world, it is not hard to imagine that Glazunov must have enjoyed this opportunity to make a connection with two musical figures from the past that he so admired.

The year 1912 also brought him two significant commissions for incidental music – projects that provided him with the opportunity to collaborate with some of the most gifted artists in Russia. In the summer of that year he was busy composing music for a production of *Masquerade*, a play by Mikhail Lermontov (1814–1841). Directed by the revolutionary, Vsevolod Meyerhold, with designs by Alexander Golovin, it would not reach the stage until 25 February/10 March 1917, after an extraordinary five years of rehearsal! In the words of Solomon Volkov '*Masquerade* was a typical romantic melodrama from the life of Petersburg high society, in which the hero, the jealous Arbenin, poisons his wife.'[49]

In addition to his own music, including a disquieting leitmotif representing Evgeny Arbenin, and an affecting *Romance* for Arbenin's wife, Nina, he also included music by Glinka, a contemporary of Lermontov. In Act Three, for example, Glinka's *Valse-Fantasie* is employed, although Glazunov neatly weaves the Arbenin theme into the older composer's elegant waltz. There is also an orchestration of Glinka's song, *Venetian Night*. As many numbers in the score are very short, Glazunov did not bring out a suite, publishing only *Nina's Romance* as his Opus 102. Nonetheless, his incidental music does convey the splendour of the aristocratic world of the play, as well as suggesting the darker undercurrents of jealousy and murder. Indeed, the sinister scoring of the *Chiming Clock* could stand as a symbol for time running out on Russia's Imperial age – as it happened, the play's audiences in 1917 were quite likely to find themselves being shot at, as they made their way home from the Alexandrinsky Theatre.

Sir Thomas Preston, who attended a performance of *Masquerade* in that year, left the following account of his experience:

> One of the most beautiful works, produced for the first time during the early days of the revolution (under the Kerensky régime), was Lermontieff's *Mascarade*, with incidental music by Glazounoff. It was extraordinary to see with what enthusiasm the audience of workers, Soviet bureaucrats, employees and Chekists watched the performance on the stage of a story of the aristocratic life of St. Petersburg of the thirties [1830s].[50]

This remarkable production ran for almost 500 performances.[51]

Returning to the winter of 1912, Glazunov received another request for incidental music when he was visited in the St Petersburg Conservatory by P. W. Daniltschenko, a Captain in the Ismailov regiment, and Nikolai Nikolayevich Arbatov, a theatrical producer. It transpired that Grand Duke Konstantin Konstantinovich Romanov, a grandson of Tsar Nicholas I and an enthusiastic amateur poet and dramatist, had written a play – *The King of the Jews* – on the events surrounding Christ's trial and crucifixion. Although amateur performers were to be involved, with the Grand Duke himself taking the role of Joseph of Arimathea, the choreography was created by Mikhail Fokine and Glazunov had the services of the Court Orchestra, conducted by Hugo Warlich, at his disposal.

Initially, his reaction to the project was not particularly enthusiastic. However, when it was explained to him that, to avoid any problems with the censor, the Grand Duke had decided that Christ would not be represented by an actor – his presence being conveyed by the reactions of the performers – Glazunov's interest was aroused. He explained to Daniltschenko and Arbatov that he could not compose the music until the summer of 1913, when he would have a break from his responsibilities at the Conservatory, but the Grand Duke's two emissaries were only too happy to leave the text of the drama with him. As Glazunov later commented:

> While attending to my work at the Conservatory, I began to think of the characterization of Christ. A melody came to my mind, in which I later perceived the figure on the cross. The entirety of the music was based on this theme, which appears in all possible variations.[52]

Glazunov's imagination was clearly stimulated by the fact that, as Christ was not to be represented by an actor, the music would need to carry much of the expressive burden of the text. In addition, the musical challenge he set himself – developing the score from one principal theme – was something that strongly appealed to his creativity. After completing the music by the autumn of 1913, Glazunov arranged a meeting with the Grand Duke at the Pavlov Palace:

> I played my music for him on the piano, and he was enthusiastic about it. As a result, I decided to arrange the orchestration in such a way that the music could be used for a concert-like performance… The première took place at the Imperial Eremitage Theater on January 9, 1914. Since then, the music to *The King of the Jews* has been performed under my direction in many cities.[53]

This beautiful and deeply felt score contains eleven numbers, starting with an *Introduction and Chorus*, in which the melody, representing Christ, unfolds with a calm dignity, building towards the spirited entry of the chorus hailing Christ's procession into Jerusalem. Indeed, the development of the Christ theme gives the music an inner logic that is not generally a feature of scores that are conceived as part of a theatrical production. Some of the transformations are particularly appealing, showing that Glazunov's melodic gifts had, if anything, become richer with the passing years. This is particularly true of the *Entr'acte* to Act II (*The Palace of Pontius Pilate*) and the *Entr'acte* to Act IV. The score also contains a wonderful Syrian Dance, a memorable evocation of the decadence and sensuality of Christ's tormentors. Glazunov's skilful use of the orchestra even impressed an otherwise unsympathetic Prokofiev. In his diary for 13 December 1914 the younger composer noted that the piece contained 'wonderful effects, you could not tell how they were achieved, such as far-off echoes from Pilate's feasting as Christ was being led to his execution'.[54]

Glazunov also mentioned that the *Song of the Singers of Psalms* 'had made a tremendous impression upon the officers of the Ismailov

Regiment… for they often remembered it in the days of the Great War'.[55] This is an interesting comment as it reveals something of the impact that his music could have on receptive listeners and thereby provides another caveat for those who tend to dismiss him as a composer who produced nothing more than graceful and pleasing music.

The world that produced *The King of the Jews* was soon to disappear in the chaos of war and revolution. When Russia entered the First World War, in August 1914, St Petersburg was renamed Petrograd. (In 1924 its name would be changed again, this time to Leningrad, following the death of the country's first communist leader, before switching back to St Petersburg in 1991.) Glazunov responded to the outbreak of hostilities by writing his *Paraphrases on the National Anthems of the Allies*. Initially composed for two pianos, four hands, this ingenious occasional piece, which contains the anthems of no less than seven nations – Russia, Serbia, Montenegro, France, Britain, Belgium and Japan – was orchestrated in the following year and, in addition to performances in Russia, was heard at two war-time Promenade Concerts in London, conducted by Sir Henry Wood. Dimitri Tiomkin, who attended the first performance of the orchestral version of the *Paraphrases* in Petrograd, vividly remembered the work's 'thundering resonance of brass and fine contrapuntal effects. It had its première at a huge concert for war charities and stirred a thrilling patriotic ovation.'[56]

On a personal level, 1914 was a particularly sad year for the composer, as it marked the death of his father. Moreover, he also lost one of his most important musical friends with the passing of Anatoliy Lyadov on 15/28 August 1914. Another link with the past was broken in the following year, with the death of Sergey Taneyev on 6/19 June 1915. These melancholy events can only have increased Glazunov's sense of responsibility to the tradition of which he was now one of the last important representatives. In the year before Taneyev's death, for example, Glazunov composed his Prelude and Fugue in D minor for Organ, Op. 98, returning to a form which demanded the highest level of contrapuntal ingenuity.[57] Taneyev had been fascinated by counterpoint and his insights into the subject are propounded in his two-volume work: *Convertible Counterpoint in the Strict Style*. The D minor Prelude and Fugue can be seen as a powerful statement of the musical values shared by these two outstanding musicians.

It is significant that Glazunov would return to the form of the prelude and fugue on no fewer than five further occasions over the next few years. As these were particularly difficult and depressing years for the composer, it seems clear that, far from being mere exercises in technical virtuosity, these works embodied Glazunov's troubled reaction to a time of political chaos and social disintegration, expressed in a way that also demonstrated his faith in the traditions of Western music as he understood them to be. They certainly contain some of his most profound and searching music and, in a real sense, stand as an imposing expression of his musical credo, at a time when the world that he knew was vanishing disconcertingly before his eyes.

Glazunov, as already indicated, composed his *Karelian Legend* in 1916, although few concert-goers at the time could have imagined that this would prove to be his penultimate orchestral work. The only other new piece from this year was a setting, for voice and piano, of Shakespeare's Sonnet 66: *Tir'd with all these, for restful death I cry*, in a Russian translation by A. Kremlev. In the words of Yuri Serov, 'The piece definitely contains a special inner strain.'[58] Glazunov's sense of unease is not to be wondered at, given the continuing deterioration of conditions in Petrograd and, in 1917, the year of revolutions, the bitterness and discontent that had been gathering for so long finally broke out in armed opposition to the government.

Despite the continuing war and the violent political upheavals of 1917, Glazunov was remembered by the French government with the award of the Cross of the Legion of Honour.[59] In the same year, he completed three works. For one of them, the *Theme and Variations* in G minor, he returned to a composition which he had originally written for string quintet in 1895, and arranged it for string orchestra. The theme, which is rather like a stately dance from an earlier time, has a haunting quality and the variations skilfully exploit both the potential of the melody and the resources of the string orchestra. A much more exuberant piece is the *Mazurka-Oberek* for violin and piano. Glazunov dedicated this work to the violinist, Paul Kochanski, and later provided a version for violin and orchestra. As with the *Variations* mentioned above, the *Mazurka-Oberek* appears to have been mainly composed some years before, as Glazunov refers to it in a letter to Felix Blumenfeld as an early piece but one he had just now completed, no doubt for an upcoming tour of cities on the River Volga that he was about to undertake.[60] A spirited and tuneful work, it would provide violinists with an excellent encore piece to follow the Violin Concerto.

The most significant new work composed in 1917, however, was the Piano Concerto No. 2 in B major, Op. 100. For this piece he seems to have elaborated on a theme he had used many years before in his *Cortège Solennelle*, Op. 50, perhaps realising that it contained far more potential for development than its treatment in a short orchestral work allowed. Glazunov then follows the pattern established by Liszt, as he derives all the principal ideas in the Concerto from the opening melody.

The one continuous movement contains four main sections which function as an opening movement (*Andante sostenuto – Allegro*), slow movement, scherzo and finale. The first two sections have a rich, autumnal character but, with the playful scherzo and the triumphant finale, Glazunov draws this remarkably fresh sounding work to a lively conclusion. The unison statement of the melody in the final bars seems to act as a resolute QED, as if Glazunov is indicating that the thematic and structural opportunities provided by his material have now been fully realised.

The Concerto received its premiere at a concert given in the Petrograd Conservatory on 29 October/11 November, with S. V. Bentser as soloist. Remarkably this was only four days after the Revolution in which the

Bolsheviks had overthrown the Provisional Government of Kerensky. Over the next few years Glazunov would have to face not only the challenges provided by deteriorating conditions in Petrograd, but also the problems posed by the new government. For one thing, this was a regime with very decided ideas on the role that cultural institutions would have to play in the radical new world order it intended to create.

Chapter eight

1918–28: The end of an era

The winter of 1917–18 was one of the most severe since the year of 1812 when Napoleon invaded Russia. In the words of Ludmila Korabelnikova:

> People used furniture for fuel and went to bed wrapped up in furs. Daily bread rations were reduced to a quarter of a pound, and even for that the emaciated Petrograders had to stand in line. A Russian music critic bartered his grand piano for twelve pounds of black bread... Glazunov, the beloved director of the Petrograd Conservatory, whose corpulent figure was a sightseeing landmark in Russian musical circles, lost half of his impressive avoirdupois in a single year.[1]

As a member of the bourgeois intelligentsia, Glazunov belonged to a class that was inimical to the Bolsheviks. On the other hand, he had a number of important factors in his favour, including his stance in support of the rebellious students in 1905. This had certainly not been forgotten and his efforts on behalf of the student body ever since had ensured that he enjoyed their continuing respect.

In the years following the end of the First World War he was, in any case, the most famous composer left in the country. The exodus of talent from Russia at this time is probably unparalleled in the history of music. The careers of Grechaninov, Lourié, Lyapunov, Medtner, N Nabokov, Obukhov, Prokofiev, Rachmaninoff, Stravinsky and Vishnegradsky,

Glazunov showing the strain of the years of war and revolution

for example, would all now be forged in Europe and America. Lenin's government was therefore glad enough to have retained a figure of Glazunov's stature.

In this respect Lenin's appointment of Anatoliy Lunacharsky to the office of People's Commissar of Public Education on 28 October/8 November 1917 is highly significant. As Boris Schwarz notes, Lunacharsky 'guided the arts in the emerging Soviet state with imagination and flexibility. In ideological matters, he could be firm, but he was not dogmatic.'[2]

Glazunov was fortunate indeed to have the support of this highly intelligent and cultured man. This is clearly illustrated by Schwarz when he goes on to explain:

> Among the older serious composers, the figure of Alexander Glazunov stands out. He guided the Petrograd Conservatory through the difficult years of readjustment and transition. Obviously he enjoyed the respect and affection of Lunacharsky; in fact, a personal directive of Lunacharsky (dated 9 March 1918), protected Glazunov from having his apartment on Kazanskaya Street requisitioned by the government.[3]

In Tsarist times the conservatories were under the aegis of the Directorate of the Russian Musical Society, although a degree of independence was achieved following the 1905 disturbances. After the February Revolution in 1917 the conservatories sought to achieve full independence from government control but the Provisional Government did not respond to their request. The situation changed dramatically with the Bolshevik Revolution and, on 12 July 1918, a decree was promulgated which, in effect, brought the conservatories under the control of the Soviet government. One most welcome improvement, arising from this development, was the decision of Lunacharsky to come to the aid of the hard-pressed Petrograd Conservatory, by providing 225,000 roubles towards its running costs. At the same time this payment also helped to define the relationship between the Conservatory and the government. Lunacharsky made this clear when he wrote to Glazunov, pointing out that, as the People's Commissariat of Public Education was funding the Conservatory, it would have the right to involve itself in the drive to open up the institution to members of the working class.[4]

Glazunov's reply to Lunacharsky's letter is revealing, as it gives a clear indication of the fundamental values which guided his conduct. He certainly felt able to defend the record of the Conservatory by insisting on its adherence to what were essentially liberal values:

Glazunov at his desk in the Conservatory

Students are admitted prevailingly from the poorer classes of the population, unconditionally and without consideration of national origin. The sole criterion for admission was, and is, exclusively the degree of talent and a certain degree of preparation (though there have been cases where exceptionally gifted individuals have been admitted 'in the raw'). The only wish one could express in the interest of a broader service of the Conservatory towards the musical needs of the working population is the lowering of the tuition [fees], an increase in scholarships, and an improvement in the material status of the faculty.[5]

As was soon apparent, the government had a much more radical plan in mind to increase the access of workers and peasants to all the institutions of higher education in the country. To this end Lenin ordered the abolition of all admission tests, as these exams were seen clearly to favour those applicants from the middle and upper classes. Glazunov was concerned that this would lead to a fall in the standards of the conservatories but, once again, Lunacharsky came to the rescue, by ensuring that they would be exempt from the new regulations.

Despite the marked decline in his living standards over these years, Glazunov still managed to produce some of his most interesting and significant piano music. The two remarkable *Prelude-Improvisations*, for example, contain some strikingly dissonant harmonies, in addition to his characteristic lyricism, as he briefly inhabits a more recondite musical landscape. Indeed, these pieces provide further evidence of the 'inner strain' to which Serov referred in connection with the Shakespeare song setting of 1916.

Even more significant are the Four Preludes and Fugues for Piano, Op. 101, which Glazunov dedicated to his friend, Alexander Winkler, a distinguished Piano Professor at the Petrograd Conservatory. All four pieces are based around the key of C: No. 1 in A minor, No. 2 in C sharp minor, No. 3 in C minor and No. 4 in C major, so that Glazunov, in effect, creates a four-movement work, with the final C major Prelude and Fugue providing a powerful sense of culmination at the end of the set. And while the technical skill on display is of a very high order indeed, the expressive power of these pieces should not be overlooked. Their depth of feeling, allied to the complexity and subtlety of musical thought, ensure that they deserve a high place in any assessment of his compositions.

The suffering and disquiet that appears in many pages of the Preludes and Fugues is hardly to be wondered at. By 1919, life became even more difficult for the inhabitants of Glazunov's native city. Solomon Volkov vividly describes the level to which many people were reduced at that time: 'The history of the culture of the twentieth century will note that in 1919 in Petrograd… the plumbing had frozen, public transportation had stopped, and a horse that had fallen on the street was stripped down to the carcass by hungry citizens…'[6]

The conditions in which Glazunov lived are made clear in the reminiscences of Rimsky-Korsakov's son-in-law, Maximilian Steinberg, who was a professor at the Petrograd Conservatory:

> Glazunov, who all his life was used to living in a large flat with all conveniences, was now housed in one smallish room heated by a small stove; here he worked, composed, slept. In the next room was his mother, almost eighty years old. In the other rooms the temperature was freezing; some time later other people moved in. Under such circumstances, creative work was difficult… In this crowded room Glazunov received some of the most famous foreign musicians… I remember the conductor Hermann Abendroth. Entering the room, I saw Abendroth in a fur coat listening to the Second Piano Concerto of Glazunov, played by the composer, also in a fur coat.[7]

Elizabeth Wilson makes a revealing point when she notes that, in 1918 and 1919, a number of institutions simply ceased to function because of the chaotic state of the country at that time. Classes continued at the Petrograd Conservatory, however, as Glazunov was bravely persistent in applying to the authorities for the necessary support. These years, unsurprisingly, took a considerable toll on his health.[8]

H. G. Wells, who met Glazunov when he visited the Soviet Union in September/October 1920, confirms the statements of Steinberg and Wilson, by again emphasising the physical and psychological strain on the composer:

> All musical people in England know the work of Glazounov; he has conducted concerts in London and is an honorary doctor both of Oxford and Cambridge. I was very deeply touched by my meeting with him. He used to be a very big florid man, but now he is pallid and very much fallen away, so that his clothes hang loosely on him. He came and talked of his friends Sir Hubert Parry and Sir Charles Villiers Stanford. He told me he still composed, but that his stock of music paper was almost exhausted. 'Then there will be no more.' I said there would be much more, and that soon. He doubted it. He spoke of London and Oxford; I could see that he was consumed by an almost intolerable longing for some great city full of life, a city with abundance, with pleasant crowds, a city that would give him stirring audiences in warm, brightly-lit places. While I was there, I was a sort of living token to him that such things could still be. He turned his back on the window which gave on the cold grey Neva, deserted in the twilight, and the low lines of the fortress prison of St. Peter and St. Paul. 'In England there will be no revolution – no? I had many friends in England – many good friends in England…' I was loth to leave him, and he was very loth to let me go.[9]

When Glazunov told Wells that he was still composing, he may have been referring to the *Fantasy* in F minor, Op. 104, for two pianos. This substantial composition in three movements opens with a *Moderato tranquillo* in A flat major, to be followed by a Scherzo (*Allegro*) which, in an arresting and novel gesture for the composer, seems to break off in mid-flight, and a finale (*Moderato*). The themes of the opening movement are imaginatively reworked throughout the rest of the composition and, as might be expected, contrapuntal, harmonic and rhythmic ingenuity are much in evidence. The *Fantasy* is an impressive contribution to the literature for two pianos – a genre that was greatly enriched by Glazunov's contemporaries Arensky, Medtner and Rachmaninoff.

Following these years in which the composition of piano music had been his main creative focus, Glazunov turned again to the string quartet. It had been over two decades since he had completed his String Quartet No. 5 in D minor and, considering the quality of that composition, it is perhaps surprising that he had waited so long to return to the genre. The reason for this hiatus may well be found in the death of Belyayev, whose musical evenings had been such a vital stimulus to Glazunov's composition of chamber music.

In 1919, however, a new source of inspiration appeared when the members of the Petrograd Quartet renamed themselves as the Glazunov Quartet.[10] It was for this highly distinguished group of players that he composed his String Quartet No. 6 in B flat major, Op. 106, completed in 1921. Despite its darker moments, the piece has an overall confidence and buoyancy of spirit – something that had not been a feature of his music since the composition of the Second Piano Concerto.

In the opening movement, for example, the first subject seems to gain in assurance with each new statement and, although the contrasting material (*sostenuto poco*) is of a more pensive nature, the movement ends with a joyful flourish. The second movement, *Intermezzo rusticano,* has a delightfully asymmetrical rhythm (3/8 + 2/8 + 3/8), clearly demonstrating that Glazunov still possessed a genuine freshness of invention. In addition, there are some telling examples of his technical skill in writing for the string quartet. The wonderful section *sul ponicello*, for example, with its delicate suggestion of folk instruments, is a case in point.

The slow movement, *Andante piangevole,* provides an expressive note of sorrow and introspection, adding to the emotional range of the composition as a whole, while the finale, which is a theme with ten variations, is surely one of the most successful conclusions in all of Glazunov's chamber music. The theme is short and presented initially in a spare fashion with all the strings in unison, although it soon proves to be a fertile source for his creativity. In the final variation, the opening theme from the first movement is recalled, rounding off the quartet in a jubilant manner – a fact that is all the more remarkable, considering the circumstances under which the work was written. It is an admirable testament to the resilience of Glazunov's spirit.

In the past, the Sixth Quartet's reputation suffered from critics who were wedded to the view that Glazunov's later works were inferior to those of his youth. Even a highly perceptive commentator such as Boris Schwarz writes that it 'showed traces of creative decline…'[11] and it is barely mentioned in an essay devoted to Glazunov's string quartets by the otherwise sympathetic critic, Edwin Evans.[12] It is therefore encouraging to note that some recent assessments of the work are much more responsive to its very real qualities. Klaus Burmeister, for example, is surely closer to the mark when he explains that the Sixth Quartet is '… a truly monumental work. It reflects everything that makes Glazunov's music unique: absolute formal control, intellectual concentration, profundity and finely nuanced colours.'[13]

The fact that there was now a string quartet named in his honour was the first of a number of compliments paid to Glazunov as the fortieth anniversary of his career as a composer was celebrated in 1922. He travelled to Berlin where, on 22 March, his Eighth Symphony was performed by the Berlin Philharmonic. During his stay in the German capital he met Lola Kinel. She had been charged with the task of trying to persuade him to sign a contract to conduct fifteen concerts in America for a fee of $10,000. In her memoirs she describes Glazunov as possessing:

> … a typical Russian face: broad, shapeless, bulbous yet somehow full of character and kindliness. I recalled the many stories I had heard about him in Petrograd. He had one great failing: he was too kind and this was so well known that occasionally pupils took advantage of it.[14]

In spite of this tempting offer, he could not be induced to sign the contract. He told Kinel that he was 'just too old, too ill' and he was clearly concerned that English was not one of the foreign languages with which he was familiar. It is also revealing that he mentions his concerns for the students at the Conservatory: '– all so hungry, no clothes' and alludes yet again to the shortage of music paper.

Her meeting with Glazunov left a deep impression on Kinel and she seems to have been affected in much the same way as H. G. Wells. When she left Glazunov she noted: 'I felt terribly sorry for this kindly, pudgy Russian, as great and true an artist as ever lived. A few days later I read in the paper that Glazounov returned to Russia: to poverty, hunger and cold.'[15]

Despite the widespread suffering, the Soviet Union was beginning to emerge from the civil war of 1918–21 and it showed its appreciation of Glazunov's continued presence at the Conservatory by marking the fortieth anniversary of his career as a composer in some style. He was awarded the title 'People's Artist of the Republic' on 6 September 1922 and, on 29 October, a concert in his honour was held in the Great Hall of the Moscow Conservatory. Proceedings got under way with a speech delivered by Lunacharsky, in which he drew attention to Glazunov's international renown by mentioning that the composer had recently been elected a Member of the Berlin Academy.[16] A celebratory cantata, written especially for the occasion by Pavel Chesnokov, to words by Valery Bryusov, was performed and Glazunov's works heard that evening included the Seventh Symphony, conducted by the composer, and the Violin Concerto.[17]

The anniversary also gave rise to a flurry of musicological activity, with a number of articles, pamphlets and journals devoted to various aspects of Glazunov's career, including the first edition of the journal *Muzyka.* Most significant of all, perhaps, was *A K Glazunov* by Victor Belyayev (no relation of M. P. Belyayev), the first major study of the composer since that of Alexander Ossovsky: *Alexander Konstantinovich*

Glazunov: His Life and Creative Work, published in 1907.

On a personal note, 1922 was also a significant one for Glazunov, as he married Olga Nikolaevna Gavrilova. The couple departed in secret to Pskov where they were married according to the ordinances of the Russian Orthodox Church.[18] Given the anti-clerical campaign launched by the Bolsheviks after the Revolution, the secrecy surrounding these proceedings is hardly surprising. Olga already had a daughter, Elena, by her previous marriage. Elena was a talented pianist and throughout her career Glazunov's piano music would remain an integral part of her repertoire. The composer adopted Elena as his own daughter and, in 1926, he dedicated his richly textured *Idylle* for solo piano, Op. 103, to her. As Stephen Coombs writes:

> It is an extraordinary piece for this period. Despite the appalling conditions in which the composer lived (disappointments and frustrations, crushing poverty and illness), this piece has an almost joyful quality together with a heart-rending beauty… This is a wonderful swan-song with all the traits of Glazunov's musical character – melodic invention, harmonic sophistication and a wealth of contrapuntal detail.[19]

The *Idylle*, together with the powerful Prelude and Fugue in E minor from the same year, constitute Glazunov's last works for solo piano.[20]

An insight into the life that he led with Olga and Elena is provided by his friend, Sir Thomas Preston, who was a regular visitor to the Glazunov apartment during the 1920s. He notes that Olga and Elena 'had kept the house of the great musician for many years' and describes the impressions he received from his first visit to the composer's home:

> It was then about 4.30 in the afternoon and I only left his house well after midnight. From this day onwards, for the many years that I was to spend in Soviet Russia, Alexander Constantinovich became my dearest friend and hardly a week passed without our meeting, either at our respective houses, or at some concert or musical entertainment. The hours I spent with Glazounoff I count amongst the happiest of my life… The fascination of Glazounoff was not only due to his monumental knowledge of all things musical. He could and would talk on any subject. But it was probably kindness of heart, sincere modesty and almost childlike simplicity, that endeared this great man to everybody who had the good fortune to meet him.[21]

Preston goes on to describe a meal he shared with the family consisting of black bread, raw herring, homemade vodka – 'a preparation concocted by the Professor himself' – Russian cutlets (a Sunday treat!) homemade jam and tea without milk or lemon, the latter being too expensive at the time. After the meal Elena entertained the company with some piano music, played on an old upright piano, as Glazunov could not afford to heat the rooms in the flat that contained his three grand pianos.

When Prokofiev returned to Russia with his wife, Lina, in 1927, for a concert tour, he called on Glazunov. The composer was out but he did meet Olga and Elena, both of whom made a favourable impression on him. At the time Prokofiev was not sure whether Glazunov had married the mother or the daughter, but the uncertainty relating to Glazunov's marital status has already been explained in part by the secrecy surrounding the ecclesiastic service in Pskov in 1922. Later, Glazunov and Olga took part in a civil marriage ceremony, which was performed in the Russian Embassy in Paris, after they left the Soviet Union in 1928.[22]

The flat visited by Prokofiev was in fact the home in which Glazunov had lived his entire life, surrounded by the careful ministrations of his mother. She seems to have treated her eldest son as if he were still a boy right up to the time of her death and there are a number of stories indicating her well-meaning but somewhat smothering attentions. If Glazunov ordered a cab to take him to the Conservatory, his mother would apparently express concern over whether the horse was calm enough to ensure the safety of her son's journey.[23] Nonetheless, when his mother died on 6 September 1925,[24] he had one less compelling reason for remaining in his homeland.

At the Conservatory, matters were also developing in a way that increased the strain on the ageing composer. With the death of Lenin, in 1924, and the subsequent rise of Stalin, Glazunov must have felt that he was living in a world that was almost entirely alien to his nature. Through the years of war, revolution, famine and the rise of a new order, he had remained steadfast in support of his beliefs. This is true not only of the music which he composed but also of his dealings with those in authority. When, in 1924, for example, many students were expelled from the universities and conservatories because they were not members of the proletariat, Glazunov, according to Preston, 'made a brave stand, [so] that a number of the more talented ones were allowed to remain'.[25]

Schwarz sums up the difficulty of Glazunov's position at this time:

> The internal squabbles were particularly abhorrent to Glazunov who continued to enjoy the confidence of all the factions. An old-time liberal who had sided with the students in 1905, he suddenly found himself caught between resentful professors and rebellious, often arrogant, students.[26]

Glazunov in 1925

Fittingly, his approaching departure from the Soviet Union is associated with an Elegy. Mikhail Kurbanov, who had been a member of the Belyayev group in earlier days, suggested to Glazunov that he should write a funeral march for string quartet to mark the twenty-fifth anniversary of Belyayev's death: 'No one in the world has yet written a funeral march for quartet! It will be magnificent!' The Elegy, in D Minor, for String Quartet, Op. 105 which Glazunov completed on 9 November 1928, not long after his arrival in Paris, is a short but moving tribute to one of his most loyal admirers.

In this piece Glazunov returns for the last time to the 'Belyayev theme' of the 1880s, embedding the motif in the musical texture. This occurs mainly in the viola part, Belyayev's preferred instrument. Towards the end, the music settles into an *alla marcia funebre,* the Belyayev motif appearing in the viola (pizzicato) over which the highly expressive lament unfolds one last time. As Gerald Abraham notes, it is both 'very personal' and 'very expressive'. In marked contrast to the 'cheerful, effective, extrovert' Belyayev pieces of the 1880s, it provides a vivid indication of how dramatically the circumstances of his life had changed over the intervening years.[27]

By 1928 Glazunov had achieved all that he could in resisting those aspects of change with which he was profoundly unhappy – at least some of which were motivated by political, rather than musical, considerations. When he left the Soviet Union to travel to Vienna, as a representative of his country at the Schubert centenary celebrations, he was, as it turned out, leaving the land of his birth for the last time. He would remain nominally in charge of the Conservatory until 1930, but his departure from the Soviet Union was indeed the end of an era.

CHAPTER NINE

1929–36: Concert tours and Paris

Glazunov travelled to Vienna on 15 June 1928[1] where, as part of the programme to mark the Schubert centenary, he chaired the committee charged with the task of awarding the prize offered by the Colombia Gramophone Company of New York for a contemporary work written in the spirit of Schubert. Some remarkable compositions were submitted to the competition including Havergal Brian's *Gothic Symphony,* Franz Schmidt's Symphony No. 3 in A and Hans Gál's Symphony No. 1 in D, although the first prize was eventually awarded to Kurt Atterberg for his melodious and colourful Symphony No. 6 in C.

Glazunov and his wife Olga were settled in Paris by the end of September at 39, Rue Singer but sadly his remaining years would be marked by ill health. This made his attempts to earn a living by giving concerts increasingly difficult, as he suffered from angina, rheumatism and gout. He was not without friends in Paris, however, as the French capital was home at this time to many Russian émigrés.

One of them was Nikolai Cherepnin, who had been a colleague of Glazunov's at the St Petersburg Conservatory for many years. Greatly to his credit, Cherepnin took steps to aid the ailing composer. He approached Nikolai Artsybushev, a long-standing member of the Belyayev group and now the manager of the M. P. Belaieff publishing house, to see if he could make arrangements to ensure the publication of Glazunov's new works. In August 1928 Cherepnin wrote to his wife:

> Yesterday… visited Glazunov in the afternoon and brought him some Russian books to read, which pleased him very much. His health is still unsatisfactory… but his mood is good. On his table lies a letter from Auer, who is now in Paris [and] asks Glazunov to visit him, since he cannot venture out. This means these old friends will not manage to see each other, although they have much to reminisce about… I managed to convince [Artsybushev]… of the necessity of putting together a life for Glazunov in Paris: to allow him to search for opportunities, on the one hand, and to satisfy his needs, on the other; and to immediately grant him an adequate monthly stipend from the accounts of the Belaieff Publishing House!!![2]

Glazunov returned to the concert hall on 19 December, conducting a programme of his own works at the Salle Pleyel in Paris. This included his *Overture Solennelle*, the symphonic poem *Stenka Razin*, the Second Piano Concerto, with Elena as soloist, and the Seventh Symphony.

As it turned out the concert created some critical controversy in the musical press. Paris in 1928 was at the centre of musical modernism and, to some of the radical critics of the day, Glazunov's conservative idiom represented an approach to composition that they rejected out of hand. A case in point was the vicious review of the concert, printed in the Russian language newspaper, *Latest News*, on 30 December. It was written by Boris de Schloezer, the brother of Tatyana, Scriabin's second wife:

> '… one cannot say that his [Glazunov's] is a star whose lustre age has dimmed; new and young it never was… All he did was construct endless autonomous aural systems that moved under their own motive power in accordance with their own purely private specific musical laws, bereft of psychological influences or the slightest admixture of alien poetical or visual stimuli…'[3]

Glazunov at the time of his tours to America and Europe

Here Glazunov's music is dismissed simply because it does not comply with the assumptions that define the critic's personal aesthetic. What does such as vague phrase as 'psychological influences' actually mean? Why should *all* music require an 'admixture of alien poetical or visual stimuli'? His case is not helped by the fact that he does not appear to know how many string quartets Glazunov had composed by this time, as elsewhere in his article he gives the number as four when in fact it should be six. Unsurprisingly, this infuriated a number of Glazunov's admirers who were not prepared to allow Schloezer's partisan attack to go unanswered. A letter was sent to the editor of *Latest News*, signed by a number of prominent Russian musicians, including Medtner, which insisted that Glazunov was 'a figure of such stature whose achievements in the history of Russian music are so incontrovertible that no criticism of him can possibly diminish his significance'.[4]

In 1929, after an absence of twenty-two years, Glazunov returned to England to conduct a concert of his own works at the BBC. The programme, which was broadcast on 9 June, following two rehearsals of two-and-a-half hours each, comprised the *Lyric Poem*, the *Carnaval Overture* and *The Seasons.* The composer was impressed with the BBC Wireless Orchestra – and with his fee of £50!

The music critic of the *Daily Express*, Gordon Beckles, provides the following sketch of the Russian visitor:

> Traditional pictures of the composer show a face of Oriental intensity. All that is now gone. When I entered the broadcasting studio a dear old man… was wandering about the players examining the band parts. Around his neck was what appeared to be an untidy piece of handkerchief: it was a stiff collar melted into disorder. Then he approached a high slant-seated chair, ensconced himself thereon, and, with legs dangling and left hand resting on the thigh, he waved the beat.[5]

While in London Glazunov also made his only recording of an orchestral work – *The Seasons* – for the Columbia Record Company.[6] Although Beckles makes no direct reference to Glazunov's state of health in his article, the composer's appearance was of immediate concern to Joe Batten, the company's recording manager, when he met Glazunov prior to the sessions at the Portman Rooms in Baker Street: 'I shall never forget meeting him, tall, elderly, so frail and ill with gout and rheumatism that I wondered if he could stand the physical strain of three or four hours of intensive recording. But he did, and produced a performance of sheer beauty.'[7]

In a letter to Steinberg, Glazunov explained how the three recording sessions proceeded. Although only *Winter* was taped during the first, greater progress was made in the second, so that by the end of the final four-hour session, the project was completed. Glazunov's only regret was that the *Saytr* variation, which was added to *Autumn* in 1907, could not be included, as not all of the players had the requisite parts.[8]

Although Glazunov was not always admired as a conductor, his performance of *The Seasons*, captured in Columbia's recording, is excellent. He was certainly fortunate to be working with instrumental players of a very high calibre but, even so, Batten must have been surprised by the energy captured in *Winter*. In the *allegro* movements, for example, such as Variation 1 (Hoar frost) and Variation 3 (Hail), the tempi are brisk. This then helps to highlight the contrast with the more lyrical sections, such as Variation 2 (Ice), where the melody is given time to unfold gracefully. The same contrasts are also apparent in *Spring* whose appearance is remarkably light-footed.

Glazunov's visit to London was undoubtedly a successful one. In addition to his broadcast concert and the recording, he was able to attend a performance of his Violin Concerto on his day off. This was part of a concert at the Royal Academy of Music, conducted by Sir Henry Wood, a man who was one of the most loyal advocates of the composer's music in England.

Returning to France, Glazunov spent some time in Antibes in August, prior to setting out on a tour of America in November. This was under the auspices of the leading impresario, Sol Hurok, whose wife, Emma, had been a pupil of the composer.

In his memoirs, *Impresario*, Hurok mentions that he had met Glazunov in Paris in 1929, and offered to organise a tour of America for him. Hurok explained to the composer that he 'did not expect to make money out of his tour', but that he would be 'proud and grateful' to bring Glazunov to America.[9] Earlier in the decade Glazunov had declined an offer to tour the United States. Clearly his lack of English, in addition to his various health problems, had discouraged him from undertaking this venture. However, now that he had left the Soviet Union, he needed to earn a living and he also hoped, no doubt, that his presence in America might stimulate further interest in his music. Therefore, in early November 1929, Glazunov and Olga, accompanied by Elena and her husband, Sergey Tarnovsky, sailed across the Atlantic on the French liner *Rochambeau*. Hurok provides the following account of the composer's arrival at New York on 5 November, explaining that to him, 'it was a moving moment when the old man… a world of kindness in his wrinkled face under the shaggy white hair, stepped off the boat onto American soil'.[10]

Hurok was able to hire the Metropolitan Opera House and Orchestra for the first concert in New York, which took place on 3 December. The programme, which Glazunov conducted, contained the *Overture Solennelle*; the Piano Concerto No. 2 in B major (with Elena as soloist); four Songs, (sung by the famous Russian soprano, Nina Koshetz); Glazunov's orchestral version of the *Song of the Volga boatmen* and the Symphony No. 6 in C minor.

Before the concert began, Walter Damrosch, the famous conductor and staunch supporter of Russian music, made a speech introducing Glazunov to the audience and presenting him with a floral lyre. In a review published in *The New York Times*, Olin Downes describes the scene, which clearly had something of a festive atmosphere about it:

> The audience, which greeted Mr Glazounoff when he appeared on the stage with impulsive and heartfelt cordiality, included in its ranks celebrated musicians and Russians prominent in many professions and other walks of life, and emanated, as it seemed, something of a day more romantic and gallant than this one, richer in its colour, perhaps more sentimental, but also more brilliant and more youthful in its mood than ours.[11]

Glazunov also received a warm reception when he attended a concert at the Carnegie Hall on 29 December. In honour of his presence, the New York Philharmonic Orchestra concluded their programme with his Fourth Symphony. Willem Mengelberg was due to conduct this performance but, due to ill health, his place was taken at short notice by Hans Lange. At the end of the Symphony, 'Mr Lange turned and applauded the composer who rose and bowed to the members of the orchestra who also paid their tribute. They were soon joined by the entire house with enthusiasm.'[12]

While in America Glazunov demonstrated a degree of curiosity in contemporary music by expressing a desire to hear Gershwin's *Rhapsody in Blue.* After attending a performance of this piece, given by the New York Philharmonic with Gershwin as soloist, Glazunov went to see the famous American composer in the artists' room. He was accompanied by the distinguished Russian musician, Vladimir Drozdoff, who acted as interpreter.

Gershwin started the conversation by saying that he had long desired to study orchestration with Glazunov. The latter remarked to Drozdoff, however, that Gershwin could not think of studying orchestration seriously until he had an understanding of counterpoint. Although initially rather cast down by this comment, Gershwin clearly gave it some serious thought for, the next day, he contacted Glazunov at his hotel and asked if he could recommend a teacher. And so, with the aid of Drozdoff, it was arranged that Gershwin would study with Joseph Schillinger.[13]

This incident reveals something significant about the character of the two men. Glazunov, for his part, treated all musical matters with the utmost sincerity and honesty. It would have been very easy for him to make up some flattering observation – a compliment that would have pleased Gershwin without, of course, being of any service to him. By telling Gershwin what he genuinely thought about his idea of studying orchestration, Glazunov actually demonstrated his respect for him. For his part, Gershwin had the strength of character to consider the implications of Glazunov's comment and to take steps that would enable him to develop more fully his range as a composer. As Walter Rimler notes, Gershwin thanked Glazunov for being completely honest with him.[14]

Although Glazunov's concerts were well received by audiences, his health was no longer anything like robust enough to cope with the combined strain of travel and conducting, particularly in the middle of a North American winter. Hurok also notes how some of Glazunov's friends had to come to his aid with financial support:

> The Detroit Symphony offered only $500 for Glazounov's performance as guest conductor, but Ossip Gabrilowitsch added another $500 out of his own pocket to the fee.
>
> Serge Koussevitzky gave him a glowing welcome in Boston. When he left Chicago, Frederick Stock and a group of his friends got up a fund of between $7000 and $8000. This they presented to him as royalties – so they said – for the many performances of his works in this country.[15]

The *Chicago Tribune* had also welcomed Glazunov's arrival in the city on 18 December, by noting that:

> The Chicago Symphony Orchestra did something yesterday it does not often do. It interrupted its recording of phonograph records to welcome a visitor, and played a number in his honor.
>
> The guest was Alexander Glazounow, a Russian composer who blew into Chicago yesterday in a gale that parallels, he says, the weather in his far northern homeland. The composer was ceremoniously introduced to Chicago's symphony, which he will direct tomorrow and Saturday in concert at Orchestral Hall. Then the players struck up the Triumphal March, written by Glazounow for the 1893 World's Fair, much to that gentleman's delight.[16]

The programme for the first concert, on Friday 19 December, was planned along similar lines to that of the New York performance, with the *Triumphal March*, Op. 40, the first movement (Prelude) of the Suite *From the Middle Ages*, the Violin Concerto (with Jacques Gordon, the Concert Master of the Chicago Symphony Orchestra, as soloist) and the Symphony No. 6 in C minor.

Following the first concert, the *Chicago Tribune* commented:

> Mr Glazounoff was immensely popular with audience and orchestra alike. A wave of enthusiasm swept through the house at his first appearance that took several minutes to subside, and at the conclusion of the concert, the orchestra joined with the applause of the audience by giving him the fanfare technically known as a "tusch". And this is no ordinary or frequent token of appreciation.[17]

Glazunov revealed to the paper that he was impressed by Chicago's 'great buildings and the swiftly moving Americans. Even jazz… received a kind word when Glazounow said he found it new and interesting.' As the *Chicago Tribune* explained, Glazunov was due to give a second concert in the city on Saturday 21 December, but the cold weather had already undermined his health and when he was visited by Dr Maurice A. Bernstein he was far from well. Bernstein told the paper that, when he entered Glazunov's room in the Congress Hotel, the composer was dressed for the concert and determined to carry out his engagement, regardless of the Doctor's opinion.[18] Bernstein was understandably concerned that Glazunov's fever and bronchitis might well develop into pneumonia and so he insisted that the composer should take to his bed. In his place, the concert was conducted by Eric De Lamarter.

In the New Year, Glazunov's appearance in Boston was celebrated with a generous article in the *Boston Evening Transcript* written by a former student of the St Petersburg Conservatory, Nicolas Slonimsky. He suggested that Glazunov was being welcomed to America 'with a measure of sincere admiration and awesome respect that no other composer of universal fame has heretofore received.' The article concludes by summing up Glazunov's career as 'a noble life in art'.[19]

Unfortunately, the health problems that were apparent in Chicago continued to trouble the composer as Hurok's memoirs confirm: 'The old man was not well. He was ill for a while in Chicago. When he recovered, I brought him back to New York by way of Niagara Falls. He saw the ice caves… and he said, 'If I don't live a day more, it was worth the trip to see Niagara Falls.'[20]

Towards the end of his tour, a number of events were organised which give some indication of the affection that many musicians felt for Glazunov. Clearly his efforts on behalf of Russian music and musicians were still appreciated:

> Walter Damrosch, who was musical director of the National Broadcasting Company at the time, gave a reception in Glazounov's honour at his home. He had played Glazounov's Third Symphony over the air that night, a special broadcast.

> Kadroff's Quartet of Russian singers sang at the party, to Glazounov's delight. Damrosch, who himself has done so much to spread the gospel of good music to America, could not do enough for Glazounov.
>
> Before the composer left these shores his former pupils in New York gave a banquet in his honour at the Hotel Commodore. There were six hundred guests, and one by one his pupils among them rose and told what this gentle old man had done for them.[21]

At the conclusion of his North American tour, Glazunov boarded the French liner *Rochambeau* once again for his return journey to France. As the voyage proceeded he was soon at work on what would prove to be his final piece of chamber music for strings: the String Quartet No. 7 in C major, Op. 107. In a letter to L. V. Nikolaev, dated 21 February 1930, Glazunov informs his correspondent that he has already completed the first movement and has conceived the ideas for the other three.[22]

The suggestion that he compose a string quartet may have originated with Jacques Gordon who, as noted above, played the solo part in a performance of Glazunov's Violin Concerto, given in Chicago. The new work bears the dedication 'To the Gordon String Quartet' and was published by M. P. Belaieff in 1932.

Each movement of the Seventh Quartet has a title. The first, *Homage to the Past*, opens with an *Adagio* introduction, presenting the principal theme of the main *Allegro giocoso* section. What is remarkable here is that, even so late in his career, Glazunov could produce music with such rhythmic vitality and freshness of invention. Clearly the recollection of the past was for him a powerful creative stimulus. The second movement, *The Breath of Spring*, is more pensive in character; the music has a melancholy quality, as if the composer were seeking to recapture, in old age, the sense of joy that he had experienced in his youth. This is followed by *In the Mysterious Forest,* an ingenious

Scherzo, which evokes a magical, enchanting world – one that had always appealed to Glazunov's imagination. Its shifting rhythms and imaginative exploitation of texture make this a memorable movement.

The Russian Festival finale which follows provides an exultant celebration of the composer's homeland. The opening theme of this rondo has a distinctly Russian character and Glazunov treats it with affection and skill, varying its rhythmic shape and sonority; as elsewhere in the quartet, he is able to draw on a lifetime's experience of writing for this medium. Towards the end, for example, there is a particularly striking passage in which each instrument is required to play *pizzicato* chords in a style Glazunov describes as 'quasi balalaika'. The striking syncopations of the final bars bring the quartet to a brilliant conclusion, rounding off a work that stands as a beautifully crafted, imaginative and touching summation of his contribution to the genre.

In addition to composing the Seventh String Quartet, 1930 also brought a number of conducting engagements. Glazunov travelled to Poland, Czechoslovakia and Estonia to give concerts of his works, while in the summer he had a holiday in Saint-Claude in the Jura mountains where he started composing his Cello Concerto – the *Concerto Ballata*.[23] Then, in the winter of 1930-1, he was in Berlin to attend the first German production of Borodin's *Prince Igor*.

By October 1931, Glazunov had settled at Boulogne-sur-Seine. This would be his home for the rest of his life. The following month he made his last visit to England where, on 26 November, he conducted the Eastbourne Municipal Orchestra in *Winter* from *The Seasons*, the Second Piano Concerto, with Elena again as soloist, and the Seventh Symphony.

The English composer, Eric Coates, happened to see Glazunov in an Eastbourne hotel during this visit and left this affectionate – though far from flattering! – description of him:

> I ran across him in Eastbourne, where he was due to conduct one of his Symphonies and his Piano Concerto. He was sprawling over a writing-desk in the lounge of the hotel where we were both staying, scribbling on a piece of paper, the while puffing furiously at a huge cigar. His bulky frame obtruded through the framework of the arm-chair in which he was sitting, which looked as if it might collapse at any moment, and as he wrote he grunted and snorted like a grampus. I did not disturb him, lest he might not 'recapture the first wild careless rapture' of the phrase which had just come into his mind. So I remained in my chair by the fireside and watched and listened to the great man in the first agonies of delivering an embryo masterpiece.[24]

Glazunov's concert was well received by the critic of the Eastbourne Chronicle – even his conducting was praised: 'Glazounov electrifies the orchestra, much as Sir Thomas Beecham – certainly it did not want for lack of impetus and his conducting, though dignified like that of Nikisch, is full of vigour and a grace that is infectious.'[25]

As both 'vigour' and 'grace' are unquestionably present in his recording of *The Seasons,* this compliment may well have been fully justified. It does provide further evidence that, over the years, Glazunov became a more than competent conductor of his own music.

The year 1931 also saw the completion of the *Concerto Ballata* for cello and orchestra, in C major, Op. 108. It was dedicated to Pablo Casals who, during his tours of Russia, had become acquainted with Glazunov, as well as a number of other Russian composers.[26] However, the first performance of the concerto, which took place in Paris on 14 October 1933, with Glazunov conducting, was entrusted to one of Casals' pupils, Maurice Eisenberg.

The piece is in three main sections played without a break and, as with the Violin Concerto, the soloist has a cadenza leading straight into the finale. Glazunov explained that the slow movement was in the style of a ballad and for this reason he chose the title *Concerto Ballata* for this composition. In fact, the idea of a ballad – a narrative with the cello soloist as narrator – fits the overall concept of the concerto very well, as the piece is more episodic and fluid in structure in comparison with his other concertos.

The work opens impressively with an eloquent theme in the lower register of the cello and this beautiful melody appears in various guises as the composition unfolds. The first movement (*Allegro commodo*) becomes increasingly animated before a transition into the melancholic slow movement (*Adagio, con tristessa*). The cello then leads the orchestra into the lively and sunny finale (*Allegro marciale*). Although the musical argument has a somewhat rhapsodic, and occasionally repetitive, character – perhaps a reflection of his wanderings after leaving the Soviet Union – the Concerto possesses some affecting and powerful episodes, and Glazunov writes at all times with real sensitivity and skill for an instrument that he clearly loved.

His fondness for the *Concerto Ballata* is reflected in his anxiety to have it performed. This is clear from a letter which he wrote a few years later to the conductor, Ivan Gregorevich Boutnikoff on 1 August 1935. Here the composer indicates that, of the two programmes of his works that Boutnikoff suggested for a concert in Vienna, Glazunov preferred the one containing the Cello Concerto. He went on to explain that a performance of this piece would be 'very dear' to him.[27]

The phase of creativity that saw the composition of the Seventh String Quartet and the *Concerto Ballata* was, unfortunately, impaired in his last years by his deteriorating health. In other letters to Boutnikoff, Glazunov complains of ailments affecting his leg, shoulder and stomach and later he mentions a severe bout of rheumatism, brought on by a cold. He also mentions concerns about his health in a letter he wrote to Rachmaninoff. After thanking Rachmaninoff for help with his finances, he explains: 'Yesterday morning, following your advice and taking advantage of a warm, sunny day, I took a rather long walk in the Bois de Boulogne. Because of the beautiful weather my "excursion" brought me no punishment, but what will happen on a bad day?'[28]

Despite these problems, a new and totally unexpected source of interest arrived in 1932 when Glazunov heard a performance of the Quatuor des Saxophones de la Garde Republicaine. This group was led by its founder, Marcel Mule, who had formed the quartet in 1928.[29] Impressed by both the sonority of the instruments and the virtuosity of the players, Glazunov resolved to write his Saxophone Quartet in B flat major, Op. 109, which he duly dedicated to the group. It has ever since been regarded as a seminal work in the saxophone quartet repertoire: a piece that is both demanding and rewarding. The first of its three movements has a mellow mood, the principal melodies helping to establish the appealing lyrical quality of the *Allegro*. This is followed by a *Canzona variée* – a theme with five variations, the last of which is a brilliant Scherzo, very much in Glazunov's best vein. The Finale is also a lively movement with something rather insouciant and French about the principal theme and there is certainly no lack of energy in the scintillating coda.

The composer had to wait until April 1933 to hear his quartet and, in a letter to Ia. A. Vol'fman, he expressed his satisfaction with the skill of the performers and the full and novel sound that the quartet of saxophones produced.[30]

The public premiere of the work eventually took place on 14 December of that year. In the audience was the virtuoso saxophonist, Sigurd Rascher. He later recorded his impression of the performance and his enthusiastic response to his meeting with Glazunov:

> Overflowing with excitement, eventually even I made it into the artists' room. I had difficulties expressing myself in common language, so I held the master's hand and asked simply, 'May I play for you?' 'Young man', he said in a fatherly tone, 'the saxophone I have known for fifty years!'[31]

Glazunov nonetheless acceded to the request and so the very next day Rascher presented himself at the composer's home to demonstrate the potential of the saxophone to him. Duly impressed, Glazunov immediately complied with Rascher's request to write a concerto for the instrument and, over the next three months, worked on his Concerto in E flat major for Alto Saxophone and String Orchestra, Op. 109.

Rascher, to whom the Concerto is dedicated, visited the composer again, prior to the work's premiere:

> With great patience he [Glazunov] entered into all details. These were unforgettable hours: even today, more than half a century later, not only what he said about music is clear in my memory, but also the master's voice, his facial expression, and even the furnishings of the room.[32]

Rascher gave the first performance of the Concerto on 26 November 1934, in the Church of St Nicholas, Nykoping, Sweden, when he was accompanied by the Norrkoping Symphony Orchestra, directed by Tord Benner. The same programme was repeated immediately on 27 November, in Norrkoping. Other performances soon followed: the French premiere took place in Paris, on 20 January 1935, with Marcel Mule as soloist, while Rascher introduced the Concerto to London on 14 January 1938.

The most compact of all Glazunov's concertos, it falls into three sections, played without a break. The principal theme is introduced at once by the strings in unison (*Allegro moderato*) before being taken up and embellished by the soloist. It is noticeable how he achieves a beautiful texture throughout the piece by dividing the strings, while the singing tone of the saxophone is most memorably displayed in the second section (*Andante*) which contains two new themes, both of which have a wistful character. Glazunov characteristically places the cadenza between the *Andante* and the final section.[33] In this concluding *Allegro*, the saxophone launches into a lively fugato, the strings following the soloist's lead. The themes from the *Andante* and the first movement are recollected before the tempo speeds up, as the piece gathers momentum towards its high-spirited conclusion.

In the Saxophone Quartet and the Saxophone Concerto, Glazunov shows his respect for the saxophone by treating it in his own way, although his experiences of hearing the instrument played in America and France can be detected in both works. Of these pieces Marcel Mule observed: 'I hold a wonderful memory of this great composer who welcomed the interest in the saxophone, and who dedicated two works of supreme quality which magnificently enrich the repertoire of the saxophonists.'[34]

Glazunov's last orchestral work also dates from this time: the *Epic Poem* (*Poème épique*), Op. posthumous. Started at the end of 1933 and completed on 3 February 1934,[35] it is dedicated to the Academie des Beaux Arts de l'Institut de France. The principal theme of the piece is derived from the letters of *Academie:* a-c-a-d-e-e (mi)-e and, as Mundy explains, 'this modal tune conjures up images of Russian chant and the middle ages'.[36]

The theme in question certainly freed Glazunov's imagination to return to the epic world of knights, martial conflict and romantic love that was of absorbing interest to him. The *Epic Poem* can be placed, therefore, within a sub group of Glazunov's orchestral works, which includes the ballet *Raymonda*, the *Ballade* and the Suite *From the Middle Ages,* although it has a more sombre character than that of the earlier pieces. With its strongly contrasted themes and rich instrumentation, it provides a fitting farewell to Glazunov's highly productive career as a composer of orchestral music. The work was first heard in Paris, in 1935, although the score was not published until 1965, on the hundredth anniversary of Glazunov's birth.

During his final years in Paris, Glazunov was no longer at the centre of a large and talented group of musicians, artists and writers, as he had been in his St Petersburg heyday. Yet despite these changing circumstances, he did have friends and colleagues whose presence must have been a comfort to him: as already mentioned, Nikolai Cherepnin exerted himself on Glazunov's behalf and another friend in exile was the illustrious Russian writer, Yevgeniy Zamyatin, the author of the celebrated novel, *We*. Indeed, Stanley Dale Krebs describes Glazunov as 'one of his [Zamyatin's] few friends in exile'.[37] And there were occasional visits from some of his old students from the St Petersburg Conservatory, such as the great violinist, Efrem Zimbalist, who called on the composer when passing through Paris.[38]

Of the French musicians, with whom Glazunov made contact, few were of greater significance than the leading composer and organist, Marcel Dupré. It was he who encouraged Glazunov to write what would be his last composition, the *Fantasy*, in G minor, for Organ, Op. 110, the manuscript of which contains the following dedication: '*Au grand musician virtuose maître Marcel Dupré en souvenir de nos recontres chez lui, chez moi et a le Cathedrale St Sulpice, le 12 Avril 1935, Paris.*' Dupré would later edit Glazunov's organ works for the firm of M.P. Belaieff.

The *Fantasy* contains a series of freely evolving variations on the famous plainchant, *Dies Irae.* The initial presentation of the theme is derived from the clarinet solo which occurs towards the end of the Lento (*Variation IV*) of Liszt's *Totentanz,* a work which received its first performance in 1865, the year of Glazunov's birth. The opening *Moderato,* solemn and dignified, gives way to the delicate *Allegretto pastorale,* which in turn leads into a resolute fugue. Towards the end of the fugue, as Ute Schalz-Laurense observes, the 'continual increase in musical density permits a layering of the theme in three different rhythmic sizes and a drastic, grating harmonisation'.[39] There is real courage in the concluding bars, as Glazunov sets aside the years of illness and increasing neglect to conclude his life's work with this splendid final peroration.

Glazunov's health continued to decline during the rest of the year and in a letter to Boutnikoff, dated 1 August 1935, he writes:

> I conclude from your letter that rumours concerning my illness did not reach you. In April I caught a cold and an acute rheumatism, from which I am still suffering. The weather does not help: it is still cold. I feel ashamed to admit it, but in many ways I cannot do without constant assistance. Although I can still move my fingers, I have a great deal of trouble playing and even writing… My life is very unpleasant. I am quickly irritated and lose my patience.[40]

The final remark is particularly revealing, as Glazunov's temperament was, by nature, calm and imperturbable. The end was clearly not far away and it came on 21 March 1936, the very day on which a concert was to be given in his honour by the Lamoureaux Orchestra.[41] Only some hours before the composer's death, brought about by uraemic poisoning, the publisher, Alphonse Leduc, had personally delivered to Glazunov's apartment a copy of the first edition of the Saxophone Concerto.[42]

Towards the end of his life, Glazunov had been hoping that his health would improve sufficiently to enable him to return to Leningrad.[43] However, what he could not accomplish in life was finally fulfilled in death when, in 1972, his remains were disinterred from the cemetery in Neuilly, where he had been buried in 1936, and re-interred in

Leningrad's Alexander Nevsky Cemetery, where he now rests beside many of the great composers with whom he is most closely associated: Borodin, Chaikovsky and Rimsky-Korsakov.[44]

Chapter ten

Epilogue

Following Glazunov's death on 21 March 1936, a number of important obituaries appeared in the press throughout the world. In England, Havergal Brian provided the article which was printed in the May edition of *Musical Opinion*. Brian had met Glazunov when the latter visited England in 1928 and, at that time, the aforementioned journal asked him to interview the Russian visitor. Glazunov evidently expressed an affection for England and Brian noted: 'I think he was quite sincere when he said he cherished the memory of Parry and Stanford, and his face glowed when I mentioned his visits to the Royal College of Music, the Royal Philharmonic Society and the Leeds festival.'[1]

Commenting also on Glazunov's character, Brian wrote that he was 'impressed by the unassuming modesty of his demeanour' and expressed the hope, alas unfounded, 'that nothing in worldly affairs had made the closing days of a kindly man unhappy'.[2]

It is perhaps to be expected that, as an important symphonist himself, Brian should focus much of his obituary on this aspect of Glazunov's output – and he was surely right to do so. His concluding remarks are also significant, as they provide an insight into the nature of Glazunov's achievement – something that has been largely ignored ever since: 'I feel it impossible to say what the position of Glazounoff and his music will be; however, we must agree that, of all the Russian composers, he is the one genius who expressed himself naturally and easily in classical moulds.'[3]

The view that Glazunov's symphonies were at the core of his achievement is supported by comments made in the memoirs of

Sir Henry Wood: *My Life in Music*. Wood, who refers to Glazunov as an 'old friend', conducted a memorial concert in the composer's honour. He goes on to explain:

> Madame Glazounoff wrote to me after the concert, to which she had listened by wireless in her Paris home, and marvelled at the reception accorded to her husband's works. At the same time she thanked me for my long friendship and the many presentations of Glazounoff's compositions. I feel that his three Symphonies the Fourth, Fifth and Sixth will now take their place in the repertoire and, perhaps, the F minor piano concerto, which I produced in August of 1913.[4]

Across the Atlantic the notices of the composer's death adopted a similar tone. In the obituary published in *The New York Times*, for example, Glazunov's character and reputation are neatly summarised, echoing the comments of Brian: 'He was known in Russia not only as a creator of important symphonies and stage works and an incomparable pedagogue, but also as a friend of the poor and the outcast – a modest, unassuming man with a most magnanimous personality.'[5]

Glazunov's achievement as a symphonist is further emphasised when the writer comments: 'Of his symphonies, the Eighth is considered by many of his admirers the apex of his expression in the classic form. But the Sixth has always been the most popular of his symphonic works.'[6]

Glazunov's passing was also marked by a memorial concert held in New York's Steinway Hall on 15 May 1936. This was organised by the newly formed Glazounoff Association whose President, Vladimir Drozdoff, had acted as Glazunov's interpreter during his American tour of 1929–30. The names of honorary members make impressive reading and, in their own way, indicate the high esteem in which Glazunov was held: Mischa Elman, Ossip Gabrilowitsch, Leopold Godowsky, Alexander Grechaninov, Jascha Heifitz, Josef Hofmann, Serge

Koussevitzky, Joseph Lhevinne, Mischa Mischakoff, Michel Piastro, Toscha Seidel, Alexander Siloti, Nikolai Sokolov and Efrem Zimbalist.

Yet despite these promising signs, Glazunov was to suffer the fate of many composers with the marked decline of his reputation that occurred following his death. Indeed, this process was well under way even before the end of his life.

In part this can be explained by the extraordinary rapidity of his development which meant that he was left as one of the last prominent figures of a musical age that was no longer considered relevant. In this respect, it is interesting to compare his compositional progress with two of his exact contemporaries: Sibelius and Nielsen. Glazunov had reached his Symphony No. 6 (1897) about three years before Sibelius completed his Symphony No. 1 (1900), while Glazunov's Seventh Symphony, of 1902, coincides with Nielsen's Second. Although these three great composers shared the same year of birth, in terms of composition Glazunov really belonged to an earlier generation. To emphasise this idea, it is perhaps worth pointing out that his last completed symphony, the Eighth, dates from 1906, the year *before* Rimsky-Korsakov finished work on his last opera, *The Golden Cockerel*.

This aspect of his career is therefore particularly significant when considering Glazunov's relationship with the composers who were coming to prominence in the early twentieth century. While he continued to uphold the traditions that he loved and valued, many of the younger generation were seeking out new techniques with which to express the spirit of a very different age.

The tension between Glazunov and the young musicians of the next generation is at its most acute in his relationships with three of the leading composers of the twentieth century: Prokofiev, Shostakovich and Stravinsky. That it has taken Glazunov's reputation so long to recover – in so far as it has – is due, in no small measure, to the undeniably vivid but often negative descriptions found in Prokofiev's writings and the dismissive remarks made by Stravinsky.

GLAZUNOV and PROKOFIEV

Prokofiev certainly never denied that Glazunov was an important figure in the early part of his career. Indeed, things between them proceeded smoothly at first, as it was Glazunov who, in 1904, persuaded Prokofiev's mother to allow her son to enter the St Petersburg Conservatory. When she suggested that it might be better for him to study to become a civil engineer or an architect, Glazunov replied:

> If a child with abilities like your son's shouldn't be sent to the Conservatory, then who should be? At the Conservatory his talent will be fully developed, and there is every chance he will become a genuine artist. But if he is trained as a civil engineer he'll be an amateur musician, and he'll never be able to realize his potential completely.[7]

As a sign of his admiration for Prokofiev's talent, Glazunov sent him two scores by Glinka, in one of which he inscribed the words: *From A Glazunov to his dear colleague, Serezha Prokofiev*. However, by 1908, Prokofiev comments that Glazunov's 'interest in the boy… was giving way to an irritating impression produced by that adolescent who had grown into a young man and begun to compose very unseemly pieces'.[8]

Clearly the dissonant harmonies and often acerbic tone of many of the works in Prokofiev's modernist phase were extremely uncongenial to Glazunov. Nevertheless, when Prokofiev went to seek Glazunov's permission to perform some of these compositions at a concert given at one of the Evenings of Contemporary Music, the older composer consented. As Prokofiev observes: 'He took no interest in the pieces, but he didn't want to put obstacles in the way of a young composer.'[9]

Anthony Phillips encapsulates the situation particularly well in his introduction to the first volume of Prokofiev's diaries, as he explains that Conservatory's focus on producing thoroughly trained students, with a secure grasp of the traditional forms of composition, was always likely to be irksome to Prokofiev, a highly ambitious young genius with a fiercely independent spirit. Phillips goes on to comment:

> Even the jaundiced eyes of the author of the *Diaries* cannot altogether obscure either Glazunov's essential generosity of spirit, or that at least he recognised his unruly charge's special gifts… The notorious incident of Glazunov's discomfort at being obliged, as Director, to announce… the award of the Rubinstein Prize for a performance of a work with which he so cordially disagreed, [Prokofiev's First Piano Concerto] may be forgiven when it is remembered that the prize was supposed to be for playing the piano, not for innovative composition.[10]

And yet, despite these eminently fair remarks, the Rubinstein Prize is one of a number of incidents which certainly contributed to the negative attitude surrounding Glazunov. This is not altogether fair, particularly in the light of Prokofiev's own comments on his approach to the competition: 'While I might not be able to compete successfully in performance of a classical concerto there was a chance that my own might impress the examiners by its novelty of technique; they simply would not be able to judge whether I was playing it well or not!' [11]

In his diary entries, however, Prokofiev skilfully casts Glazunov in the role of antagonist, when he describes the memorable scene: 'Mumbling, Glazunov announced that the grand piano had been awarded to a student of the distinguished Professor Yesipova, Sergey Prokofiev, then without pausing went on to read out the marks.'[12] The use of the word 'mumbling' looks like a telling point, as it suggests Glazunov's disapproval in the face of Prokofiev's triumph. In fact, this is not actually as significant a detail as it appears to be, given that Glazunov habitually spoke quietly- something that Prokofiev had already noted in an earlier diary entry. Glazunov, he remarked, 'mumbled in his usual indistinct fashion'.[13]

When this incident is mentioned it is also rarely pointed out that it was Glazunov who had suggested to Prokofiev that he should perform the Concerto for the Professors at the Conservatory prior to the competition.[14] Indeed, when Prokofiev had played the Concerto to Glazunov, the latter was not entirely negative about it. Prokofiev gives the following account of their conversation:

> He approved of the form, the logic, the technique, found much temperament and admirable sonorities, but the music itself… strange… incomprehensible… of course, your ears are different from mine… It turned out that Glazunov must have heard from somewhere or other of the existence of the Second Concerto. I played him the *Intermezzo*.
>
> 'Very interesting. Splendidly done. But the music… very strange… especially the middle section.'
>
> I explained the logic of the middle section, and then played him the first movement. Glazunov liked the mood of the opening and generally considered the Concerto to be a significant development over the First. Very individual and interesting piano style, but the music![15]

Even though Prokofiev is obviously having fun at Glazunov's expense, with the repetitions of 'but the music', he nonetheless reveals that the older composer was far from being entirely dismissive of the scores he heard. Indeed, the remarks that Glazunov made about the First Concerto's 'admirable sonorities' and the fact that the Second Concerto represented real progress, in comparison with the First, are perceptive. As is generally the case in life, there is more than one side to any given story.

Perhaps even more significant in this respect is the episode that occurred in January 1916 when Glazunov left the hall during a performance of Prokofiev's *Scythian Suite*, a work which may well represent Prokofiev's attempt to rival Stravinsky's *The Rite of Spring*. Following the concert,

Alexander Aslanov, who had been in the audience, informed Prokofiev that Glazunov had 'ostentatiously' walked out during *The Procession of the Sun*, the final movement of the Suite.[16] A point that is sometimes made concerning this incident is that Glazunov had made a public demonstration of his disapproval of Prokofiev's composition.

As in the case of the Rubinstein Prize, the negative interpretation of Glazunov's conduct may not be entirely justified. For one thing, taking into account Glazunov's height and bulk, it is hard to imagine how he could possibly have left the hall in an unostentatious manner. Prokofiev also later pointed out that Glazunov's departure coincided with the work's 'penultimate page,' which in Prokofiev's own words sounded 'truly... overwhelming'.[17] As the end of the work is hardly more dissonant than much of the rest of the piece, it is certainly possible that Glazunov left the hall because of the cumulative effect of the sheer volume of the music. When, at one point in the second movement, the timpani player burst a drum skin, Prokofiev noted in his diary that it was 'sadly not ear-splitting enough'![18] As already mentioned, Glazunov had experienced problems with ear infections and his heightened concern for his hearing may well account for his conduct in this instance.[19]

It should also be remembered that Glazunov, as a Russian gentleman, was not given to public expressions of his feelings. Prokofiev himself provides evidence of the elderly composer's courteous behaviour. On the day following his visit to Glazunov's apartment in Leningrad, during his 1927 tour of the Soviet Union, he discovered that, on returning to his hotel, Glazunov had called on him in his absence. 'Like the gentleman he was' the older composer had left two calling cards. This put Prokofiev in mind of an occasion, nearly a quarter of a century earlier, when 'with the same courtesy' Glazunov had visited Prokofiev's mother a few days after she had taken her young son to see the famous composer.[20]

No doubt Glazunov disliked the music of the *Scythian Suite* but it does not follow from this that he was making a public statement when he left the hall just before the end of the piece. In this context, it is worth noting that, in 1926, Glazunov attended the premiere of the nineteen-year-old Shostakovich's First Symphony, a work that, in many ways, is far more forward-looking and radical in tone than Prokofiev's *Suite*. Yet, as Solomon Volkov explains, 'The audience kept looking over at Glazunov, who sat in his usual sixth-row-aisle seat. He had no intention of quitting the hall (as he had with Prokofiev); on the contrary, he smiled and applauded…'[21]

Although the relationship between Glazunov and Prokofiev always contained an undeniable element of strain, it is heartening to note that in 1928, Prokofiev was photographed sitting between Glazunov and Winkler when the three met up in Paris.[22] And very much to his credit, Prokofiev also signed the greetings sent to Glazunov in 1932, to mark the fiftieth anniversary of his composing career.[23]

GLAZUNOV and SHOSTAKOVICH

Glazunov's connection with another central figure in twentieth century music, Dmitry Shostakovich, evolved along somewhat similar lines to his relationship with Prokofiev. Once again, it was Glazunov who strongly supported the idea that the future composer should take the entrance exam for the Petrograd Conservatory. In this case he confided to Sofiya Vasilyevna, Shostakovich's mother, that 'I cannot recall a time when there were children as gifted as your son at the Conservatory.'[24]

When Shostakovich sat the entrance exam in 1919, it was soon known within the walls of the institution that, in the opinion of its Director, the thirteen-year-old applicant possessed a talent that was 'on a level with Mozart's'.[25] In the years that followed, Glazunov paid close attention to the progress made by Shostakovich and, in his comments on the young man's performances in examinations, he reveals his consistent admiration for his outstanding abilities. One such note reads: 'Exceptional gifts which have blossomed early. Something to be astonished and delighted at. Fine technical workmanship, interesting and original content.'[26]

In the difficult years following the Civil War of 1918-21, Glazunov secured grants of money and rations to help maintain Shostakovich's health, which was by no means robust. On more than one occasion, he wrote directly to Lunacharsky to appeal for aid, ending one of his letters with: 'The death of such a man would be an irremediable loss for the arts the world over.'[27]

The most revealing incident of all, however, occurred at a meeting in the Conservatory at which the possibility of Shostakovich's expulsion was raised. It may seem extremely odd, to put it mildly, that such an idea could be contemplated but, in those dangerous times, it was noted that the Shostakovich family belonged to the despised liberal intelligentsia. Moreover, there was also the fact that neither Shostakovich nor his mother was a member of the Communist Party. Mikhail Gnesin, the composer and Conservatory professor, explains what took place when Shostakovich's name was mentioned. At the suggestion made by the Conservatory's assistant director, that financial support should be removed from Shostakovich, Glazunov uncharacteristically lost his temper and pointed out that if the name of Shostakovich meant nothing to this man then he had no business working at the Conservatory. Glazunov went on to insist that Shostakovich was one of the most promising composers of his generation and one of the best hopes for the future of music.[28]

Glazunov's unwavering appreciation of Shostakovich's genius did not mean, of course, that the music of the young composer was any more appealing to him than that of Prokofiev. When looking through the score of Shostakovich's First Symphony, for example, he suggested some alterations to the harmony at the end of the opening movement's first phrase, as he found the original chords to be too harsh. In the end, Shostakovich remained true to his initial intention but, as noted above, Glazunov still welcomed the work's first performance. Indeed, during his tour of North America, in 1929, he continued to draw attention to the achievement of his brilliant countryman. In an article published in *The*

New York Times, he identified Shostakovich among 'the leading modern Russian composers whose works have made the deepest impression,' citing the opera *The Nose,* based on the satirical short story by Gogol, as one of Shostakovich's finest compositions to date.[29]

GLAZUNOV and STRAVINSKY

A more problematical relationship was that of Glazunov and Stravinsky, despite – or perhaps because – of the fact that they had both started out as private pupils of Rimsky-Korsakov. Indeed, these two great composers stand at almost opposite ends of Rimsky-Korsakov's teaching career. In the early stages of his activity as a composer, Stravinsky made a piano transcription of Glazunov's Fourth String Quartet and the older composer's influence can certainly be detected in Stravinsky's early Piano Sonata and the Symphony in E flat major. The brilliant rhythmic transformation of the folk theme at the end of *The Firebird* may also stem from Glazunov, as it exemplifies a technique of which he too was very fond; it is a significant element in the finale of his Sixth Symphony, for example. Nonetheless, Glazunov looked on askance when Stravinsky found his own voice in seminal works such as *Petrushka* and *The Rite of Spring*. Richard Taruskin is one of the leading critics who has commented on the strong antipathy that existed between the two composers.[30]

One does wonder, however, if the animosity that existed between the two men was felt more strongly on Stravinsky's side than on Glazunov's. A revealing incident is recounted in Prokofiev's diary entry for 3 June 1929, in which he describes a chance encounter with Stravinsky. A few days before, Glazunov had given a performance of his ballet, *The Seasons*, with the Orchestre Symphonique de Paris, following which Stravinsky had gone to the artists' room to see Glazunov. Stravinsky then provided Prokofiev with the following account of this encounter:

> … but Glazunov, apparently deliberately, did not recognise him. 'Alexander Konstantinovich, look, it's me, Stravinsky!' he cried, at which Glazunov coldly shook his hand and turned away. In a most uncharacteristic manner, Stravinsky added resentfully that it was a long time since he had felt so discomfited as after this incident.'[31]

It is only fair to point out that, in a letter to Maximilian Steinberg written shortly afterwards, Glazunov provides a significantly different version of the same meeting:

> 'Stravinsky unexpectedly appeared and asked me whether I remembered him. Of course I recognised him immediately. He expressed his pleasure in the music of my ballet, and perhaps sincerely at that, since once long ago he asked me to give him the score to examine and didn't return it for a long time.'[32]

Because of Stravinsky's status as, arguably, the most influential composer of the twentieth century, his accounts of events are widely accepted. Nonetheless, the above anecdote suggests that, once again, a great deal more caution needs to be exercised in this connection. In the same way, Stravinsky's assertion that Glazunov's music was 'academic' has been repeated down the years by a number of music critics. But what appeared 'academic' to Stravinsky can be seen, on the other hand, as a complete mastery of the art of a more traditional style of composition. Clearly Stravinsky intended to suggest that Glazunov's music was dry, cerebral and lacking in inspiration but well prepared performances and recordings of Glazunov's best pieces should reveal that this criticism is a highly misleading generalisation – and one that has inhibited the dissemination of some very fine music.

In truth, this type of conflict is not at all unusual when one artistic age gives way to another. Consider, for example, the aggressively dismissive attitude of the novelist Henry James when, as a young man, he reviewed *Our Mutual Friend*, the last completed novel of Charles Dickens. James wrote that the 'poverty' of the novel arose from 'permanent exhaustion', before going on to describe *Bleak House* as 'forced' and *Little Dorrit* as 'laboured'.[33] The key point here is that James was already well aware of the fact that he was going to write a very different *type* of novel, so it is hardly surprising to find that he was totally out of sympathy with the aesthetic approach exemplified by Dickens. Modern readers can appreciate these differences and still enjoy the work of both writers.

In much the same way, Glazunov's style of composition was rejected by the composers who were at the forefront of a drive to create a new musical language. Montagu-Nathan illustrates this idea rather neatly. Assessing Glazunov's position in relation to Russian composers at the time of the First World War, he comments:

> And among them towers Glazunof, rooted deep in the soil of music, and spreading his branches in almost every direction. And the more shade he brings upon the field the more the younger growths lean away from the shade, stretching eagerly towards the light that gives them life.[34]

GLAZUNOV and TWENTIETH CENTURY CRITICS

Of the music critics who took their lead from Stravinsky, one of the most important was Gerald Abraham, a leading authority on Russian music. Some, if certainly not all, of his writings exemplify a negative attitude to Glazunov[35] and, even allowing for the fact that the best critics cannot be expected to appreciate the style of every individual composer, it is important to consider Abraham's argument, as expressed in his essay '*Glazunov. The End of an Episode.*'[36]

He starts by describing the generation of composers who followed the Mighty Handful as a 'generation of epigones' of which 'Glazunov was only the most important figure'. As defined in the *Collins dictionary*, an 'epigone' is 'an inferior follower or imitator' and, given that Glazunov was born in 1865, discovered by Balakirev (born in 1837) and taught by Rimsky-Korsakov (born in 1844), he can, of course, be seen as a 'follower' – everyone has to start somewhere, after all. However, here is another case in which the astonishing speed with which Glazunov's compositional career evolved needs to be taken more fully into account. His First Symphony, for example, received its premiere in 1882, some sixteen years *before* Balakirev's first venture into the genre reached the concert hall. It should also be noted that works such as *Stenka Razin* (1885), the Second Symphony (1886), the *Oriental Rhapsody* (1889) and *The Kremlin* (1890) form a significant, rather than an inferior, contribution to the final flowering of orchestral music from the Nationalist composers that occurred in the 1880s: Borodin's *In the Steppes of Central Asia* (1880), Balakirev's *Tamara* (1883), Rimsky-Korsakov's *Capricio Espagnole* (1887), *Sheherazade* (1888) and the *Russian Easter Festival Overture* (1888).

Further evidence of the importance of Glazunov's contribution to the cause of the Mighty Handful can be discovered in the field of chamber music. The Third String Quartet in particular exemplifies Balakirev's pan-Slavonic ideas more fully than any other chamber work by a member of the Kutchka, combining, in its finale, *A Slavonic Festival*, melodies in the style of several Slav nations. In similar vein, there is no more vivid evocation of the sound of Tartar musicians than in the *Orientale* from the Suite for String Quartet, Op. 35.[37]

Glazunov, therefore, did not provide a pale imitation of the previous generation but created works which undoubtedly helped to enhance the reputation of the Nationalist movement. This is clearly demonstrated by the very positive reaction of leading French musicians to his Second Symphony and the tone poem *Stenka Razin,* when these works were programmed as part of Belyayev's Paris concerts in 1889.[38]

The accusation of inferiority can certainly be called into question by considering a piece such as *Stenka Razin.* Here the creative imagination that Glazunov brings to the development of the *Song of the Volga boatmen* is extremely impressive, as it generates a real sense of symphonic growth – hardly a strong point in the orchestral works of the Mighty Handful. As already indicated, the theme is explored in a variety of imaginative ways and it is questionable if any other Russian composer of the time made better use of a single folk tune. Indeed, it was Abraham himself who elsewhere expressed the view that compositions such as *Stenka Razin* and *The Kremlin* 'suggested the advent of a considerable master'.[39] It is hard to square this with his assertion that Glazunov was no more than an epigone.

At the core of his argument, however, is the suggestion that Glazunov's best work was done in his ballet scores and in theme and variation movements, rather than in the form of the symphony. Yet, while praise for Glazunov's ballet music and variation technique is both welcome and deserved, Abraham goes on to suggest that a 'Glazunov symphony is just an uninterrupted flow of melodious ideas, laid out according to the classical or neo-romantic (Lisztian) forms, lusciously harmonised and beautifully orchestrated. But nothing ever happens to these ideas.'

Abraham's characterisation of a Glazunov symphony as 'just an uninterrupted flow of melodious ideas' is hardly the most devastating observation ever made about a composer's work. Nonetheless, the assertion that 'nothing ever happens to these ideas' is a serious criticism and one that should not go unchallenged. The Second Symphony, for example, explores the potential of the principal theme in an imaginative way, to reveal strongly contrasting aspects of its character, while the tremendous energy generated in the first movements of the Fifth and Sixth symphonies would not be attainable *without* the masterful development of their ideas. Examine, also, the finales of the Fourth and Seventh Symphonies in which all the themes from the previous movements reappear. Importantly, the melodies are not simply repeated, rather they are transformed and combined in new ways, thereby providing an exhilarating kaleidoscope of ideas that constitutes an achievement unique to Glazunov in the history of Russian symphonic music.

Abraham then proceeds in his attempt to undermine Glazunov's claim to be a major symphonist by advancing the idea that he could have been a 'first-rate miniaturist', listing the theme and variations from the Suite for String Quartet, Op. 35, as part of his evidence for this view. Anyone wishing to test this theory would do well to play the theme and variations followed by, say, the first movement of the Sixth Symphony. Most listeners would surely be struck by the contrast between the rather colourless variations and the impressive combination of power and beauty that the symphonic movement provides. Here it would seem that the examples are being forced into a preconceived argument, rather than the argument evolving from a careful appreciation of the music.

The essay concludes with the following summation: '… as a youth he had promised so much more. The rose-strewn career of Balakirev's 'Little Glinka,' wealthy *enfant gâté* of Russian music, with its record of uninterrupted outward success, remains after all a tragedy of brilliant promise only half fulfilled.'

It is certainly fair to suggest that Glazunov's early career was 'rose-strewn' as he received every encouragement from men of the stature of Balakirev, Rimsky-Korsakov, Stasov, Borodin and Belyayev. As a member of a wealthy family he could pursue his passion for music untrammelled by financial cares. At the same time it must also be acknowledged that not everyone who is provided with great opportunities in life has the energy, dedication and genius to take advantage of them. Glazunov's career proves that he had all of these qualities.

Having granted that, it is simply extraordinary to suggest that Glazunov enjoyed a career of 'uninterrupted outward success'. The fact that he was Director of the St Petersburg/Petrograd/Leningrad Conservatory would indeed suggest a degree of recognition but Abraham's remarks completely ignore the enormous strain that the role placed on Glazunov:

trying to maintain the independence of the Conservatory, in his dealings with various forms of highly authoritarian government; mediating in the disputes between gifted but temperamental members of staff and their talented but often rebellious students; enduring, with his fellow Russians, the terrible privations of the years of war, revolution and famine, followed by years of ill health. Abraham has absolutely nothing to say of this crucial aspect of the composer's life – a life that was, in the end, anything but 'rose-strewn'.

To sum up his argument, Abraham suggests that Glazunov's 'brilliant promise' was 'only half fulfilled' – a viewpoint that can only be entertained by overestimating compositions such as the First Symphony while, at the same time, seriously undervaluing a master work such as the Eighth Symphony. Consider, for example, how the themes of the first movement of the Eighth are developed with far greater conviction, giving the symphony an emotional depth that is not to be found in Glazunov's first essay in the genre, however engaging it may be. If anything, the contrast is even more pronounced in the two slow movements. The rather bland *Andante* of the First Symphony lacks the profound impact of the Eighth Symphony's *Mesto* – a movement that explores new emotional territory for the composer. The contrast between the two works is apparent even in the scherzos. While the scherzo of the First Symphony is undoubtedly a lively and attractive movement, it is not subtly integrated into the overall structure of the composition as is that of the Eighth. A comparison between the two finales is also instructive. The cheerful, folk-inspired finale of the First is entirely in keeping with the approach of the Nationalist school. In contrast, the polyphonic textures and subtle thematic transformations found in the last movement of the Eighth are uniquely characteristic of Glazunov's own mature vision. His craftsmanship enables him to capture in a moving way the triumph of hope over anxiety and despair. As Montagu-Nathan observes, the 'later symphonies have shown that he can write music that, far from being less interesting than his programmatic works, have a strength and beauty that have yet to be estimated at their true value as examples of Russian music'.[40]

Indeed, far from a decline into mediocrity, Glazunov's re-evaluation of his style in the early 1890s, encouraged by his friendships with Chaikovsky and Taneyev, heralded the most productive period of his activity as a composer. It is therefore refreshing to turn from the negative attitude of Abraham to consider some contrasting opinions on the value of Glazunov's compositions. The composer and conductor, Eugene Goossens, a noted admirer of Stravinsky and a passionate advocate of new music, was a musician of broad sympathies and in comparing Glazunov with the French master, Saint-Saëns, he writes that their 'creative fertility stemmed from real genius, but I think that their chief claim to fame lies in their fine craftsmanship. Both were cunning workmen.'[41]

The distinguished Dutch pianist and musicologist, Alex van Amerongen, makes a similar point but also helps to highlight the fact that Glazunov's technical skill was at the service of his creativity – not a substitute for it:

> It is my opinion that Glazounov's music has lost nothing of its freshness and spontaneity. We can without doubt be more objective in our judgement about his art… It is now a matter of indifference to us that Glazounov persevered in his aesthetic views from before 1900 and continued to compose in the style with which he was familiar and which was part of himself. He was against every revolutionary impulse and expressed his great creative talent in that musical language which came to him most naturally and freely. We find the admirable result of this tenacity to principle in the richness of his work, which has remained full of life because of its perfect harmony of form and subject.[42]

CONCLUSION

Glazunov once likened himself to the character of Kotchubai from Pushkin's poem *Poltava*, who claimed to have three treasures in his life.[43] In a life possessed by music, Glazunov's three treasures were: giving concerts, directing the St Petersburg Conservatory, and composing music. When he drew this analogy, during the 1920s, he was deeply depressed for it seemed to him that the only option left open to him was to conduct his own music.

Assessing his career as a conductor, it is evident that he belonged to the age in which composers were expected to give performances of their own music. The figure of the professional conductor, as it is understood today, was emerging as a significant force towards the end of the nineteenth century but Glazunov lacked the ability of men such as Hans von Bülow, Hans Richter, Hermann Levi or Arthur Nikisch. The distinguished conductor, Nikolai Malko, explains that when Glazunov conducted the works of other composers, 'it was not interesting. He was often quite helpless.'[44] The failed premiere of Rachmaninoff's First Symphony is undoubtedly the most significant example of this.

With time, and a great deal of experience, however, he did become a fine interpreter of his own compositions. Again, it is worthwhile recalling the words of Malko when he suggests that, in his own music, Glazunov 'could impart to the orchestra precisely that which was characteristic of the work, and it would reach the musicians and through them the listener'.[45] In later years Glazunov wisely limited himself to performing only his own pieces and, as a result, he enjoyed greater success. Evidence of this can be found in the excellent recording he made of *The Seasons* in 1929.

Glazunov's role as a teacher and administrator of the St Petersburg/Petrograd/Leningrad Conservatory represents a much more significant contribution to the musical life of Russia and, indeed, to that of the world beyond its borders. His time as Director coincided with probably the greatest political and social upheaval the country had ever witnessed but, as is often the case, it was also a period characterised by exceptional brilliance. As a key figure in the cultural life of the time, Glazunov was in a position to examine the early scores of great composers such as Nikolai Myaskovsky, Serge Prokofiev and Dmitry Shostakovich. While walking along the corridors of the Conservatory, he would also have heard some of the twentieth century's most outstanding virtuosi as they practised: performers of the calibre of Jascha Heifetz, Vladimir Horowitz, Nathan Milstein and Efrem Zimbalist.

Glazunov contributed his vast expertise in orchestration and composition to his students, but it is in the role of Director that the true stature of the man is most fully revealed. He endeavoured, very honourably, to maintain the independence of the Conservatory in the face of government intervention. He also personally assisted many poor but able students with guidance and, more often than not, financial support. The efforts he made on behalf of Jewish musicians, who frequently faced appalling anti-Semitism, provide yet further confirmation of Glazunov's essential decency. And all this was achieved despite bouts of depression and heavy drinking. Therefore, Mundy's conclusion that Glazunov 'was, without doubt, a great man' seems to be a just assessment.[46]

Dr Sigrid Neef also makes a revealing comment when she describes the composer as a 'colossal, impassive-seeming figure, [whose] physical mass concealed a sensitive, empathetic nature'.[47] Significantly, Elizabeth Stutsman's description of Glazunov also focuses on the difference between the physical appearance and the essential character of the man:

> His enormous stature mainly gave the impression of an imperturbable and composed personage, which contrasted with his extraordinarily vivacious spirit. The fundamental straightforwardness of his character and his warm sympathy radiated, inspiring in all who approached him respect and affection.[48]

Further insight into Glazunov's nature is provided by Dmitri Tiomkin, who writes:

> Like all men of personality Glazunov has his individual peculiarities… Either he is very lively or very silent… Utter modesty and spiritual democracy were his watch words at home and in school. As a rule, he spoke little in society, but when he was aroused on a particular subject he could be brilliantly conversational… There is in him much of the hospitable Russian merchant who loves to entertain his visitors, or, in the good old days, treat them to a glass of tea or vodka.[49]

Perhaps there were those who could not – or would not – see past Glazunov's self-contained demeanour and so failed really to appreciate the many qualities of his nature. In turn, this may have contributed to some of the misunderstandings which have subsequently clouded his reputation.

In the end, however, it is as a major Russian composer that Glazunov has the strongest claim on our attention. As Boris Asafyev notes, 'The work of Glazunov puts a crown on an immense and fruitful period'.[50] His ballet music has remained popular: to this day *Raymonda* is part of the repertory of the Mariyinsky and the Bolshoi companies, while *The Seasons*, although rarely given in the theatre, is performed in the concert hall and has received many fine recordings. These scores constitute the last great flowering of the romantic tradition in Russian ballet. And yet other aspects of his rich and varied output are still neglected, with the result that audiences have very limited opportunities to experience Glazunov's finest works with the excitement that only well prepared live performances can engender. It is true that the Violin Concerto and the Saxophone Concerto are occasionally programmed but audiences are very unlikely to encounter many of the works that represent Glazunov at his best.

My own list would include the mature symphonies from the Fourth to the unfinished Ninth and the two piano concertos. There is also a wealth of fine music in the shorter orchestral works: *Lyric Poem*, *Stenka Razin*, *The Forest*, *The Sea*, *Oriental Rhapsody, The Kremlin, Spring* (Op. 34), *Carnaval Overture,* Concert Waltz No. 1, *Scènes de Ballet, From Darkness into Light, Raymonda Suite, Overture Sollennelle, Ballade, Preludes* (Op. 85) and the *Prelude in Memory of Gogol*. In the chamber music the string quartets from the Second to the Seventh can be recommended together with the delightful *Novelettes*, String Quintet, *Elegy* (Op. 105) and Saxophone Quartet. An excellent indication of the range and quality of his piano music can be found in pieces such as the *Barcarolle and Novelette*, Three Études, *Grand Concert Waltz*, Preludes and Fugues, Variations, Op. 72, Piano Sonatas, *Prelude-Improvisations* and the *Idylle.*

Glazunov was a remarkable composer. If Chaikovsky is the Tolstoy of Russian music and Musorgsky the Dostoevsky, then Glazunov may be likened to Turgenev. Both Glazunov and Turgenev were gentlemen with a liberal political outlook, whose origins in Russian culture were enriched by a sophisticated knowledge of European traditions. In the work of the composer and the novelist it is apparent that inspiration is served by a high level of craftsmanship. And so, in summing up Glazunov's achievement, it can be said that he combined several compositional qualities, including a gift for distinctive melody, a protean genius for developing themes, an impressive mastery of counterpoint and symphonic construction and a degree of skill in orchestration that even Rimsky-Korsakov greatly admired.[51] His best music has a freshness and strength that belies the claim that it is merely 'academic'. The range and quality of his piano music, together with the works for string quartet undoubtedly merit further exploration. It is also to be hoped that the generous flow of melody and rhythmic energy found in his ballet scores will continue to engage the attention of leading dance companies. In the concert hall, programmes would be refreshed with the introduction of the vivid colours of Glazunov's many shorter orchestral pieces but, above all, well prepared performances of the symphonies of his maturity, with their distinctive combination of craftsmanship, vitality and beauty, would undoubtedly enhance his reputation.

Catalogue of works

For a very full list of works, including dedications and student pieces, see D. Gojowy and H. Günther, *Alexander Glasunow, Sein Leben in Bildern und Dokumenten* (Munich: List Verlag, 1986), pp 155–158.

Orchestral works

Opus.

5. Symphony No 1, in E major (1881 rev. 1885 and 1929).
3. Overture on Three Greek Themes, No. 1 in G minor (1882).
6. Overture on Three Greek Themes, No. 2 in D major (1883).
7. Serenade No. 1, in A major (1883).
9. *Characteristic Suite*, in D major (1884).
11. Serenade No. 2, in F major (1884).
12. *Lyric Poem*, in D flat major (1884).
8. Elegy *To the Memory of a Hero*, in C sharp minor/D flat major (1885).
13. *Stenka Razin*, symphonic poem, in B minor (1885).
14. Two Pieces for Orchestra 1. *Idylle*, in D major 2. *Rêverie Orientale*, in A minor (1886).
16. Symphony No. 2, in F sharp minor (1886).
19. *The Forest*, fantasy for orchestra, in C sharp minor (1887).
18. Mazurka, in G major (1888).
26a. *Slavonic Holiday,* symphonic sketch from the finale of the String Quartet No 3 (1888).
21. *Wedding March*, in E flat major (1889).
28. *The Sea*, fantasy for orchestra, in E major (1889).
29. *Oriental Rhapsody*, in G major (1889).
30. *The Kremlin*, symphonic picture, in C major/E flat major (1890).

33. Symphony No. 3, in D major (1890).
34. *Spring*, musical picture, in D major (1891).
40. *Triumphal March*, for the World Fair in Chicago, in E flat major (1892).
45. *Carnaval Overture*, with Organ ad lib., in F major (1892).
46. *Chopiniana Suite*, based on four pieces by Chopin (1893).
47. Concert Waltz No. 1, in D major (1893).
48. Symphony No. 4, in E flat major (1893).
50. *Cortège Solennelle*, in D major (1894).
51. Concert Waltz No. 2, in F major (1894).
52. *Scènes de Ballet*, suite for orchestra, in A major (1894).
53. *From Darkness into Light*, fantasy for orchestra, in B minor/C major (1894).
55. Symphony No. 5, in B flat major (1895).

None. *Oriental Suite* for Orchestra (1895).

58. Symphony No. 6, in C minor (1896).

57a. Suite from the ballet *Raymonda* (1898).

68. *Characteristic Dance* (*Pas de caractère*), in G major (1899).
69. *Romantic Intermezzo*, in D major (1900).
73. *Overture Solennelle*, in D Major (1900).
76. *March on a Russian Theme*, in E flat major (1901).
77. Symphony No. 7, in F major (1902).
78. *Ballade*, in F major (1902).
79. *From the Middle Ages*, suite for orchestra, in E major (1902).
81. *Ballet Scene* (*Scene dansante*), in A major (1904).
83. Symphony No. 8, in E flat major (1906).

None. Solemn Procession in G (1907).

85. Two Preludes for Orchestra: No 1, in A minor, In Memory of Stasov (1906); No 2, in E minor, In Memory of Rimsky-Korsakov (1908).
86. *Russian Fantasy,* for balalaika orchestra, in A major (1906).
84. *The Song of Fate*, Dramatic Overture, in D minor (1908).
87. *In Memory of Gogol*, Symphonic Prologue, in C major (1909).

88. *Finnish Fantasy*, in C major (1909).
None. Symphony No. 9 (1910, unfinished), in D minor (first movement orchestrated by G. Yudin in 1948; revised 1986).
91 *Cortège Solennelle*, in B flat major (1910).
89. *Finnish Sketches* for Orchestra: No. 1 *From the Kalevala*; No. 2 *Cortège* (1912).
96. *Paraphrases on the National Anthems of the Allies* (1915).
99. *Karelian Legend*, in A minor (1916).
None. Theme and Variations in G minor for String Orchestra (1917).
None. *Epic Poem* (*Poème épique*), in A minor (1933).

Stage works
57. *Raymonda*, ballet in Three Acts (1896–7).
61. *Les Ruses d'amour*, ballet in One Act (Pastoral after Watteau) (1898).
67. *The Seasons*, ballet in One Act (1899).
90. Introduction and Dance for Oscar Wilde's *Salome* (1908).
95. Incidental Music for Grand Duke Konstantin Romanov's play *The King of the Jews* (1913).
None. Incidental Music for Lermontov's play *Masquerade* (1913).

Works for solo instrument and orchestra
20. Two Pieces for Cello and Orchestra: No. 1 Melody; No. 2 Spanish Serenade. (1888).
71. Minstrel's Song (*Chant du Ménestrel*), in F sharp minor, for Cello and Orchestra (1900).
82. Violin Concerto, in A minor (1904).
92. Piano Concerto No. 1, in F minor (1911).
100. Piano Concerto No. 2, in B major (1917).
108. Concerto Ballata, for Cello and Orchestra, in C major (1930).
109. Concerto for Alto Saxophone and String Orchestra, in E flat major (1933).

Works for solo instrument and piano

17. Elegy: *Une Pensée a François Liszt* for Cello and Piano, in D flat major (1886).
24. *Rêverie* for Horn and Piano, in D flat major (1890).
32. Meditation for Violin and Piano, in D major (1891).

None. Arab Melody for Cello and Piano, in F sharp minor, (arr. from Op. 4, No. 5) (1891).

44. Elegy for Viola and Piano, in G minor (1893).

None. Album Leaf for Trumpet and Piano, in D flat major (1899).

None. Mazurka-Oberek for Violin and Piano, in D major (1917).

Chamber music

None. Five Pieces for String Quartet (1879-1881).

None. Fugue in D (unpublished) (1881).

1. String Quartet No. 1, in D major (1882).
10. String Quartet No. 2, in F major (1884).
15. *Five Novelettes*, Suite for String Quartet (1886).

None. *El Pano*, Spanish Melody arranged for String Quartet (1886).

None. Finale for '*B-la-F*' String Quartet (1886).

None. Fugato on the name '*B-la-F*' (1887).

None. First Movement, *Christmas Singers (Les Chanteurs de Noel)* for *Name Day Quartet* (*Jour de fête)* (1887).

26. String Quartet No. 3, in G major, (*Slavonic*/*Quatuor Slave*) (1888).
35. Suite for String Quartet, in C major (1887–1891).
38. *In modo religioso,* in E flat major, for Brass Quartet (1892).
39. String Quintet for two violins, viola and two cellos, in A major (1892).
64. String Quartet No. 4, in A minor (1894).

None. Theme and Variations for String Quintet (unpublished and later arranged for string orchestra in 1917) (1895).

None. Three Pieces from the *Fridays* (*Les Vendredis*): No. 1 Prelude and Fugue; No. 2 Courante; No. 3 Polka (with Sokolov and Lyadov) (1895).

70. String Quartet No. 5, in D minor (1898).

None. Variation Three from *Variations on a Russian Theme* (1898).

106. String Quartet No. 6, in B flat major (1921).

105. Elegy, in D minor, *In Memory of M. P. Belyayev* for String Quartet (1928).

107. String Quartet No. 7, in C major (1930).

109. Saxophone Quartet, in B flat major (1932).

Piano music

None. Easy Sonata (?1880).

None. Sonatina (?1880).

None. Miniature, in C major, (1883).

2. *Suite on the Theme S-a-s-c-h-a*: 1. Introduction 2. Prelude 3. Scherzo 4. Nocturne 5. Waltz (1883).

None. *Barcarolle sur les touches noires* (1887).

25. Prelude and Two Mazurkas (1888).

22. Two Pieces: 1. Barcarolle, in D flat major; 2. Novelette, in D major (1889).

37. Nocturne, in D flat major (1889).

23. *Waltz on the Theme S-a-b-e-l-a*, in B flat major (1890).

31. Three Études: No. 1 in C major; No. 2 in E minor; No. 3 in E major (*Night*) (1889).

36. Little Waltz, in D major (1892).

41. Grand Concert Waltz, in E flat major (1893).

42. Three Miniatures: No. 1 Pastoral; No. 2 Polka; No. 3 Waltz (1893).

43. Salon Waltz, in C major (1893).

49. Three Pieces: No. 1 Prelude, in D flat major; No. 2 Caprice-Impromptu, in A major; No. 3 Gavotte, in D major (1894).

54. Two Impromptus: No. 1 in D flat major; No. 2 in A flat major (1896).

None. *Four Improvisations* (with Arensky, Rachmaninoff and Taneyev) (1896).
62. Prelude and Fugue, in D minor (1899).
72. Theme and Variations, in F sharp minor (1900).
74. Piano Sonata No. 1, in B flat minor (1901).
75. Piano Sonata No. 2, in E minor (1901).
None. First Prelude-Improvisation, in E minor (1917).
None. Second Prelude-Improvisation, in G minor (1918).
101. Four Preludes and Fugues: No. 1 in A minor; No. 2 in C sharp minor; No. 3 in C minor; No 4. in C major (1918–1919).
104. Fantasy for Two Pianos, in F minor (1920).
103. *Idylle*, in F sharp major (1926).
None. Prelude and Fugue, in E minor (1926).
None. Two Pieces for Piano: 1. Lullaby; 2. Dance (1928).

Organ music
93. Prelude and Fugue No. 1, in D major (1906).
98. Prelude and Fugue No. 2, in D minor (1914).
110. Fantasy, in G minor (1935).

Choral works
56. Coronation Cantata for Soloists, Choir and Orchestra, in D major (1896).
63. Festival Cantata (for the Centenary of the Pavlovsk Institute), for Soloist, Female Choir and Two Pianos, Eight Hands (1898).
65. Commemorative Cantata (for the Centenary of the Birth of Pushkin), for Soloists, Choir and Orchestra (1899).
66. *Hymn to Pushkin*, for Female Choir a cappella, (Piano ad libitum) (1899).
None. Cantata in Memory of M. Antokolsky (with Lyadov) (1902).
94. *Love* (words by Shukovsky) for Choir a cappella. (1907).
None. Prelude-Cantata (for the Fiftieth Anniversary of the

St Petersburg Conservatory) for Soloists, Choir and Orchestra (1912).

None. *Down Mother Volga*, Russian Folk Song arranged for mixed choir a cappella (1921).

Songs for voice and piano

4. Five Songs: 1. Romance (Heine) 2. The Nightingale (Kol'stov) 3. Romance (Heine) 4. Spanish Song 5. Arabian Melody (1882).

None. From Hafiz (Pushkin) (1888).

27. Two Songs: 1. Why are the voices silent? (Pushkin) 2. Oriental Romance (Pushkin) (1888).

None. The Belle (Pushkin). (1890).

59. Six Songs: 1. The Muse (Pushkin) 2. From Petrarch (Korinfsky, after Petrarch) 3. From Petrarch (Korinfsky, after Petrarch) 4. If you will love (Korinfsky, after Petrarch) 5. Delia (Pushkin) 6. The Silver-shining Heavens (Maikov) (1898).

60. Six Songs: 1. Drinking Song (Pushkin) 2. A wish (Pushkin) 3. The sea-nymph (Pushkin) 4. The dream (Pushkin) 5. Life still lies before me (Maikov) 6. By the majestic towers of Venice (Pushkin) (1898).

80. Duet, for Soprano and Contralto: My free song (A. G. Seversky) (1900).

None. Russian Song ('Masha is told not to cross the river') (1905).

102. Nina's Romance from *Masquerade* by Lermontov (1916).

None. Shakespeare's Sonnet 66 (Tir'd with all these…) (1916).

Bibliography

Abraham, G., *The Concise Oxford History of Music* (Newton Abbot, Devon: Readers Union, by arrangement with Oxford University Press, 1979).

_______, *On Russian Music* (New York: Johnson Reprint Corporation, 1970, originally published by William Reeves, London).

_______, *Rimsky-Korsakov A Short Biography* (London: Gerald Duckworth & Co. Ltd.)

_______, *Slavonic and Romantic Music* (London: Faber and Faber Limited, 1968).

Asafev, B. V., *Russian Music From the Beginning of the Nineteenth Century* (trans. A. J. Swan) (Ann Arbor, Michigan*: Edwards Brothers, Inc, 1953*).

Bacharach, A. L., (ed.) *The Musical Companion* (London: Victor Gollancz Ltd, 1947).

Balanchine, G., and F. Mason, *Balanchine's Complete Stories of the Great Ballets,* revised and enlarged edition (New York: Doubleday & Company Inc., 1977).

Benois, A., *Reminiscences of the Russian Ballet* (trans. M. Britnieva) (London: Putnam, 1945).

Bertensson, S., & J. Leyda, *Sergei Rachmaninoff: A Lifetime in Music* (Bloomington, Indiana: Indiana University Press, 2001. Originally published by New York University Press, 1956).

Binyon, T. J., *Pushkin* (London: Harper Perennial, 2002).

Bowers, F., *Scriabin A Biography of the Russian Composer* (Tokyo and Palo Alto: Kodansha International Ltd., 1970).

Buckle, R., *Diaghilev* (London: Weidenfeld & Nicolson, 1993).

Bullock, P. R., *Rosa Newmarch and Russian Music in Late Nineteenth and Early Twentieth-Century England* (England: Ashgate Publishing Limited, 2009).

Calvocoressi, M. D., *A Survey of Russian Music* (England: Penguin Books, 1944).

_________, and G. Abraham, *Masters of Russian Music* (New York: Tudor Publishing Company, 1944, originally published by Alfred A. Knopf, Inc., 1936).

Campbell, S., (ed. and trans.) *Russians on Russian music, 1880-1917* (United Kingdom: Cambridge University Press, 2003).

Casals, P., and A. E. Kahn, *Joys and Sorrows* (London: Macdonald and Co. (Publishers) Ltd, 1970).

Coates, E., *Suite in Four Movements* (London: Thames Publishing, 1986).

Davis, R. B., '*The Beauty of Belaieff: A Catalogue of Details of Selected Publications (1885-1900) of M. P. Belaieff*' for the Barbican Exhibition of 3rd February to 9th March 1987.

Dianin, S., (trans. R. Lord) *Borodin* (London: Oxford University Press, 1963).

Dubal, D., *Evenings with Horowitz: A Personal Portrait* (New Jersey: Amadeus Press, LLC, 2004).

Ewen, D., *Composers of Today* (New York: The H. W. Wilson Company, 1936).

Fifield, C., *True artist and true friend. A Biography of Hans Richter* (Oxford: Clarendon Press, 1993).

Figes, O., *Natasha's Dance: A Cultural History of Russia* (London: Penguin Books, 2003).

Frolova-Walker, M., *Russian Music and Nationalism* (New Haven and London: Yale University Press, 2007).

Garden, E., *Balakirev: A critical study of his life and music* (London: Faber and Faber Limited, 1967).

Gojowy, D. and H. Günther: *Alexander Glasunow, Sein Leben in Bildern und Dokumenten* (Munich: List Verlag, 1986).

Goossens, E., *Overture and Beginners* (London: Methuen & Co., Ltd., 1951).

Gottlieb, R., *George Balanchine The Ballet Maker* (New York: Harper Perennial, 2004).

Grigorovich, Y. & V. Vanslow (trans. A. Kroll), *The Authorized Bolshoi Ballet Book of Raymonda* (USA: T.F.H. Publications, Inc., with the cooperation of VAAP Copyright Agency of the Soviet Union, 1987).

Hanson, L. & E., *Prokofiev The Prodigal Son* (London: Cassell & Company Ltd, 1964).

Harrison, B., (ed. P. Cleveland-Peck) *The Cello and the Nightingales* (London: John Murray (Publishers) Ltd, 1985).

Homans, J., *Apollo's Angels: A History of Ballet* (London: Granta Books, 2010).

Hurok, S., and R. Goode, *Impresario* (London: Macdonald & Co., (Publishers) Ltd., 1947).

Kinel, L., *Under Five Eagles* (London: Putnam, 1937).

Kolodin, I., *The Musical Life* (New York: Alfred A. Knopf, 1958).

Korabelnikova, L., (trans. A. Winestein, ed. S. Hershman-Tcherepnin) *Alexander Tcherepnin The Saga of a Russian Emigré Composer* (Bloomington and Indianapolis: Indiana University Press, 2008).

Krebs, S. D., *Soviet Composers and the Development of Soviet Music* (London: George Allen and Unwin Ltd, 1970).

Lebrecht, N., *The Companion to 20th Century Music* (London: Simon & Schuster Ltd, 1992).

Leonard, M., *Slobodskaya* (London: Victor Gollancz Ltd, 1979).

Leonard, R. A., *A History of Russian Music* (London: Jarrolds Publishers Limited, 1956).

Letellier, R.I. (ed.), *The Ballets of Alexander Glazunov: Scènes de Ballet, Raymonda and Les Saisons* (Newcastle upon Tyne: Cambridge Scholars Publishing, 2012).

MacDonald, M., (ed.) *Havergal Brian on Music Volume Two: European and American Music in his Time* (London: Toccata Press, 2009).

Maes, F., *A History of Russian Music: From Kamarinskaya to Babi Yar* (trans. A. J. and E. Pomerans) (Berkeley: University of California Press, 2006).

Malan, R., *Efrem Zimbalist A Life* (New Jersey: Amadeus Press, LLC, 2004).

Malko, N., *A Certain Art* (New York: William Morrow & Co., Inc., 1966).

Milstein, N. and Volkov, S., *From Russia to the West* (trans. A. W. Bouis) (London: Barrie & Jenkins Ltd, 1990).

Monsaingeon, B., (trans. S. Spencer) *Sviatoslav Richter. Notebooks and Conversations* (London: Faber and Faber Limited, 2005).

Montagu-Nathan, M., *An Introduction to Russian Music* (London: Cecil Palmer & Hayward, 1916).

_________, *Contemporary Russian Composers* (Connecticut: Greenwood Press, Publishers, 1970, a reprint of London: Cecil Palmer & Hayward, 1917).

Mundy, S., *Alexander Glazunov: Russia's great musical conciliator* (London: Thames Publishing, 1987).

Norris, C., (ed.) *Shostakovich: the Man and his Music* (London: Lawrence and Wishart Ltd, 1982).

Norris, Geoffrey, Rakhmaninov (London: J. M. Dent & Sons Ltd, 1976).

Norris, Gerald, *Stanford The Cambridge Jubilee and Tchaikovsky* (London: David & Charles (Publishers) Limited, 1980).

Pougin, A., (trans. L. Haward) *A Short History of Russian Music* (London: Chatto & Windus, 1915).

Poznansky, A., *Tchaikovsky: The Quest for the Inner Man* (Great Britain: Lime Tree, an imprint of Reed Consumer Books Ltd, 1993).

_________ (ed.) (trans. R. C. Burr Jr. & R. Bird) *Tchaikovsky Through Others' Eyes* (Bloomington & Indianapolis: Indiana University Press, 1999).

Preston, T., *Before the Curtain* (London: John Murray, 1950).

Prokofiev, S., *Prokofiev by Prokofiev* (ed. F. King, trans. G. Daniels) (New York: Doubleday and Company Inc., 1979. London: Macdonald and Jane's Publishers Limited, 1979).

_________, *Soviet Diary 1927 and Other Writings* (trans. & ed. O. Prokofiev, associate ed. C. Palmer) (London: Faber and Faber Limited, 1991).

_________, *Diaries 1907-1914 Prodigious Youth* (trans. and annotated A. Phillips) (London: Faber and Faber Limited, 2006).

_________, *Diaries 1915-1923 Behind the Mask* (trans. and annotated A. Phillips) (London: Faber and Faber Limited, 2008).

_________, *Diaries 1924-1933 Prodigal Son* (trans. and annotated A. Phillips) (London: Faber and Faber Limited, 2012).

Rimler, W., *George Gershwin: An Intimate Portrait* (Urbana and Chicago: University of Illinois Press, 2009).

Rimsky-Korsakov, N., (trans. J. A. Joffe) *My Musical Life* (London: Ernst Eulenburg Ltd, 1974, originally published by Alfred A. Knopf, Inc., 1923).

Rimsky-Korsakov, T., (trans. L. Timofeeva, ed. M. J. Crocker & M. Maksotskaya), *Rimsky-Korsakov Letters to his Family and Friends* (Milwaukee: Amadeus Press, 2016).

Sabaneyeff, L., *Modern Russian Composers* (London: Martin Lawrence Limited, 1927).

Schwarz, B., *Music and Musical Life in Soviet Russia 1917-1970* (London: Barrie & Jenkins Ltd, 1976).

Slonimsky, N., *Music Since 1900* (New York: Schirmer Books, Fifth Edition, 1994).

______, *Perfect Pitch: A Life Story* (Oxford: Oxford University Press, 1988).

______, *Writings on Music Volume One. Early Articles for the Boston Evening Transcript* (New York and London: Routledge, Taylor & Francis Group, 2004).

Sollertinsky, D. and L., (trans. G. Hobbs and C. Midgley) *Pages from the Life of Dmitri Shostakovich* (London: Robert Hale, 1981).

Stasov, V. V., (trans. F. Jonas) *Selected Essays on Music* (London: Barrie & Rockliff, 1968).

Steane, L., *Glazounov: An assessment of the value of Glazounov's orchestral music, with tributes from various sources* (Coventry: Parbury Bros. Ltd., 1967).

Stravinsky, I., *An Autobiography* (New York: Simon and Schuster, Inc., 1936).

Swan, A. J., *Russian Music and its sources in chant and folk-song* (London: John Baker, 1973).

Taruskin, R., *Defining Russia Musically* (Princeton, New Jersey: Princeton University Press, 1997).

Tawaststjerna, E., (trans. R. Layton) *Sibelius* (London: Faber and Faber Ltd, 2008).

Taylor, P. S., *Anton Rubinstein: A Life in Music* (Bloomington and Indianapolis: Indiana University Press, 2007).

Tchaikovsky, P. I., *Letters to His Family* (trans. Galina von Meck, with additional annotations by P. M. Young) (New York: Cooper Square Press, 2000).

Tiomkin, D., and P. Buranelli, *Please Don't Hate Me* (New York: Doubleday & Company, Inc., 1959). Tovey, D. F., *Essays in Musical Analysis Volume 3 Concertos* (London: Oxford University Press, 1978).

Venturini, D. J., *Alexander Glazounov: His Life and Works* (Delphos, Ohio: Aero Printing, 1992).

Vodarsky-Shiraeff, A., *Russian Composers and Musicians* (Milton Keynes, UK: Lightning Source UK Ltd, n.d. Originally published in 1940).

Volkov, S. (trans. A. W. Bouis), *Testimony: The Memoirs of Dmitri Shostakovich, as related to and edited by Solomon Volkov* (London: Hamish Hamilton, 1979).

_______, (trans. A. W. Bouis), *St. Petersburg: A Cultural History* (New York: Simon & Schuster Inc., 1997).

Walsh, S., *Igor Stravinsky: A Creative Spring: Russia and France 1882–1934* (London: Pimlico, Random House, 2002).

Wells, H. G., *Russia in the Shadows* (New York: George H. Doran Company, 1921).

Wilson, E., *Shostakovich: A Life Remembered* (New Edition) (London: Faber and Faber Limited, 2006).

Wood, H. J., *My Life of Music* (London: Victor Gollancz Ltd, 1946).

Yastrebtsev, V. V., *Reminiscences of Rimsky-Korsakov*, (ed. & trans. F. Jonas) (New York: Columbia University Press, 1985).

Journals

Chicago Tribune

The Daily Express

The Eastbourne Chronicle

The Alexander Glazounov Society Quarterly Newsletter Volumes 1–17. (Delphos, Ohio: Aero Printing, Inc., 1985–2002).

Musical Opinion

The Musical Times

The New York Times

Notes

Preface

1. S. Mundy, *Alexander Glazunov: Russia's great musical conciliator* (London: Thames Publishing, 1987), p 5.
2. E. Coates, *Suite in Four Movements* (London: Thames Publishing, 1986), p 153.
3. W. Golding, *An Egyptian Journal* (London: Faber and Faber Ltd, 1985), p10.

Chapter one

1. H. Günther, 'Alexander Glazounov – An Appreciation' (trans. S. Kruger) in *The Alexander Glazounov Society Newsletter*, Volume 2, Number 3 (Delphos, Ohio: Aero Printing, 1987).
2. For details in this chapter about the Glazunov family history and the early years of the composer, I am indebted to D. Gojowy and H. Günther, *Alexander Glasunow, Sein Leben in Bildern und Dokumenten* (Munich: List Verlag, 1986) (trans. Ernst Pories) in *The Alexander Glazounov Society Newsletter* (Delphos, Ohio: Aero Printing, 1987). See, in particular, Volumes 9, Number 3; Volume 9, Number 4; Volume 10, Number 1 and Volume 11, Number 1.
3. T. J. Binyon, *Pushkin* (London: Harper Perennial, 2002), p 595.
4. *The Alexander Glazounov Society Newsletter,* Volume 9, Number 3.
5. M. Montagu-Nathan, *Contemporary Russian Composers* (Connecticut: Greenwood Press, Publishers, 1970 (reprint of London: Cecil Palmer & Hayward, 1917), p 83.
6. D. J. Venturini, *Alexander Glazounov: His Life and Works* (Delphos, Ohio: Aero Printing, 1992), p 49.

7. N. A. Rimsky-Korsakov, *My Musical Life* (trans. J. A. Joffe) (London: Ernst Eulenberg Ltd, 1974, originally published by Alfred A. Knopf, Inc., 1923), p 231.
8. L. Ferder, 'How do you spell genius?' in *The Alexander Glazounov Society Newsletter*, Volume 3, Number 4.
9. D. Gojowy and H. Günther, *Alexander Glasunow*, in *The Alexander Glazounov Society Newsletter,* Volume 9, Number 4.
10. E. Garden, *Balakirev: A Critical Study of His Life and Music* (London: Faber and Faber Limited, 1967), pp 221–2.
11. D. Gojowy and H. Günther, *Alexander Glasunow*, in *The Alexander Glazounov Society Newsletter,* Volume 10, Number 1.
12. F. Maes, *A History of Russian Music From Kamarinskaya to Babi Yar* (trans. A. J. and E. Pomerans) (Berkeley: University of California Press, 2006), p 67.
13. O. Figes, *Natasha's Dance: A Cultural History of Russia* (London: Penguin Books, 2003), p xxviii and p xxxi–xxxii.
14. A. Glazunov quoted in T. Rimsky-Korsakov (trans. L. Timofeeva, ed. M. J. Crocker & M. Maksotskaya), *Rimsky-Korsakov Letters to his Family and Friends* (Milwaukee: Amadeus Press, 2016), p 96.
15. N. A. Rimsky-Korsakov, *My Musical Life*, p 231.
16. G. Abraham, 'Glazunov and the String Quartet', in *Slavonic and Romantic Music* (London: Faber and Faber Limited, 1968), pp 218–19. The pieces were finally published in 1951 in an edition by A. M. Rivkin.
17. D. Gojowy and H. Günther, *Alexander Glasunow*, in *The Alexander Glazounov Society Newsletter,* Volume 9, Number 4.
18. D. Gojowy and H. Günther, *Alexander Glasunow*, in *The Alexander Glazounov Society Newsletter,* Volume 10, Number 1.
19. N. A. Rimsky-Korsakov, *My Musical Life*, p 256.
20. D. J. Venturini, *Alexander Glazounov*, pp 6 & 7.
21. S. Mundy, *Alexander Glazunov,* p 14.

22. S. Dianin, (trans. R. Lord), *Borodin* (London: Oxford University Press, 1963), p 126.
23. N. A. Rimsky-Korsakov, *My Musical Life*, p 257.
24. R. B. Davis, '*The Beauty of Belaieff: A Catalogue of Details of Selected Publications (1885–1900) of M. P. Belaieff*' for the Barbican Exhibition of 3rd February to 9th March 1987.
25. S. Mundy, *Alexander Glazunov*, p 17.
26. See, for example, the section from 29 bars after letter H to letter N, in the M. P. Belaieff study score, pp 180–190.
27. S. Campbell, (ed. and trans.), *Russians on Russian Music 1880-1917* (United Kingdom: Cambridge University Press, 2003), p 145.
28. D. Gojowy and H. Günther, *Alexander Glasunow*, in *The Alexander Glazounov Society Newsletter,* Volume 9, Number 2.
29. A. Ossovsky, quoted by G. Abraham in 'Glazunov: the End of an Episode' from *On Russian Music* (New York: Johnson Reprint Corporation, 1970, originally published by William Reeves Bookseller Limited, London), p 234.
30. V. V. Stasov, (trans. F. Jonas) *Selected Essays on Music* (London: Barrie & Rockliff, 1968), p 114.
31. D. Gojowy and H. Günther, *Alexander Glasunow*, in *The Alexander Glazounov Society Newsletter,* Volume 9, Number 2.
32. P. I. Tchaikovsky, *Letters to His Family* (trans. Galina von Meck, with additional annotations by Percy M. Young) (New York: Cooper Square Press, 2000), p 295.

Chapter two

1. N. A. Rimsky-Korsakov, *My Musical Life*, p 261.
2. Compare the melody's initial presentation starting at six bars after Letter F with its transformation at Letter S, in the *Musikproduktion Hoeflich* Study Score 899.

3. D. Gojowy and H. Günther, *Alexander Glasunow*, in *The Alexander Glazounov Society Newsletter,* Volume 10, Number 3.
4. N. A. Rimsky-Korsakov, *My Musical Life*, p 231.
5. Ibid, pp 274 & 285.
6. Ibid, p 275.
7. N. Malko, *A Certain Art* (New York: William Morrow & Co., Inc., 1966, an imprint of HarperCollins Publishers), p 75.
8. D. Gojowy and H. Günther, *Alexander Glasunow*, in *The Alexander Glazounov Society Newsletter,* Volume 11, Number 2.
9. D. Gojowy and H. Günther, *Alexander Glasunow*, in *The Alexander Glazounov Society Newsletter,* Volume 11, Number 1.
10. Ibid.
11. N. A. Rimsky-Korsakov, *My Musical Life*, p 269.
12. Ibid, p 270.
13. I Kolodin, *The Musical Life* (New York: Alfred A. Knopf, 1958), p 4.
14. Other examples include the *Meditation* for Violin and Piano or Orchestra, Op. 32 and the *Elegy* for Viola and Piano, Op. 44.
15. L.& E. Hanson, *Prokofiev The Prodigal Son* (London: Cassell and Company Ltd, 1964), p 219.
16. N. Malko, *A Certain Art,* p 75.
17. V. V. Stasov, *Selected Essays on Music*, p 115.
18. M. D. Calvocoressi, *A Survey of Russian Music* (England: Penguin Press, 1944), p 75.
19. D. Gojowy and H. Günther, *Alexander Glasunow*, in *The Alexander Glazounov Society Newsletter,* Volume 11, Number 4.
20. S. Campbell, *Russians on Russian Music*, p 100.

Chapter three

1. M. D. Calvocoressi, *A Survey of Russian Music,* p 75.
2. S. Mundy, *Alexander Glazunov,* p 23.

3. B. Schwarz, *Music and Musical Life in Soviet Russia 1917–1970* (London: Barrie & Jenkins, 1976), p 410.
4. Per Skans, liner note to *A Russian Birthday: Collective Works by Russian Composers*. Compact Disc. Olympia. OCD 575. 1995.
5. N. A. Rimsky-Korsakov, *My Musical Life*, p 282.
6. A. L. Bacharach, (ed.), *The Musical Companion* (London: Victor Gollancz Ltd, 1947), p 527.
7. D. Gojowy and H. Günther, *Alexander Glasunow*, in *The Alexander Glazounov Society Newsletter,* Volume 13, Number 3.
8. S. Campbell, *Russians on Russian Music,* p 145.
9. A year later he contributed two further pieces to the repertoire of the 'cello with the *Melody*, Op. 20, No. 1 and the *Spanish Serenade*, Op. 20, No. 2.
10. N. A. Rimsky-Korsakov, *My Musical Life*, p 283.
11. M. Malkiel & A. Barry, liner note to *Borodin: Prince Igor*. 1995. Compact Discs. Phillips 442 537–2, p 14.
12. S. Dianin, *Borodin*, p 155, note 1.
13. G. Abraham, *On Russian Music,* p165. This is from Abraham's translation of Glazunov's account written in 1896 for the 'Russian Musical Gazette'.
14. S. Dianin, *Borodin*, p 155, note 1.
15. M. Malkiel and A. Barry, liner note to *Borodin: Prince Igor*, p 13.
16. N. A. Rimsky-Korsakov, *My Musical Life,* p 283.
17. S. Dianin, *Borodin*, p 155.
18. Ibid, pp 217–18. Glazunov also orchestrated the piano pieces of Borodin's *Petite Suite* in 1889. The suite originally ended with a Nocturne but Glazunov added his orchestration of Borodin's Scherzo in A flat to enhance the sense of a finale. In Glazunov's version, the Nocturne appears as the middle section of the Scherzo. In addition, he provided an orchestral accompaniment for Borodin's atmospheric Pushkin setting, 'For the Shores of a Distant Homeland'.

19. N. A. Rimsky-Korsakov, *My Musical Life*, p 300.
20. During the period when Glazunov was concentrating on important orchestral works (1888–1890) he did find time to compose a number of shorter piano compositions. The *Prelude and Two Mazurkas*, Op. 25 of 1888 together with the pieces from 1889, such as the *Barcarolle and Novelette*, Op. 22 and the *Nocturne* in D flat, Op. 37, have a fresh and genuinely charming character. However, it is the *Three Études*, Op. 31, from the same year, that provide the clearest indication of how Glazunov's mature piano style would develop: No. 1 in C major is energetic and confident, while No. 2 in E minor is more passionate and romantic in nature. Finally, No. 3 in E major, subtitled *Night*, with its clarity and elegance, provides a fine example of his superb craftsmanship in writing for the piano.
21. D. Gojowy and H. Günther, *Alexander Glasunow*, in *The Alexander Glazounov Society Newsletter,* Volume 12, Number 2.
22. Iosif Raiskin, (trans. by M. Berridge and M. George), liner note to *Glazunov: String Quartets No.3 & No.5.* 2004. Compact Disc. MDG 603 1236–2. 2004.
23. Per Skans, liner note to *Glazunov String Quartets No.3 & No.5.* Compact Disc. Olympia OCD 525. 1992.
24. D. J. Venturini, *Alexander Glazounov*, p 14.
25. N. A. Rimsky-Korsakov, *My Musical Life*, p 299.
26. W. Eggerking (trans. B. Robinson), *The Sea*, Study Score 767 (Munich: Musikproduktion Hoeflich, 2008), p v.
27. N. A. Rimsky-Korsakov, *My Musical Life*, p 298.
28. See L. Foreman, liner note to *Kalinnikov Symphony No.1 c/w Glazunov The Sea* and *Spring* for Glazunov's programme. Compact Disc. Chandos CHAN 8611. 1988.
29. M. D. Calvocoressi, *A Survey of Russian Music,* p 75.
30. D. Gojowy and H. Günther, *Alexander Glasunow*, in *The Alexander Glazounov Society Newsletter,* Volume 12, Number 3.
31. N. A. Rimsky-Korsakov, *My Musical Life*, pp 301–2.

32. D. Gojowy and H. Günther, *Alexander Glasunow*, in *The Alexander Glazounov Society Newsletter,* Volume 12, Number 3.
33. S Campbell, *Russians on Russian Music,* p 135.
34. Ibid, p 132.
35. R. A. Leonard, *A History of Russian Music* (London: Jarrolds Publishers Limited, 1956), p 208.
36. N. A. Rimsky-Korsakov, *My Musical Life*, p 305.
37. D. J. Venturini, *Alexander Glazounov*, p 16.
38. S. Mundy, *Alexander Glazunov,* p 34.
39. M. MacDonald (ed.), *Havergal Brian on Music: Volume Two: European and American Music in his Time* (London: Toccata Press, 2009), p 304.
40. S Campbell, *Russians on Russian Music,* p 153.
41. V. V. Stasov, *Selected Essays*, p 115.
42. G. Abraham, *The Concise Oxford History of Western Music* (Newton Abbot, Devon: Readers Union by arrangement with the Oxford University Press, 1979), p 699.

Chapter four

1. N. A. Rimsky-Korsakov, *My Musical Life*, pp 308–9.
2. D. Gojowy and H. Günther, *Alexander Glasunow*, in *The Alexander Glazounov Society Newsletter,* Volume 11, Number 4.
3. Ibid.
4. G. Abraham, 'Glazunov: The End of an Episode' in *On Russian Music*, (New York: Johnson Reprint Corporation, 1970), p 235.
5. D. J. Venturini, *Alexander Glazounov*, p 16.
6. M. D. Calvocoressi, *A Survey of Russian Music,* p75.
7. Leon Ferder in *The Alexander Glazounov Society Newsletter, Volume 9, Number 2*.

8 Glazunov also made successful transcriptions for cello and piano of two of Chopin's Études: Op. 10 No. 3 and Op. 25 No. 7.

9. A. Poznansky (trans. R.C. Burr, Jr. & R. Bird), *Tchaikovsky Through Others' Eyes* (Bloomington & Indianapolis: Indiana University Press, 1999), p 209.
10. A Poznansky, *Tchaikovsky The Quest for the Inner Man* (Great Britain: Lime Tree, an imprint of Reed Consumer Books Ltd, 1993), p 577.
11. A. Poznansky, *Tchaikovsky Through Others' Eyes*, p 253.
12. Ibid, p 141.
13. S. Mundy, *Alexander Glazunov,* p 37.
14. G. Abraham, 'Glazunov and the String Quartet', in *Slavonic and Romantic Music,* p 222.
15. M. D. Calvocoressi, *A Survey of Russian Music,* p 76.
16. Letter F and Letter M respectively, in the M. P. Belaieff Study Score (Bel. Nr. 525 a).
17. G. Abraham, 'Glazunov and the String Quartet', in *Slavonic and Romantic Music,* p 222.
18. D. J. Venturini, *Alexander Glazounov*, p 19.
19. S. Mundy, *Alexander Glazunov,* p 39.
20. S. Campbell, *Russians on Russian Music,* p 153.
21. N. A. Rimsky-Korsakov, *My Musical Life*, p 363.
22. M. MacDonald (ed.), *Havergal Brian on Music: Volume Two*, pp 304–5.
23. Glazunov met Rachmaninoff when they were invited to dinner by Arensky in the autumn of 1896. Taneyev was also a guest and, after dinner, all four composers worked collaboratively on the *Four Improvisations* for Piano. Each composer started a variation and contributed to the other three. See Anastasia Belina's excellent liner notes to *Taneyev Piano Music* Toccata Classics TOCC 0042. 2006.
24. Cui quoted in S. Bertensson & J. Leyda, *Sergei Rachmaninoff: A Lifetime in Music* (Bloomington & Indianapolis: Indiana University Press, 2001, originally published by New York University Press, 1956), pp 71–2.

25. Ibid, p 73.
26. Ibid, p 72.
27. Ibid, p 72.
28. Ibid, p 68.
29. S. Mundy, *Alexander Glazunov,* p 43.
30. S. Bertensson & J. Leyda, *Sergei Rachmaninoff*, p 71.
31. Ibid.
32. N. Malko, *A Certain Art*, p 79.
33. Geoffrey Norris, *Rakhmaninov*, (London: J. M. Dent & Sons Ltd, 1976), p 39.
34. S. Bertensson & J. Leyda, *Sergei Rachmaninoff*, p 175.
35. D. J. Venturini, *Alexander Glazounov*, p 40.
36. N. Milstein and S. Volkov (trans. A. W. Bouis), *From Russia to the West: The Musical Memoirs and Reminiscences of Nathan Milstein* (London: Barrie & Jenkins, 1990), p 110.

Chapter five

1. Gerald Norris, *Stanford The Cambridge Jubilee and Tchaikovsky* (London: David & Charles (Publishers) Limited, 1980), p 493.
2 Ibid, p 494.
3. C. Fifield, *True Artist and True Friend: A Biography of Hans Richter* (Oxford: Clarendon Press, 1993), p 502.
4. Y. Grigorovich & V. Vanslow (trans. A. Kroll), *The Authorized Bolshoi Book of Raymonda* (USA: T.F.H. Publications, Inc., with the cooperation of VAAP Copyright Agency of the Soviet Union, 1987), p 19.
5. J. Homans, *Apollo's Angels: A History of Ballet* (London: Granta Publications, 2010), p 272.
6. A. Benois, *Reminiscences of the Russian Ballet* (trans. M. Britnieva) (London: Putnam, reprint 1945), p 140.
7. N. Malko, *A Certain Art*, p 84.

8. Fortunately this production has been recorded on DVD: Olesia Novikova (Raymonda); Friedemann Vogel (Jean de Brienne); Mick Zeni (Abderahman). Choreographic revival and staging Sergej Vikharev. Orchestra and Corps de Ballet of Teatro alla Scala. Conductor Michail Jurowski. Arthaus Musik 101 630. (2011). The finest audio recording of the ballet is that made by Evgeny Svetlanov and the Bolshoi Theatre Orchestra – one of the best recordings of any work by Glazunov.
9. The final Hymn is omitted in the Gregorovich version of the ballet. It is replaced by the *Entr'acte* from Act One.
10. G. Balanchine & F. Mason, *Balanchine's Complete Stories of the Great Ballets,* revised and enlarged edition (New York: Doubleday & Company Inc., 1977), p 411.
11. Ibid, pp 471–2.
12. N. Malko, *A Certain Art*, p 87.
13. J. Homans, *Apollo's Angels*, p 288.
14. A. Benois, *Reminiscences of the Russian Ballet*, p 140.
15. Interestingly the *Gavotte,* Op. 49 No. 3 was the one piece by Glazunov that Prokofiev recorded, although his diaries reveal that he was also impressed by the Second Piano Sonata. His characterful performance of the *Gavotte* can be heard on CD: DAL SEGNO DSPRCD038.
16. There is also the ten-minute Ballet Scene (Scènes dansante), Op 81, of 1904. It is dedicated to Maria Petipa, the daughter of Marius Petipa, who, as prima ballerina, was a significant member of the Mariyinsky Theatre in her own right. The work is based on Russian folk songs and it is evident that Glazunov enjoyed working with these melodies in this fresh sounding and delicately scored piece. The brief scenario, faintly reminiscent of *Raymonda*, revolves around a young girl's vision and her dance with the son of a nobleman. It was first performed at a concert in December 1904, held to raise funds in aid of indigent musicians. See *The*

Alexander Glazounov Society Newsletter, Volume 9, Number 1.

17. R. I. Lettelier (ed.), *The Ballets of Alexander Glazunov: Scènes de Ballet, Raymonda and Les Saisons* (Newcastle upon Tyne: Cambridge Scholars Publishing, 2012), p xvii.
18. A. Benois, *Reminiscences of the Russian Ballet*, p 295.
19. In 1881–2, he had written his Five Songs, Op. 4. These belong to the tradition of Glinka and Chaikovsky; they possess an attractive fluency, warmth and charm. The two Pushkin settings of 1888, published as Glazunov's Op. 27, are two of his best songs. The first of these, '*Why are the voices silent?*' (sometimes referred to as the '*Bacchic Song*') is a celebration of the power of reason. The second song, the *Oriental Romance*, in contrast, employs exotic, 'Eastern' sounding harmonies to convey the sensual nature of Pushkin's verse.
20. D. J. Venturini, *Alexander Glazounov*, p 23.
21. Iosif Raiskin, (trans. by M. Berridge and M. George), liner note to *Glazunov: String Quartets No.3 & No.5*. Compact Disc. MDG 603 1236–2. 2004.

Chapter six

1. D. J. Venturini, *Alexander Glazounov*, p 23.
2. B. Harrison (ed. P. Cleveland-Peck), *The Cello and the Nightingales* (London: John Murray (Publishers) Ltd, 1985), p 56.
3. T. Greenawalt, 'The Piano Sonatas of Glazounov' in *The Alexander Glazounov Society Newsletter,* Volume 3, Number 3.
4. S. Taneyev (trans. L. Ferder) in *The Alexander Glazounov Society Newsletter,* Volume 15, Number 1.
5. R. Stevenson, 'The Piano Music' in C. Norris (ed.), *Shostakovich: The Man and his Music* (London: Lawrence and Wishart, 1982), p 87.
6. *The Alexander Glazounov Society Newsletter,* Volume 7, Number 4.

7. S. Prokofiev, *Diaries 1924–1933* (trans. and annotated A. Phillips) (London: Faber and Faber Limited, 2012), p 754.
8. S. Campbell, *Russians on Russian Music,* p 157.
9. S. Taneyev quoted in I. Martynov, liner note to *Glazunov Symphony No.7 c/w Glazunov Symphony No.1.* Compact Disc. Olympia OCD 100. 1987.
10. In the *Ballade* Glazunov provides further evidence of the considerable imagination that he brings to the composition of shorter orchestral pieces. It is cast in three sections (ABA). The first contains an ardent melody which increasingly reveals the passionate side of its character. The central section is in a livelier tempo, with fanfares evoking the world of knights engaged in heroic action, before returning to a beautifully elaborated re-statement of the opening theme, into which an echo of the fanfare motif is woven. The Suite *From the Middle Ages* is richly orchestrated and contains some memorable melodies, particularly in the first and third movements. The second movement scherzo is a magical little piece but the Finale is perhaps not on quite the same level as the rest of the work.
11. N. Slonimsky, *Music Since 1900*, 5th edition. (New York: Schirmer Books, an imprint of Macmillan Publishing Company, 1994), p 37.
12. *The Alexander Glazounov Society Newsletter,* Volume 15, Number 3.
13. Glazunov (trans. L. Ferder), *The Alexander Glazounov Society Newsletter,* Volume 15, Number 3.
14. S. Volkov, *St. Petersburg A Cultural History* (New York: Free Press Paperbacks. A Division of Simon & Schuster Inc., 1997), p 362.
15. *The Alexander Glazounov Society Newsletter,* Volume 4, Number 3.
16. S. Mundy, *Alexander Glazunov,* p 52.

17. N. Milstein and S. Volkov, *From Russia to the West*, p 11.
18. N. Malko, *A Certain Art*, p 66.
19. N. Slonimsky, *Music Since 1900*, p 48.
20. N. A. Rimsky-Korsakov, *My Musical Life*, p 475.
21. Ibid, p 412.
22. S. Prokofiev (ed. F. King, trans. G. Daniels), *Prokofiev by Prokofiev: A Composer's Memoir* (New York: Doubleday and Company Inc., 1979. London: Macdonald and Jane's Publishers Limited, 1979), p 190.
23. N. A. Rimsky-Korsakov, *My Musical Life*, p 414.
24. Ibid, p 413.
25. V. V. Yastrebtsev, (ed. and trans. F. Jonas) *Reminiscences of Rimsky-Korsakov* (New York: Columbia University Press, 1985), p 528, note 38.
26. N. A. Rimsky-Korsakov, *My Musical Life*, p 420.
27. Ibid, p 419.
28. Ibid, p 419.
29. V. V. Yastrebtsev, *Reminiscences of Rimsky-Korsakov*, p 177.
30. N. A. Rimsky-Korsakov, *My Musical Life*, p 419.
31. V. V. Yastrebtsev, *Reminiscences of Rimsky-Korsakov*, p 371.
32. D. Nice, liner note to *Glazunov Symphony No.8*. Compact Disc. CHANDOS. CHAN 996. 2003.
33. Stasov quoted in Mundy, *Alexander Glazunov*, p 56.
34. V. V. Yastrebtsev, *Reminiscences of Rimsky-Korsakov*, p 395.
35. M. D. Calvocoressi, *A Survey of Russian Music*, p 77.

Chapter seven

1. S. Prokofiev, *Prokofiev by Prokofiev*, p 106.
2. N. A. Rimsky-Korsakov, *My Musical Life*, p 431.
3. Quotation from the *Russian Musical Gazette* (Nos. 5–6, 1907) in N. A. Rimsky-Korsakov, *My Musical Life*, p 431.
4. D. J. Venturini, *Alexander Glazounov*, p 30.

5. Ibid, p 2.
6. T. Preston, *Before the Curtain* (London: John Murray, 1950), p 194.
7. M. Leonard, *Slobodskaya A Biography* (London: Victor Gollancz Ltd, 1979), pp 49–50.
8. Ibid, p 50.
9. N. Slonimsky, *Perfect Pitch: A Life Story* (Oxford: Oxford University Press Inc., 1988), pp 16–17.
10. Ibid.
11. S. Volkov, *St. Petersburg*, p 362.
12. N. A. Rimsky-Korsakov, *My Musical Life*, p 266.
13. R. Taruskin, *Defining Russia Musically* (New Jersey: Princeton University Press, 1997), p 454.
14. D. Tiomkin and P. Buranelli, *Please Don't Hate Me* (New York: Doubleday & Company, Inc., 1959), p 12.
15. N. Malko, *A Certain Art*, pp 70–1.
16. S. Prokofiev, *Prokofiev by Prokofiev*, p 150.
17. D. Tiomkin, *Please Don't Hate Me*, p 12. That Glazunov was able to impress musicians of the first rank is further borne out by the legendary pianist, Vladimir Horowitz who, in conversation with David Dubal, remarked, 'And Glazunov was a great, great musician.' See David Dubal, *Evenings with Horowitz: A Personal Portrait,* p 91.
18. N. Malko, *A Certain Art*, p 73.
19. D. Tiomkin, *Please Don't Hate Me*, p 43.
20. M. Leonard, *Slobodskaya*, p 50.
21. S. Prokofiev, *Prokofiev by Prokofiev,* p 107.
22. R. Buckle, *Diaghilev* (London: Weidenfeld & Nicolson, 1993), pp 96 & 101.
23. B. Schwarz, *Music and Musical Life in Soviet Russia*, p 8.
24. D. J. Venturini, *Alexander Glazounov*, p 30.
25. *The Musical Times* (48), 1 July 1907, p 454.

26. Ibid.
27. N. A. Rimsky-Korsakov, *My Musical Life*, p 435.
28. Ibid, p 446.
29. G. Abraham, *Rimsky-Korsakov: A Short Biography* (London: Gerald Duckworth & Co. Ltd., 1945), pp 125–7.
30. V. V. Yastrebtsev, *Reminiscences of Rimsky-Korsakov*, p 478.
31. G. Abraham, *Rimsky-Korsakov*, p 127.
32. A. Orga, liner note to *Glazunov Orchestral Works Volume 10.* Compact Disc. Naxos 8. 553857. 1996.
33. A. Benois, *Reminiscences of the Russian Ballet*, pp 277–8.
34. D. J. Venturini, *Alexander Glazounov*, p 31.
35. Ibid, p 6.
36. E. Tawaststjerna (trans. R. Layton), *Sibelius Volume 11: 1904–1914* (London: Faber and Faber Ltd, 2008), p 48.
37. Ibid, p 97.
38. N. Slonimsky, *Music Since 1900*, p 102.
39. See Leon Ferder's description of the programme for the tone poem in *The Alexander Glazounov Society Newsletter,* Volume 4, Number 4. This was originally given the wrong number of Volume 5, Number 2, but can be identified by the date: October 1989.
40. E. Tawaststjerna (trans. Robert Layton), *Sibelius Volume 111*, 1914–1952, p 34.
41. *The Alexander Glazounov Society Newsletter,* Volume 15, Number 3.
42. G Yudin, Study Score of *Alexander Glasunow 9. Sinfonie* (Bel. Nr. 526) (Frankfurt: M. P. Belaieff, 1987).
43. Ibid.
44. Ibid.
45. D. J. Venturini, *Alexander Glazounov*, p 32.
46. B. Monsaingeon, *Sviatoslav Richter. Notebooks and Conversations*. (London: Faber and Faber Limited London, 2005), p 144.

47. D. F. Tovey, *Essays in Musical Analysis Volume 3. Concertos*. (London: Oxford University Press, 1978), p 209.
48. Michel Stockhem, (trans. J. Drake) liner note to Alexander Glazunov: Piano Concerto No. 1/Symphony No. 5. Compact Disc. Fuga Libera Fug 521. 2006.
49. S. Volkov, *St. Petersburg*, p 200.
50. T. Preston, *Before the Curtain*, (London: John Murray, 1950), p 217.
51. S. Prokofiev, *Diaries 1915–1923*, p 174, note 1.
52. Glazunov quoted in the liner note to *Glazounov: The King of the Jews* Vox/Turnabout LP QTV 34739. 1979.
53. Ibid.
54. S. Prokofiev, *Diaries 1907-1914, Prodigious Youth* (trans. and annotated A. Phillips) (London: Faber and Faber Limited, 2006), p 796.
55. Glazunov quoted in the liner note to *Glazounov: The King of the Jews*.
56. D. Tiomkin, *Please Don't Hate Me*, p 43. To represent Britain in this piece Glazunov uses 'Rule Britannia' rather than 'God Save the King'.
57. This is Glazunov's second Prelude and Fugue for Organ. The first, in D major, Op 93, dates from 1906. In the earlier piece the melodies which dominate the brilliant and celebratory Prelude are then further developed in the expertly elaborated Fugue.
58. Y. Serov, liner note to *Glazunov Complete Songs and Romances.* Compact Disc. 2004. Northern Flowers NF/PMA 9925. 2004.
59. C. Schaper, liner notes to *Alexander Glazunov & Artur Lemba today playing their 1910 interpretations*. TACET 203, p 11. 2012.
60. D. J. Venturini, *Alexander Glazounov*, p 35.

Chapter eight

1. L. Korabelnikova, (trans. A. Winestein & ed. S-H. Hershman-Tcherepnin), *Alexander Tcherepnin The Saga of a Russian Emigré Composer* (Bloomington and Indianapolis: Indiana University Press, 2008), p 2.
2. B. Schwarz, *Music and Musical Life in Soviet Russia*, pp 11–12.
3. Ibid, p 34.
4. Ibid, p 23.
5. Ibid.
6. S. Volkov, *St. Petersburg*, p 282.
7. B. Schwarz, *Music and Musical Life in Soviet Russia*, pp 34–5.
8. E. Wilson, *Shostakovich A Life Remembered* (New Edition) (London: Faber and Faber Limited, 2006), p 28.
9. H. G. Wells, *Russia in the Shadows* (New York: George H. Doran Company, 1921). See the chapter 'Drift and Salvage'.
10. D. J. Venturini, *Alexander Glazounov*, p 36. In more recent times the members of the Moscow Conservatoire Quartet changed their name to the Glazunov Quartet. The group has recorded the string quartets of Dmitry Kabalevsky and Boris Tishchenko for Olympia. (See liner notes to *Boris Tishchenko String Quartets, Vol 1*. Olympia MKM 230.)
11. B. Schwarz, *Music and Musical Life in Soviet Russia*, p 34.
12. Edwin Evans in A. L. Bacharach, (ed.), *The Musical Companion*, pp 528–9.
13. K. Burmeister, (trans. J. & M. Berridge) liner note to *Alexander Glazunov: Complete String Quartets Volume 4*. Compact Disc. MDG 603 1239-2. 2011.
14. L. Kinel, *Under Five Eagles* (London: Putnam, 1937), p 207.
15. Ibid, p 209.
16. S. D. Krebs, *Soviet Composers and the Development of Soviet Music* (London: George Allen and Unwin Ltd., 1970), p 48.

17. *The Alexander Glazounov Society Newsletter,* Volume 15, Number 4.
18. Alexander K. Glazunov Foundation, http://www.glasunow.org/komponist/biographie. 11/2/15.
19. S. Coombs, liner note to *Glazunov: The Complete Solo Piano Music Volume 4.* Compact Disc. Hyperion CDA66866. 1996. The reference here to poverty is corroborated by Thomas Preston who refers to Glazunov's 'meagre earnings' and gives a figure of 48 Roubles a month (£4 10s) as his salary in the period after the October Revolution. See T. Preston, *Before the Curtain*, p 191 and p 194.
20. In fact, M. P. Belaieff published two short piano pieces by Glazunov – Lullaby and Dance – many years after the composer's death. The first edition ascribes these miniatures to 1928. *See* M. P. Belaieff No. 707.
21. T. Preston, *Before the Curtain*, pp 191–2.
22. Alexander K. Glazunov Foundation, http://www.glasunow.org/komponist/biographie. 11/2/15.
23. N. Malko, *A Certain Art*, pp 77–8.
24. J. Charles, (trans. B. Savoie) 'Glazounov's Compositions for Saxophone' in *The Alexander Glazounov Society Newsletter,* Volume 5, Number 2.
25. T. Preston, *Before the Curtain*, p 194.
26. B. Schwarz, *Music and Musical Life in Soviet Russia*, p 98.
27. G. Abraham, 'Glazunov and the String Quartet', in *Slavonic and Romantic Music,* p 224.

Chapter nine

1. D. J. Venturini, *Alexander Glazounov*, p 41.
2. L. Korabelnikova, *Alexander Tcherepnin*, pp 53–4.
3. S. Prokofiev, *Diaries 1924–1933*, p 753 n1.
4. Ibid.

5. L. Steane, *Glazounov: An assessment of the value of Glazounov's orchestral music, with tributes from various sources* (Coventry: Parbury Bros. Ltd., 1967). See the chapter 'English Visits (1929 and 1931)'.
6. In 1910, in St Petersburg, Glazunov made some piano recordings of his music for the Welte Mignon company: in addition to excerpts arranged from his three ballets, he included the Prelude in Db, Op 49 No.1, the Prelude in D, Op 25 No.1, and the Andante from the Piano Sonata No.1. Although the recording of the Piano Sonata No. 2 has been attributed to Glazunov, it now seems that it was made by Artur Lemba, the distinguished Estonian composer and pianist. See the highly informative note by Christian Schaper which accompanies the CD of all these recordings released on TACET 203. 2012.
7. Quoted in C. Haynes, liner note to *Glazunov conducts The Seasons*. Compact Disc. Recorded in 1929. Pearl GEMM CD 9404. 1990.
8. *The Alexander Glazounov Society Newsletter,* Volume 2, Number 4.
9. S. Hurok and R. Goode, *Impresario* (London: Macdonald & Co., Ltd., 1947), p 146.
10. Ibid, p 142.
11. Olin Downes in *The New York Times* 4 December 1929, quoted in *The Alexander Glazounov Society Newsletter,* Volume 2, Number 1.
12. Ibid.
13. Ibid.
14. W. Rimler, *George Gershwin: An Intimate Portrait* (Urbana and Chicago: University of Illinois Press, 2009), p 110.
15. S. Hurok and R. Goode, *Impresario,* p 143.
16. The *Chicago Tribune* 19 December 1929, quoted in *The Alexander Glazounov Society Newsletter,* Volume 2, Number 2.
17. Ibid.

18. Ibid.
19. N. Slonimsky, *Writings on Music Volume One. Early Articles for the Boston Transcript* (New York and London: Routledge, Taylor & Francis Group, 2004), p 81 & p 85.
20. S. Hurok and R. Goode, *Impresario,* p 143.
21. Ibid, p 144.
22. *The Alexander Glazounov Society Newsletter,* Volume 15, Number 4.
23. H. C. Worbs (trans. C. Skrine), liner note to *Alexander Glasunow Concerto Ballata* etc. Compact Disc. Koch Schwann CD 311 119 H1. 1987.
24. E. Coates, *Suite in Four Movements*, p 153.
25. D. J. Venturini, *Alexander Glazounov*, p 44.
26. P. Casals, and A Khan, *Joys and Sorrows* (London: Macdonald, 1970), p 122.
27. *The Alexander Glazounov Society Newsletter,* Volume 1, Number 1.
28. S. Bertenson & J Leyda, *Sergei Rachmaninoff,* pp 291–2.
29. S. Fancher, *Saxophone Journal*, Volume 25, Number 3, Jan/Feb 2001.
30. *The Alexander Glazounov Society Newsletter,* Volume 15, Number 4.
31. R. Back and D. Woudfull-Harris, *Glazunov Concerto in E-flat major for Alto Saxophone and String Orchestra.* Bärenreiter Urtext Score, p xi, quoting from Sigurd M. Rascher: Alexander Glazounov: Concerto pour Saxophone Alto avec l'orchestre des chords, *The Saxophone Symposium* (summer 1988), p 16.
32. Ibid, p xiii.
33. In the Bärenreiter edition of the score there are three cadenzas to choose from: two by Glazunov and one by Rascher.
34. Marcel Mule (trans. M. Martin) quoted in D. J. Venturini, *Alexander Glazounov*, p 48.

35. W. Eggerking, (trans. B. Robinson), *Poème épique*, Study Score 779 (Munich: Musikproduktion Hoeflich, 2008), p vi.
36. S. Mundy, *Alexander Glazunov,* p 76.
37. S. D. Krebs, *Soviet Composers*, p 171.
38. R. Malan, *Efrem Zimbalist: A Life* (Portland: Amadeus Press, 2004), p 230.
39. U. Schalz-Laurenze, liner note to *Symphonic Organ Music*. Compact Disc. BIS-CD-1101. 1999/2000.
40. D. J. Venturini, *Alexander Glazounov*, p 47.
41. Ibid.
42. R. Back and D. Woudfull-Harris, *Glazunov Concerto in E-flat major for Alto Saxophone and String Orchestra.* Bärenreiter Urtext Score, p xiv. The score Glazunov received just hours before his death was one for saxophone with piano reduction.
43. *The Alexander Glazounov Society Newsletter,* Volume 15, Number 4. Olga, Glazunov's widow, later took religious vows and settled in Jerusalem, living in a cell next to the Church of the Holy Sepulchre. Elena married the German writer, Herbert Günther, and died in Munich on 18 June 1999, at the age of 94. See the *Alexander Glazounov Society Newsletter*, Volume 15, Number 2. She had prviously been married to the painist, Sergey Tarnovsky. See Prokofiev, *Diaries 1924–1933 Prodigal Son,* p 754, note 1.
44. The fine bronze bust of the composer which marks the grave is by the German sculptor Karl Altenbernd.

Chapter ten

1. *Musical Opinion*, May, 1936 (pp 676-77) reprinted in M. MacDonald (ed.) *Havergal Brian on Music: Volume 2*, p 307..
2. Ibid.
3. Ibid.
4. H. J. Wood, *My Life in Music* (London: Victor Gollancz Ltd.,

1946), p 329.

5. *The New York Times* 22 March 1936, quoted in *The Alexander Glazounov Society Newsletter,* Volume 2, Number 2.
6. Ibid.
7. S. Prokofiev, *Prokofiev by Prokofiev, A Composer's Memoir*, p 49.
8. Ibid, p 151.
9. Ibid, p 152.
10. S. Prokofiev, *Diaries 1907–1914*, p xxi.
11 S. Prokofiev, *Soviet Diary and Other Writings* (trans. and ed. by O. Prokofiev, associate ed. C. Palmer) (London: Faber and Faber Limited, 1991), p 247.
12. S. Prokofiev, *Diaries 1907–1914*, p 663.
13. S. Prokofiev, *Diaries 1907–1914*, p 90.
14. Ibid, p 648.
15. Ibid, p 418.
16. S. Prokofiev, *Diaries 1915–1923*, p 75.
17. Ibid, p 600.
18. Ibid, p 74.
19. S. Volkov, (trans. A. W. Bouis) *Testimony: The Memoirs of Dmitri Shostakovich*, as related to and edited by Solomon Volkov, p 19. Glazunov also refers to recurring ear infections in a letter of 7 October 1928. See Venturini, *Alexander Glazounov*, p 41.
20. S. Prokofiev, *Soviet Diary and Other Writings*, p 81.
21. S. Volkov, *St. Petersburg*, p 355.
22. See photograph opposite p 143 in D. Gojowy and H. Günther, *Alexander Glasunow*.
23. Ibid, see photograph opposite p 147.
24. D. and L. Sollertinsky (trans. G. Hobbs and C. Midgley), *Pages from the Life of Dmitri Shostakovich* (London: Robert Hale, 1981), p 13.
25. Ibid, p 14.
26. Ibid, p 20.

27. Ibid, p 21.
28. E. Wilson, *Shostakovich: A Life Remembered*, p 32.
29. *The Alexander Glazounov Society Newsletter,* Volume 2, Number 1.
30. R. Taruskin, *Defining Russia Musically*, p 456.
31. S. Prokofiev, *Diaries 1924–1933*, p 838.
32. S. Walsh, *Igor Stravinsky: A Creative Spring: Russia and France 1882–1934* (London: Pimlico, Random House, 2002), p 482.
33. R. Gard (ed.), *Henry James The Critical Muse: Selected Literary Criticism* (London: Penguin Books, 1987), p 49.
34. M. Montagu-Nathan, *Contemporary Russian Composers* (Westport, Connecticut: Greenwood Press, Publishers, 1970. Originally published by Cecil Palmer & Hayward, London, 1917), p 91.
35. Abraham's article, 'Glazunov and the String Quartet' for example, is a detailed and far from unsympathetic account of Glazunov's achievement. He notes that, 'The only nineteenth-century Russians who took the quartet seriously enough to write a whole series of them were Glazunov and S. I. Taneyev… and their only twentieth-century successors have been Myaskovsky and Shostakovich.' *Slavonic and Romantic Music,* p 218.
36. G. Abraham, *On Russian Music*, pp 234–242.
37. V. V. Yastrebtsev, *Reminiscences,* p 407, where the *Orientale* is described as '…the most Eastern of all Eastern music'.
38. The enthusiastic response to Glazunov's music by French composers, including Delibes, is mentioned in Chapter 3. Moreover, Calvocoressi explains that both he and Ravel had a high regard for the early works of Glazunov such as the tone poems *Stenka Razin, The Forest* and the *Oriental Rhapsody*, in addition to the Second and Third Symphonies. See Roger Nichols, *Ravel Remembered* (Faber and Faber Limited: London, 1987), p 182. Glazunov was also one of the Russian composers that Debussy and Madame

Gerard De Romilly played 'enthusiastically' in piano duet arrangements. See Roger Nichols, *Debussy Remembered* (Faber and Faber Limited: London, 1992), p 55.

39. G. Abraham, *The Concise History of Music* (Newton Abbot: Readers Union, 1979), p 699.
40. M. Montagu-Nathan, *Contemporary Russian Composers*, p 93.
41. E. Goossens, *Overture and Beginners* (London: Methuen & Co., Ltd., 1951), p 80.
42. A. V. Amerongen in 'Glazounov Revalued'. See *The Alexander Glazounov Society Newsletter,* Volume 1, Number 4.
43. D. J. Venturini, *Alexander Glazounov*, p 40.
44. N. Malko, *A Certain Art*, p 79.
45. Ibid.
46. S. Mundy, *Alexander Glazunov,* p 77.
47. Dr S. Neef (trans. J. & M. Berridge), liner note to Alexander Glazunov *Raymonda*. Compact Disc. BMG 74321 49609 2. 1997 (original recording 1961).
48. Quoted by Jacques Charles in 'Glazounov's Compositions for Saxophone' (trans. B. Savoie), in *The Alexander Glazounov Society Newsletter,* Volume 5, Number 2.
49. D. Tiomkin, quoted in D. Ewen, *Composers of Today* (New York: The H. W. Wilson Company, 1936), p 90.
50. B. V. Asafyev, (trans. A. J. Swan) *Russian Music from the Beginning of the Nineteenth Century* (Ann Arbor, Michigan: Edwards Brothers, INC, 1953), p 172.
51. Rimsky-Korsakov once told Yastrebtsev, in November 1900, that 'very few contemporary composers fully satisfy me as orchestrators – only Wagner… Glazunov, and Saint-Saëns'. See V. V. Yastrebtsev, *Reminiscences,* p 268.

Recordings of Glazunov's music

I thought it worthwhile to provide the following list – even although a number of the CDs may not be currently available – given the possibility of re-issues and downloads. This is certainly not a complete discography and the absence of any recording from this list is not intended as a comment on its quality – a fact that applies particularly to a frequently recorded work such as the Violin Concerto.

1. Symphonies:

- Symphonies Nos. 1 & 4. Moscow SO/**Anissimov**. Naxos 8.553561.
- Symphonies Nos. 2 & 7. Moscow SO/**Anissimov**. Naxos 8.553769.
- Symphonies Nos. 3 & 9. Moscow SO/**Anissimov**. Naxos 8.554253.
- Symphonies Nos. 5 & 8. Moscow SO/**Anissimov**. Naxos 8.553660.
- Symphony No. 6; The Forest. Moscow SO/**Anissimov**. Naxos 8.554293.
- Symphony No. 8 c/w Tchaikovsky Symphony No. 6. Japan Shinsei SO/**Asahina**. TOBU Recordings TBRCD0001 (2 CD set).
- Symphony No. 3. London SO/**Butt**. ASV CD DCA 581.
- Symphonies Nos. 4 & 5. London SO/**Butt**. ASV CD DCA 1051.
- Symphony No. 6. London SO/**Butt**; Serenades Nos. 1 & 2; Triumphal March. Royal Philharmonic Orchestra/Butt. ASV CD DCA 699.

- Symphonies Nos. 1–8; Concert Waltz No. 1. Tchaikovsky SO of Moscow Radio/**Fedoseyev**. Relief LC 14754. CR 210312 (4CD set).
- Symphonies Nos. 6 & 7. Moscow Large SO/**Golovanov**. Arlecchino ARL A60 (from Melodiya D-0727-28 & Melodiya D-0401-02).
- Symphonies Nos. 1 & 5. Bavarian Radio SO/**Järvi**. Orfeo C 093 101 A.
- Symphony No. 2; Concert Waltz No. 1. Bamberg SO/**Järvi**. Orfeo C 148 101 A.
- Symphony No. 3; Concert Waltz No. 2. Bamberg SO/**Järvi**. Orfeo C 157 101 A.
- Symphonies Nos. 4 & 7. Bamberg SO/**Järvi**. Orfeo C 148 201 A.
- Symphony No. 6; Poème lyrique. Bamberg SO/**Järvi**. Orfeo C 157 201 A.
- Symphony No. 8; Overture solennelle; Wedding March. Bavarian Radio SO/**Järvi**. Orfeo C 093 201 A.
- Symphonies Nos. 4 & 5; The Seasons (excerpts). Leningrad Philharmonic Orchestra/**Mravinsky**. Praga Digitals PRD/DSD 350 129. (Original recordings 1948/1968/1969.)
- Symphonies Nos. 1–8; From Darkness to Light; Ballade; Mazurka. BBC National Orchestra of Wales/**Otaka**. BIS-CD-1663/64. (5 CD set).
- Symphonies Nos. 1–6+8; Violin Concerto; Coronation Cantata; Concert Waltzes Nos. 1 & 2; Characteristic Suite. Russian State Symphonic Cappella. Russian State SO/**Polyansky**/Symphony No. 7 Welsh National SO/Otaka. Raymonda Suite London SO/**Butt**. Brilliant Classics 93565 (7 CD set).
- Symphonies Nos. 1-8. USSR Ministry of Culture SO/**Rozhdestvensky**. Melodiya CD 10 01790. (5 CD set).

- Complete Symphonies and Concertos; The Seasons; The Sea; Introduction and Dance for Salome; Raymonda Suite; Meditation for Violin and Orchestra; Rêverie for Horn and Orchestra. Royal Scottish National Orchestra/Russian National Orchestra/**Serebrier**. Warner Classics 2564 66467-4 LC 04281. (8CD set).
- Symphonies Nos. 1-8; First Overture on Greek Themes; Spring, Op. 34; The Kremlin; Stenka Razin; Finnish Fantasy. USSR SO/**Svetlanov**. Warner Classics 2564 68162-2 (6 CD set).

2. Concertos:

- Violin Concerto c/w Shostakovich Violin Concerto No. 1. **Benedetti**/Bournemouth SO/Karabits. Decca 478 8758.
- Violin Concerto c/w concertos by Prokofiev and Khachaturian. **Fischer**/Russian National Orchestra/ Kreizberg. Pentatone PTC 5186591.
- Violin Concerto; Meditation; Mazurka-oberek; c/w Schoeck: Concerto quasi una fantasia. **Hanslip**/Orchestra Della Svizzera Italiana/Vedernikov. Hyperion CDA67940.
- Violin Concerto c/w Sibelius Violin Concerto & Prokofiev Violin Concerto No. 2. **Heifetz**/RCA SO/Hendl. RCA RD 8709.
- Violin Concerto (**Milstein**/Pittsburg SO/Steinberg); Raymonda Suite (Philharmonia Orchestra/Matacic); Concerto Ballata (**Rostropovich**/USSR State SO/Svetlanov); Stenka Razin (Philharmonia Orchestra/Fistoulari); Concert Waltzes Nos. 1 & 2 and The Seasons (Philharmonia Orchestra/ Svetlanov). EMI 50999 6 78398 2 7 (2 CD set).
- Violin Concerto c/w Prokofiev Violin Concerto No. 1; Shchedrin Stihira. **Mutter**/National SO/ Rostropovich. Erato ECD 75506.

- Violin Concerto c/w Kabelevsky Violin Concerto in C; Tchaikovsky Souvenir d'un lieu cher & Valse -Scherzo. **Shaham**/Russian National Orchestral/Pletnev. DG 457 064-2.
- Violin Concerto c/w Tchaikovsky Violin Concerto. **Vengerov**/Berlin Philharmonivc/Abbado. Teldec 4509-90881-2.
- Violin Concerto; Grand Adagio from *Raymonda* c/w Sibelius Violin Concerto. **Yoo**/Philharmonic Orchestra/ Ashkenazy. DG 40130/481 2157.
- Piano Concertos Nos. 1 & 2 c/w Goedicke Concertstuck. **Coombs**/BBC Scottish SO/Brabbins. Hyperion CDA 66877.
- Piano Concertos No. 1; Symphony No. 5. **Eckardstein**/ National Orchestra of Belgium/Weller. Fuga Libre FUG 521.
- Piano Concerto Nos. 1 & 2; Carnaval Overture. **Kolly**/ Slovak Radio SO/Griffiths. Pan Classics 510 084.
- Piano Concerto No. 1 c/w Prokofiev Piano Sonata No. 6. **Richter**/Moscow Youth SO/Eliasberg. Leningrad Masters LM 1324.
- Piano Concertos Nos. 1 & 2; Variations on a Russian Theme (Artsybushev et al). **Yablonskaya**/Moscow SO/Yablonsky. Naxos 8.553928.
- Concerto Ballata for Cello and Orchestra c/w Chant du Ménestrel; Two Pieces for Cello and Orchestra, Op 20; Prelude in Memory of Gogol; Elegy, To the Memory of a Hero. **Rudin**/Moscow SO/Golovschin. Naxos 8.553932.
- Concerto Ballata for Cello and Orchestra c/w Prokofiev Concertino; Tchaikovsky Rococo Variations. **Walton**/ Royal Philharmonic Orchestra/Kamu. Signum Classics SGCD 407.

- Saxophone Concerto c/w Debussy Rhapsodie; Ibert Concertino da camera; Villa-Lobos Fantasia; Bennett Concerto; Heath Out of the Cool. **Harle**/Academy of St Martin in the Fields/Marriner. EMI Classics CDC 7 54301 2.
- Saxophone Concerto c/w Larsson Concerto; Panula Adagio & Allegro. **Savijoki**/New Stockholm Chamber Orchestra/ Panula. BIS-CD-218.

3. Orchestral collections and ballet music:

- March on a Russian Theme; Oriental Rhapsody; Karelian Legend; From Darkness into Light. Hong Kong Philharmonic Orchestra/**Almeida**. Marco Polo 8.220444.
- Stenka Razin; The Sea; Spring; From the Middle Ages. Royal Scottish National Orchestra/**Järvi**. CHANDOS CHAN 7049.
- The Kremlin; From the Middle Ages; Poème lyrique; Poème épique. Moscow SO/**Krimets**. Naxos 8.553537.
- The Forest; The Sea; Oriental Rhapsody. USSR State SO/ **Svetlanov**. Melodiya SUCD 10-00156.
- Ballade; Solemn Overture; Spring; Introduction and Dance for Salomé; Romantic Intermezzo. USSR State SO/ **Svetlanov**. Melodiya SUCD 10-00158.
- Stenka Razin; Lyric Poem; Finnish Fantasy; Mazurka; Theme and Variations for Strings. **Svetlanov**. Melodiya SUCD 10-00161.
- Two Preludes, Op. 85 (To the Memory of Stasov; To the Memory of Rimsky-Korsakov); To the Memory of Gogol, Op 87; Carnaval Overture; Fortune Telling and Dance (Scène dansante); Finnish Sketches (From the Kalevala & Procession). USSR State SO/**Svetlanov**. Melodiya SUCD 10-00163.
- Scènes de Ballet; Characteristic Suite. USSR State SO/

Svetlanov. Melodiya SUCD 10-00160.

- Raymonda, Ballet in Three Acts (complete). Moscow SO/**Anissimov**. Naxos 8.553503-4 (2CD set).
- Raymonda Suite, Op. 57a; Stenka Razin. London SO/**Butt**. ASV CD DCA 572.
- Raymonda, Music from Acts 1 & 2. Scottish National Orchestra/**Järvi**. Chandos CHAN 8447.
- Raymonda, Ballet in Three Acts (complete). Bolshoi Theatre Orchestra/**Svetlanov**. Melodiya SUCD 10-00020.
- Ruses d'amour, Ballet in One Act. Roumanian State Orchestra/**Andreescu**. Naxos 8.572447.
- Ruses d'amour, Ballet in One Act. USSR SO/**Svetlanov**. Melodiya SUCD 10-00020.
- The Seasons, Ballet in One Act; Concert Waltzes Nos. 1 & 2; Stenka Razin; Schumann Carnaval (orchestrated by Glazunov et al); Orchestral works by Glinka & Liadov. L'Orchestre de la Suisse Romande/**Ansermet**. Decca Eloquence 480 0038 (2 CD set).
- The Seasons, Ballet in One Act c/w Tchaikovsky The Nutcracker. Royal Philharmonic/**Ashkenazy**. Decca 433 000-2 (2 CD set).
- The Seasons, Ballet in One Act c/w Violin Concerto; Meditation. Rosand/Malaysian Philharmonic Orchestra/**Bakels**. Vox Classics VXP 7907.
- The Seasons, Ballet in One Act. Orchestra/**Glazunov** c/w Prokofiev Piano Concerto No. 3 etc. Prokofiev/London SO/Coppola. EMI Classics 7243 5 55223 20.
- The Seasons, Ballet in One Act c/w Scarlatti-Tommasini The Good-Humored Ladies; Bach-Walton The Wise Virgins. Concert Arts Orchestra/**Irving**. EMI Classics 7243 5 65911 2 7.
- The Seasons, Ballet in One Act; Violin Concerto. Shumsky/

Scottish National Orchestra/**Järvi**. CHANDOS CHAN 8596.

- The Seasons, Ballet in One Act. USSR State Radio & Television Orchestra/**Khaikin**; Chopiniana Suite. USSR State Academic SO/Svetlanov. Melodiya MEL CD 02085.
- The Seasons, Ballet in One Act c/w Concert Waltzes Nos 1 & 2. Philharmonia Orchestra/**Svetlanov**. Works by Arensky Variations on a Theme by Tchaikovsky; Rimsky-Korsakov Sheherazade. EMI Classics 7243 5 69361 2 6 (2 CD set).
- The Seasons, Ballet in One Act c/w Scènes de Ballet. Minnesota Orchestra/**Waart**. Telarc CD-80347.

4. Chamber music:

- String Quintet c/w Tchaikovsky Souvenir de Florence. **Academy of St Martin-in-the-Fields Chamber Ensemble**. CHANDOS CHAN 9387.
- Five Novelettes, Op. 15 c/w string quartets by Titz & Tchaikovsky. **casalQuartet** Solo Musica SM 241.
- Five Novelettes, Op. 15; String Quintet. **Fine Arts Quartet**, with Nathaniel Rosen (cello). Naxos 8.570256.
- String Quartet No. 5; Five Novelettes, Op. 15. **St. Petersburg String Quartet**. DELOS DE 3262.
- String Quartet No. 1 c/w Tchaikovsky Piano Trio. **Shostakovich Quartet**/Leningrad Philharmonic Trio. Olympia OCD 157.
- String Quartets Nos. 2 & 4. **Shostakovich Quartet**. Olympia OCD 173.
- String Quartets Nos 3 & 5; Two Pieces from Les Vendredis. **Shostakovich Quartet**. Olympia OCD 525.
- String Quartets Nos. 6 & 7. **Shostakovich Quartet**. Olympia OCD 526.

- Suite for String Quartet, Op 35; Quintet; Elegy In Memory of M. P. Belyayev. **Shostakovich Quartet**. Olympia OCD 542.
- String Quartets Nos. 1 & 7. **Utrecht String Quartet**. MDG 603 1736-2.
- String Quartets Nos. 2 & 4; Elegy In Memory of M.P. Belyayev. **Utrecht String Quartet**. MDG 603 1237-2.
- String Quartets Nos. 3 & 5. **Utrecht String Quartet**. MDG 603 1236-2.
- String Quartet No. 6; Five Novelettes, Op 15. **Utrecht String Quartet**. MDG 603 1239-2.
- Suite for String Quartet, Op 35; String Quintet. **Utrecht String Quartet**, with Michael Stirling (cello) MDG 603 1238-2.
- Five Novelettes, Op. 15; Ten Pieces from Les Vendredis (Artciboucheff, Borodin et al). **Vertavo String Quartet**. SIMAX PSC 1178.
- String Quartets Nos. 3 & 4; Idyll for French Horn and Strings. **Zemlinsky Quartet**, with Christoph EB ((horn). Praga Digitals PRD/DSD 250 281.

5. Piano music:

- 'SASCHA' Suite; Three Miniatures, Op. 42; Valse de Salon, Op. 43; Grande Valse de Concert, Op. 41; Waltzes on the theme 'SABELA', Op. 23; Petite Valse, Op. 36; Piano Sonata No. 1 in B flat minor, Op. 74. **Coombs**. Hyperion CDA66833.
- Three Études, Op. 31; Two Pieces, Op. 22; Trois Morceaux, Op. 49; Nocturne, Op. 37; Miniature in C; Easy Sonata; Sonatina; Two Prelude-Improvisations; Theme and Variations, Op. 72. **Coombs**. Hyperion CDA66844.
- Prelude and Fugue in D minor, Op. 62; Four Preludes and

Fugues, Op. 101; Prelude and Fugue in E minor. **Coombs**. Hyperion CDA66855.

-
- Prelude and Two Mazurkas, Op. 25; Barcarolle sur les touches noires; Two Impromptus, Op. 54; Idylle, Op. 103; Triumphal March, Op. 40, with Holst Singers/Layton; Song of the Volga Boatmen; In Modo Religioso, Op. 38; Pas de caractère, Op. 68; Piano Sonata No. 2 in E minor, Op. 75. **Coombs**. Hyperion CDA66866.
- Piano Sonata No. 1 in B flat minor, Op. 74; Piano Sonata No. 2 in E minor, Op. 75; c/w works by Liadov & Arensky. **Cousin**. SOMM New Horizons SOMMCD 0100.
- Piano Sonata No. 1 in B flat minor, Op. 74; Piano Sonata No. 2 in E minor, Op. 75; Three Études, Op. 31; Grande Valse de Concert, Op. 41. **Damerini**. ETCETERA KTC 1118.
- Valse de salon, Op. 43; Trois morceaux, Op. 49; Two Impromptus, Op. 54; Prelude and Fugue in D minor, Op. 62; Theme and Variations, Op. 72; Two Prelude-Improvisation **Franová**. Marco Polo 8.223152.
- Piano Sonata No. 1 in B flat minor, Op. 74; Piano Sonata No. 2 in E minor, Op. 75; Grand Concert Waltz, Op. 41. **Howard**. Pearl SHE CD 9538.
- Complete Piano Music, including the Fantasy for Two Pianos in F minor, Op. 104. **Hulbert**. **Nagai** (Fantasy only). 88295 15793 (bar code of 4 CD set).
- Piano Sonata No. 1 in B flat minor, Op. 74; Three Études, Op. 31; Nocturne, Op. 37; Grande Valse dc Concert, Op. 41 c/w works by Balakirev. **Satukangas**. FINLANDIA 0630-10925-2.

6. Organ music:

- Prelude and Fugue in D major, Op. 93; Prelude and Fugue in D minor, Op. 98; Fantasy, Op. 110 c/w works by Dvořák and Sibelius. **Ericsson**. BIS-CD-1101.
- Prelude and Fugue in D major, Op. 93; Prelude and Fugue in D minor, Op. 98; Fantasy, Op. 110 c/w works by Gliere, Glinka, Grechaninov, Rachmaninov, Shostakovich and S. I. Taneyev. **Quinn**. CHANDOS CHAN 10043.
- Prelude and Fugue in D major, Op. 93; Prelude and Fugue in D minor, Op. 98; Prelude and Fugue in D minor, Op. 62 (arranged for organ by B. Sabaneev); Fantasy, Op. 110. **Zvegintseva**. Northern Flowers NF/PMA 99.

7. Incidental music:

- The King of the Jews, Op. 95. Moscow Cappella/Moscow SO/**Golovschin**. Naxos 8.553575.
- The King of the Jews, Op. 95; Introduction and Dance of Salomé, Op. 90. Russian State Symphonic Cappella/ Russian State SO/**Polyansky**. CHANDOS CHAN 9824.
- The King of the Jews, Op. 95. Russian State Symphonic Cappella/Russian State SO/**Rozhdestvensky**. CHANDOS CHAN 9467.
- Masquerade (incidental music); Two Pieces, Op. 14; Pas de caractère, Op. 68; Romantic Intermezzo, Op. 69 Gnesin Academy Chorus/Russian Philharmonic Orchestra/ **D. Yablonsky**. Naxos 8.5702.

8. Songs:

- Complete Songs and Romances. **Evtodieva**, soprano; **Shkirtil**, mezz-soprano; **Lukonin**, baritone; **Serov**, piano. Northern Flowers NF/PMA 9925.

Acknowledgements

I would like to thank United Artists who, on behalf of The Literary Executors of the Estate of H. G. Wells, gave permission to use the quotation from *Russia in the Shadows*. I am also grateful to HarperCollins for their permission to quote from *A Certain Art* by Nikolai Malko.

An early draft of the book was read by Esther Henderson, and I am indebted to her for her comments and questions, as these were of great value to me. I would also like to express my gratitude to Pat Clark and the Rev. Jack Kellet for their advice and encouragement.

Index